Anthropology, Cu

Series

Dr Jon P. Mitchell, U

Recent titles:

Land, Law and Environment
Mythical Land, Legal Boundaries
Edited by Allen Abramson and Dimitrios Theodossopoulos

Anthropology and the Will to Meaning
A Postcolonial Critique
Vassos Argyrou

Risk Revisited
Edited by Pat Caplan

Ethnicity and Nationalism
Anthropological Perspectives
Thomas Hylland Eriksen

Globalisation
Studies in Anthropology
Thomas Hylland Eriksen

A History of Anthropology
Thomas Hylland Eriksen and Finn Sivert Nielsen

Small Places, Large Issues
An Introduction to Social and Cultural Anthropology
Thomas Hylland Eriksen

What is Anthropology?
Thomas Hylland Eriksen

Anthropology, Development and the Post-modern Challenge
Katy Gardner and David Lewis

Power and its Disguises
Anthropological Perspectives on Power
John Gledhill

Corruption
Anthropological Perspectives
Edited by Dieter Haller and Cris Shore

Control and Subversion
Gender Relations in Tajikistan
Colette Harris

State Formation
Anthropological Perspectives
Edited by Christian Krohn-Hansen and Knut G. Nustad

Youth and the State in Hungary
Capitalism, Communism and Class
László Kürti

Locating Cultural Creativity
Edited by John Liep

Cord of Blood
Possession and the Making of Voodoo
Nadia Lovell

Cultivating Development
An Ethnography of Aid Policy and Practice
David Mosse

The Aid Effect
Giving and Governing in International Development
Edited by David Mosse and David Lewis

Ethnography and Prostitution in Peru
Lorraine Nencel

Witchcraft, Power and Politics
Exploring the Occult in the South African Lowveld
Isak A. Niehaus with Eliazaar Mohlala and Kally Shokane

Power, Community and the State
The Political Anthropology of Organisation in Mexico
Monique Nuijten

Negotiating Local Knowledge
Power and Identity in Development
Edited by Johan Pottier, Alan Bicker and Paul Sillitoe

Class, Nation and Identity
The Anthropology of Political Movements
Jeff Pratt

Ethnic Distinctions, Local Meanings
Negotiating Cultural Identities in China
Mary Rack

The Cultural Politics of Markets
Economic Liberalisation and Social Change in Nepal
Katharine Neilson Rankin

Bearing Witness
Women and the Truth and Reconciliation Commission in South Africa
Fiona C. Ross

Landscape, Memory and History
Anthropological Perspectives
Edited by Pamela J. Stewart and Andrew Strathern

Terror and Violence
Imagination and the Unimaginable
Edited by Andrew Strathern, Pamela J. Stewart and Neil L. Whitehead

Race, Nature and Culture
An Anthropological Perspective
Peter Wade

Claiming Individuality

The Cultural Politics of Distinction

Edited by

VERED AMIT AND NOEL DYCK

LONDON • ANN ARBOR, MI

First published 2006 by Pluto Press
345 Archway Road, London N6 5AA
and 839 Greene Street, Ann Arbor, MI 48106

www.plutobooks.com

British Library Cataloguing in Publication Data
A catalogue record for this book is available from the British Library

ISBN 0–7453–2459–2 hardback
ISBN 0–7453–2458–4 paperback

Library of Congress Cataloging in Publication Data applied for

10 9 8 7 6 5 4 3 2 1

Designed and produced for Pluto Press by
Chase Publishing Services Ltd, Fortescue, Sidmouth, EX10 9QG, England
Typeset from disk by Newgen Imaging System (P) Ltd, Chennai, India
Printed and bound in the European Union by
Antony Rowe Ltd, Chippenham and Eastbourne, England

Contents

Acknowledgements

The editors wish to thank Thomas Hylland Eriksen whose support and encouragement were crucial to bringing this project to fruition. We would also like to thank Jon Mitchell for his thoughtful comments on the manuscript.

David Castle of Pluto Press provided valuable assistance throughout the project.

Last, but by no means least, we thank the contributors for their participation in the project.

1
On Claiming Individuality: An Introduction to the Issues

Vered Amit and Noel Dyck

More than a decade ago an anthropologist authoring a book subtitled *The Individual in Cultural Perspective* reported being forewarned that this domain of study constituted a philosophical and conceptual "minefield" that evoked strong emotions within the discipline (Morris 1994:x). Our experience of charting a rather different route through this contested territory some years later suggests that, notwithstanding previous initiatives to probe the anthropology of the self and individuality (Burridge 1979; Carrithers, Collins and Lukes 1985; Mines 1994) and to reconnoiter the salience of self-consciousness (Cohen 1994; Cohen and Rapport 1995), little seems to have changed in certain respects. Conference presentations that muster the concept of individuality continue to draw fire from snipers who doggedly defend the position that "the individual" and "individuality" are unalterably "Western" cultural concepts that cannot be allowed to invade the confines of traditional, cross-cultural anthropological endeavor.

A short distance across from this deeply entrenched line of argument stands an opposing formation that, though more recently mobilized, is no less determined to fortify its ground. Indeed, in the course of finalizing our proposal for this volume we received assessments, apparently from observers situated beyond the range of the skirmishing that erupts intermittently along this front, to the effect that our undertaking might be mistimed because by now all of this *must* have been resolved: "My initial reaction ... was one of mild surprise that the argument of this book still needs to be made. I had thought – hoped, perhaps – that it had by now been done and dusted". To which we reply, would that it were so! The reality is that the notion of individuality still manages to generate roughly equal measures of controversy and confusion within anthropology, a situation more reminiscent of an ingrained stalemate than of resolution. Meanwhile, in the shadow of this standoff, individual anthropologists have been collecting ethnographic materials in highly varied locales and situations that enable perceptive interrogation of the processes and implications of individuation. Indeed, their findings cumulatively underscore the need for, as well as proffer support of, the argument mounted in this volume. In light of such promising steps, how can we account for the clinging stasis that grimly survives within this sector? What are the resources that sustain the entrenched positions provoked within anthropology by invocations or denials of individuality?

One of the most familiar grounds for the controversy attending the idea of individuality has been ideological. From this position, the distinction between individuality and individualism seems thin indeed. Individuality is tied to a particular view or version of personhood vested within philosophical preferences/aspirations for particular social arrangements. These preferences are most closely and systematically identified with the Western liberal tradition. According to Dumont, "individualism" is defined, first and foremost, by its opposition to ideologies of "holism" that valorize the social whole and neglect or subordinate the human individual (1986:279–80). Thus, individualism is understood to valorize the individual, in the sense of the independent, morally autonomous, and essentially nonsocial being. Since individualism in this sense comprises a principal feature of "modernism", Dumont designates this configuration as "individualistic, or as individualist ideology, or individualism" (ibid.:279–80).

However recently coined this particular formulation may be – according to Raymond Williams it is a product of the early nineteenth century (1983:161–5) – individuality delineated in this manner can never be simply a neutral concept. To search for it or to identify it as existing within societies and situations outside the eponymous "West" is thereby construed as promoting or, at the very least, thoughtlessly colluding with a kind of doctrinal imperialism. It is hardly surprising that this kind of correspondence should have become highly emotive and controversial in a discipline that has struggled so diligently to overcome historical accusations of colonialist complicity.

Yet this kind of ideological mapping has the effect of dividing the world into a "West vs the Rest" dichotomy that anthropologists have strenuously sought to transcend, especially during the last three decades. Sherry Ortner observes that the pervasive scholarly tendency during the 1970s to apply a relational/individualistic dichotomy in comparisons between South Asian and Western societies was part of a powerful modernization narrative: "traditional people are relational, modern people are individualistic" (1995:369). Furthermore, this kind of simplistic dichotomy "feeds into a discourse of otherness in which the Other is either inferior or romantic, but either way excluded from equality of intercourse with us" (Ortner 1995:370). In relation to her own research in Nepal, Ortner points out that Sherpa society could as readily be characterized as individualist as relationalist. Assigning terms such as these in any absolute way to any group of people is, in her terms, an "ideological charge" rather than an analytical account.

These kinds of ideological simplifications not only romanticize the "Other" but also by implication stereotype "Us" and "We". At one and the same time, they construct and conjoin two complementary essentialisms, the "West" and the "Rest". James Carrier has argued cogently that Orientalism is characteristically juxtaposed with implicit claims of Occidentalism, defining the latter as "the essentialistic rendering of the West by Westerners" (1992:199). Carrier argues that while Occidentalism has not been a frequent and explicit concern in anthropological writing, it has tended to occur when

> ... anthropologists consider Western intrusions on the societies they study. Frequently, these intrusions – wage labor, mission doctrine, plantation or mining projects – seem to be treated as local manifestations of a fairly uniform "West." And they are frequently resented, openly or covertly, in just these terms. That is, they are seen to mark the displacement of a heretofore alien, coherent, and uniform sort of social life by an equally coherent and uniform sort of social life, that of the West. (1992:199)

To Carrier's list of Western intrusions, commonly deemed to be simply "matter out of place", we can add any elements that might be designated as being "individualistic". If such elements do appear amongst peoples depicted as being *really* "collective" or "relationalist", these can be attributed to (and explained away as) intrusions of the West, also frequently typified as "modernization". Ortner also notes how Robert Desjarlais in his study of shamanism in north central Nepal identifies the prominence of "soul-loss illness" with the intrusion of modernization into Nepal, currents threatening the "corporate ways of life" of the Yolmo wa (Ortner 1995:368).

In other words, the forms of these abiding dualities can be rendered virtually impervious to any contradictory ethnographic evidence.

"Matter out of place" in the form of behaviors or social arrangements that do not readily fit with an already assigned "relationalism" can be explained away as the outcome of "Western modernization", thus preserving the tautological dualism of West/Other and the corollary "individualist"/"relationalist" distinction. In turn, this tautology neatly closes off the need for any kind of open-ended anthropological inquiry into individuality anywhere, whether in the Global "South" or "North", the eponymous "East" or "West". In the one, it is assumed to be absent a priori or, if present, only "inauthentically" so. In the other, individuality is glossed as being obvious, already fully known and therefore not requiring sustained investigation.

IT'S ALL BEEN RESOLVED

It is unlikely that this kind of dogmatic binarism served as the launching pad from which springs the other reaction to our proposal: that the case for directing anthropologists' attention to individuality no longer needs to be made. This response has arisen not out of the view that individuality is irrelevant to anthropology, but rather from an opposing stance that holds that recognition of individuality has now become thoroughly ensconced within the discipline. According to this perspective, it is no longer necessary to treat individuality as deserving or requiring any additional consideration in a volume such as this one. Whence does this reading of the state of contemporary anthropological practice derive?

It arises, we submit, from nearly three decades of sustained reconsideration and repositioning of the anthropological enterprise. During the last third of the twentieth century, the development of a processual and distributive notion of culture (Barth 1966, 1969; Goodenough 1973, 1976; Hannerz 1969, 1990), the fashioning of hermeneutic critiques of ethnographic representation (Clifford and Marcus 1986; Marcus and Fischer 1986), and the forging of feminist analyses (Ortner and Whitehead 1981; Moore 1988) all combined to call into question inclinations towards exoticism and cultural reifications judged to have underpinned too many anthropological analyses. One of the borders that these critiques sought vigorously to dismantle was a notion of "West" versus "Other". This distinction was seen as being fundamentally distorting within a world in which "the close-to-home constantly intermixes with the far-from-home, and often it is not worthwhile deciding which is which" (Fox 1991a:5).

This manner of interpolation could be both profoundly personal and epistemological, a factor of an anthropologist's own biography as well as of the intersubjective reflexivity demanded in this critical reappraisal. Hence Renato Rosaldo recounted the mundane border crossings that had been a feature of his childhood growing up "Chicano" in the United States (1989:28–9) and Lila Abu-Lughod identified herself as a "halfie", a person "whose national or cultural identity is mixed by virtue of migration, overseas education or parentage" (1991:137). Along with this kind of self-consciousness came an increasing discomfort with cultural generalization altogether. Indeed Abu-Lughod went so far as to demand that anthropologists write "against culture", arguing instead for a focus on the lives of particular individuals:

> By focusing closely on particular individuals and their changing relationships, one would necessarily subvert the most problematic connotations of culture: homogeneity, coherence and timelessness. Individuals are confronted with choices, struggle with others, make conflicting statements, argue about points of view on the same events, undergo ups and downs in various relationships and changes in their circumstances and desires, face new pressures, and fail to predict what will happen to them or those around them. (Abu-Lughod 1991:154)

In the same volume, Richard Fox argued that such an emphasis on the individual actually had a venerable pedigree within anthropology. The attempts of the early Boasians – including Sapir, Goldenweiser, Lowie, Radin, Herskovits and Boas himself – to constitute a form of cultural history revolved around debating the role of individual creativity in culture change and innovation (Fox 1991b:104). According to Fox, cultural determinism gained sway at a somewhat later stage but not during this early formative period of Americanist anthropology.

In short, late-twentieth-century anthropology featured an emphasis on a critical destabilization of the anthropologist's selfhood as well as skepticism about generalized cultural distinctions altogether, outcomes that served to focus attention upon individual lives and voices. It is, therefore, hardly surprising that this period also featured a growing disciplinary concern with autobiography and life history (e.g., Shostak 1981; Cruikshank 1990; Aman 1994). In view of this inclination, the response that greeted our proposal – namely, that the case for attending to individuality has already gained wide acceptance within anthropology – is not entirely unexpected. But neither is it persuasive. As our personal experiences and those of a number of our contributors can attest, this is a mistaken assumption. *Plus ça change* ...

The discomfort that still tends to envelop anthropological research on individuality hangs on, notwithstanding the passions generated and principled purposes declared in the course of recent maneuvers to effect radical analytical repositioning within anthropology. One reason for this would seem to be that certain longstanding formulations and presumptions that have been duly selected for demobilization and possibly even dishonourable discharge from active service in anthropological analysis have, nonetheless, been around for so long and have become so commonplace and familiar as to render them difficult for some within the discipline to relinquish. As Sherry Ortner (1995) noted in her review of anthropological studies of shamanism in Nepal, despite the articulation of compelling critiques of master narratives such as that of modernization, certain linked master oppositions stubbornly persist in otherwise highly nuanced and complex studies: for instance, tradition/modernity; shamanism/Buddhism; and individualism/relationalism. Similarly a younger colleague who conducted her doctoral fieldwork with children in two Canadian locales, secure in the conviction that distinctions between "home" and "away" were no longer pertinent in contemporary anthropology, was surprised to discover that for faculty hiring committees, these still very much mattered (Caputo 2000).

A second reason inheres in the very nature of the demand for devoting attention to individual lives that featured in calls, such as that mounted by Abu-Lughod, for anthropologists to write "against culture". The object of this exercise was to resolve issues of representation rather than to focus on particular forms of social action in their own right. The individual would no longer be conscripted to serve as an archetype for the group but would instead be assigned to act as an equivocal guide to the vagaries of participation within it. Accordingly, in the wake of this suddenly popular regard for individual stories, the particular would still be mustered to illustrate the more general but to do so cumulatively rather than prototypically. But in itself such a focus on individual histories does not necessarily recount, or have as its objective to do so, processes of deliberate individuation. It does not necessarily seek to tell us in which instances or circumstances and to what effect individuals may seek to inflect certain forms of social action by distinguishing themselves personally rather than categorically. Nor does it consider what reaction is elicited by this effort. In short, to turn one's attention to individual stories is not necessarily or automatically to take account of individuality and its social ramifications.

There is, however, another recent anthropological conceptualization of the individual which places a much more explicit focus on individuality. In this version, individuality is not simply a window onto the complexities and vagaries of social life; rather, it is considered the existential source and mainspring of all social life. For Nigel Rapport, individuality is "the human *a priori*, the physical-psychical basis on which all human knowledge of the world, all creativity within it and all activity upon it, rests (including the creation and representation of sociocultural milieux)" (2001:11342). For Rapport, therefore, individuality is not a form of social action per se. Within his schema, social action and social life more generally are epiphenomena of individuality.

Like all belief systems, such a passionate declaration of faith in the essence of the human condition is not refutable in itself: you either believe it or you don't. But more to the point of the exercise in which we are engaged in this volume, it does not provide much assistance for an anthropological *investigation* of individuality because it threatens to close off the effort before it has really begun. If the status of individuality is fixed a priori, there is little empirical need to investigate its myriad social instantiations and implications since these are in crucial ways irrelevant to its existential provenance.

> Individuality remains consequential, that is, whether or not individual consciousness is an item of collective discourse, whether or not individual reflection is publicly eschewed, and whether or not individual distinctiveness is disparaged through the institutionalization of a fund of common behaviours (concerning, for instance, notions of the person). (Rapport 2001:11342)

We would argue instead that a more agnostic attitude towards individuality is likelier to provide a productive space for comparative and open-ended exploration of personal distinctions as forms of social activity and process. And, fortunately for our enterprise, Rapport has not allowed his existentialist certainty to blunt his ethnographic curiosity.

This volume, therefore, looks back not to an existentialist anthropology but towards a longstanding effort within the discipline to interrogate sociality as being intrinsically problematic. Despite a certain tendency during the 1980s and early 1990s to castigate our anthropological forebears for producing overly determinist, timeless, homogenous and unreasonably bounded versions of the "Other", as Richard Fox (see above) has noted, there is an equally venerable tradition that has long viewed social reproduction and collective life as highly problematic. Whether it was (1) the early Boasians' effort to understand the role of individual creativity as a source of cultural innovation, (2) urban ethnographers' attempts to trace the tenuous articulations of complex metropolitan relations and networks (Mitchell 1956; Epstein 1958; Hannerz 1980), (3) programs to understand ethnicity in terms of social strategies rather than typologies (Barth 1969; Cohen 1969), or (4) more recent efforts to problematize the interaction between communality and locality, between social mobilization and collective imagination, between pressures towards deterritorialization and the harsh reinvigoration of political borders (Appadurai 1996; Gupta and Ferguson 1997; Olwig and Hastrup 1997; Amit 2002; Amit and Rapport 2003), anthropologists have clearly struggled throughout many years to apprehend the vulnerable labors of human beings engaged in the work of collective association and disassociation, of belonging, exclusion and distinction. It is the spirit of this rich legacy of disciplinary endeavor that has inspired and guided our efforts to explore in this volume a diverse range of claims of individuality.

While individuality has often been interpreted philosophically as a force for the separation and autonomy of the individual (Williams 1983:161–5), all of the chapters in this volume, although dealing with varied situations, problems and settings, treat the social expression of individuality as being inextricably linked with questions of belonging. In this respect, our examination departs from predispositions that have more commonly featured heretofore in anthropological examinations of this field. As noted above, within anthropology and related versions of cultural theory, individuality has most commonly been treated as an ideology, especially that of "individualism", and, to a lesser degree, as a question of self-consciousness (Cohen 1994; Cohen and Rapport 1995). In other words, anthropologists and their colleagues have more frequently been concerned with individualism (along with its philosophical opponents, such as communitarianism) as an ideological prescription for the appropriateness of particular forms of social arrangements. There exists a more limited literature examining the other position, that of self-consciousness. But in this volume, we are most directly concerned with yet another facet of individuality: its expression as a form of social action. For it is in its social enactments that individuality carries its most acute risks and costs. To enact forms of personal distinction or to seek recognition of particular versions of individuality is to risk social repudiation or failure. To proclaim forms of personal distinction rather than merely to think them or to prescribe them is to express, implicitly or explicitly, a dependence on others for their mutual recognition, acceptance or emulation of that endeavor. And that dependence intrinsically entails social risk. It is in the calculation and management of such risks that the cultural politics of distinction are manifested in contexts that range from the mundane to the extraordinary. Adopting this approach, the distinction with which this chapter began, namely that between relationalist and individualist societies, is rendered oxymoronic. Individuality, as a form of social enactment, is fundamentally and necessarily relational.

In charting our mission thus, we are by no means proposing that the impetus and workings of social action are inviolably demarcated from issues of ideology or consciousness. But neither can these be treated as homologous. Indeed, the tension between them underpins one of the oldest and most challenging problems pursued within the social sciences, that of social reproduction. In the continuing pursuit of this question there has been a gradual but determined theoretical shift within anthropology and its sister disciplines away from viewing social systems as general and determinative structures that exist in and for themselves and that are imposed on individuals who must abide within and through them. Instead there has been an effort to link micro and macro social levels, to consider systems processually through a generative articulation of individual action with collective structures. Individuals become purposeful agents, actively intervening in the world around them. And yet this effort to recognize individuals as active agents rather than as passive subjects must continually contend with the apparently countervailing effect of power. After all, most people appear to be relatively powerless in controlling, let alone remaking, the social systems that govern so much of their lives.

For Pierre Bourdieu, the effort at reconciling individual agency with power differentials involved a move away from structure to practice. As Ivan Karp has noted, this move helped to flesh out social systems by "providing an analytic frame which allows ethnographers to describe the complex relationships among the agents' strategies, the symbolic forms they invoke in their actions, and the distribution of power in society"(Karp 1986:132). But as Karp and others (Amit-Talai 1996; Reed-Danahay 2005; Collins 2006) have also noted, this focus on action has come at the expense of furnishing an intrinsically unreflexive and unconscious actor, who proceeds as the creature of his or her particular habitus. Bourdieu presents this as:

> Systems of durable, transposable dispositions, structured structures predisposed to function as structuring structures, that is, as principles of the generation and structuring of practices and representations which can be objectively "regulated" and "regular" without in any way being the product of obedience to rules, objectively adapted to their goals without presupposing a conscious aiming at ends or an express mastery of the operations necessary to attain them and, being all this, collectively orchestrated without being the product of the orchestrating action of a conductor. (1977:72)

Individuals are able to act because they take their social contexts as taken-for-granted givens.

In almost diametric contrast, Anthony Cohen's emphasis on self-consciousness asserts the importance of individual reflexivity but at the expense of divorcing it from social action. For Cohen, the dilemma of society is that it is comprised of individuals who, whatever their subscription to apparently common forms, can still hold widely disparate views. "Common forms do not generate common meanings" (Cohen 1994:20). Difference is reconciled with the production of collectivity through the interpretative malleability of symbols that can be stretched to accommodate a wide range of different views and meanings. For Cohen, the articulation of the individual with the social group or society is accomplished interpretatively rather than through social action per se. We might all appear to be doing the same things, but we are not all thinking the same thoughts. Notwithstanding an emphasis on the self as the ground upon which sociality is built, in Cohen's rendering individuality does not necessarily or even usually have much public expression and, therefore, can be held concomitantly without incurring much in the way of social risk. For instance, I may appear to be conforming even while indulging my individual difference in private interpretations. If, for Bourdieu, individual agency is typically exercised without reflecting on or questioning the terms of power constraining it, for

Cohen, individuals are critically reflecting on the social arrangements around them even when seemingly subscribing to them. In spite of the apparent gulf between their positions, neither places much emphasis on the individual who potentially challenges or modifies the structural terms of his or her social engagement.

In contrast to the emphasis on action without reflexivity in Bourdieu's theory of practice and of reflexivity disconnected from social action in Cohen's theory of self-consciousness, Anthony Giddens' theory of structuration attempts to integrate reflexivity with action and to render these potentially constitutive of social structure, albeit not in any simple or readily predictable manner. In this theory, the individual is a reflexive actor whose interventions in the world around her are goal directed and intentional (Giddens 1976, 1991; Karp 1986:134–5). However, interpretation or intention is not sufficient to constitute agency. Rather, agency requires the capacity to intervene as well as the intention to do so (Giddens 1976). But the structural outcomes of these actions are dislocated from the intentions motivating them. "Through this model of structure Giddens strives to show how structure is the unintended outcome of the agent's bringing about of effects at the same time as it is the medium through which those effects are achieved" (Karp 1986:135). Individuals intentionally intervene in the world around them, but they do not knowingly create or even intend to effect the structural outcomes of their interventions:

> The production and reproduction of society thus has to be treated as a skilled performance on the part of its members, not as merely a mechanical series of processes. To emphasize this, however, is definitely not to say that actors are wholly aware of what these skills are, or just how they manage to exercise them; or that the forms of social life are adequately understood as the intended outcomes of action. (Giddens 1976:160)

As Anthony Cohen has cogently noted, this is a highly compromised form of reflexivity (1994:21–2). People intervene in the world around them with intent, they reflexively monitor the outcomes of their behavior, but they do not apparently reflect on or understand the structures or systems which enable their actions and which are affected by their actions. So the actions of knowing subjects shape structure, but apparently their intentions do not!

Yet in the chapters that follow, we find people engaged in an ongoing assessment of larger institutions, systems of social relations, networks, conventions and expectations, all the while seeking to work out the implications for their own life choices. The nature and the consequences of their actions for the structures and systems through which they are operating diverge widely. Some of these actions openly confront wide-ranging social arrangements, others seek to chip away at or slide by the institutions constraining them without directly challenging them, and still others reinvest in existing forms of relations and institutions. But despite this divergence, when people are reflecting on the things that really matter to them, crucial life choices, the basis of their reflexivity fundamentally concerns the larger relations between the individual and the social. They may well miscalculate in making these assessments, but this potential for miscalculation, for getting it wrong, is itself a crucial part of the debates individuals have with themselves in making these kinds of strategic calculations. So whether or to what extent they may miscalculate in assessing the outcomes of their actions cannot be the gauge of the intrinsic ambit of their intentions or the extent of their social awareness. The decision of an Indian widow to attend a family wedding might or might not ultimately reshape the larger set of conventions shaping marriage and gender in Chennai, but as Mattison Mines' case study aptly illustrates, Kalyani's assessment of the context and implications of such an act are hardly innocent of the broader structural implications of her choice.

We therefore agree with Anthony Cohen that people's self-consciousness crucially concerns the larger social arrangements/structures/institutions in which they are implicated. But this reflexivity does have consequence because it is always inflected with the immanence of social action. Even the decision not to carry out a particular course of action is a decision about action. What further lends these considerations poignancy is a consciousness of the inherent risks as well as positive potentiality in any given instance of social action. It is in the interplay between reflexivity with intention, action and consequence (both apprehended and experienced) that social engagement becomes truly authorial and potentially fateful.

This reading of social action, although marching in step with a longstanding scholarly effort to articulate the individual with the social, does not in itself specifically pertain to enactments of individuality. Rather it is a feature of any form of sociality. To the extent that the enactment of individuality is about an engagement with the social, it is subject to the same processes, dilemmas and ambiguities of any form of sociality. But in claiming individuality, people are also engaging in forms of situated action that serve to distinguish actors personally rather than categorically from each other. In doing so, they raise their heads above the collective parapet in ways that may augment the more generic uncertainties and perils of sociality. There's nobody else to hide behind when you seek to draw attention to the particularity of yourself or to some attribute, aspiration, capacity, grievance, accomplishment, or biographical feature of yourself.

It is therefore scarcely surprising to find that claims of individuality can involve some of the most acute and self-conscious readings and working through of the relationship between oneself and the social. Accordingly, a significant theme in most of the chapters in this volume concerns issues of personal *choice* about the nature of social engagement. These include, respectively, anxieties about the limitations or possible adverse consequences of such choices, the assertion of the right to make such choices, or the effort to open up the room for maneuver in which to make them. As noted above, the intended consequences and range of these choices diverge considerably between the situations described in this volume. But all of these instances involve the experiencing of the institutional in an intensely personal manner. Here power is encountered, gauged, reflected on, challenged by individuals. Here individuals are making choices about the nature of their social interventions.

As social analysts, anthropologists continue to participate in a broader scholarly effort to situate individuals as active players in the functioning of social systems, to investigate how persons, rather than omnipotent and anonymous social forces, construct the structures and contexts they inhabit. But this attempt to probe the articulation of the individual with the social is not simply an endeavor restricted to theoreticians. It is also an aspect of our daily exertions as social actors and never more so than when we, and others, distinguish ourselves in one form or another as individuals.

The nine remaining chapters in this volume examine a broad range of cases that explore the claiming of individuality and the cultural politics of distinction. Mattison Mines' chapter examines the personal narrative of a widowed South Indian woman as well as those of three of her closest kin recounting their respective efforts to come together for protection and support following her husband's death. What their narratives or poly-biographies elucidate is not only a shared undertaking, but also in each narrator's story something of the speaker's individuality, of his or her personal character and sense of self. What interests Mines is the combined presence of these two perspectives, the collective and the individual, in the narratives and what this dual sense uncovers about the dynamics of self-awareness and agency. Mines shows that all four of the narratives reveal individuals who believe that to some extent how they conduct their lives is their own choice, but who, nonetheless, seek to show regard for others while moving little by little towards achievement of some of their goals.

Karen Fog Olwig's chapter approaches individuality through the analysis of the life stories of two young people, a brother and a sister, who have grown up on the Caribbean island of Nevis. While involving themselves in a range of relations and activities that reflect and affirm their ability to contribute in socially responsible ways to the collectivity of the family and home, these siblings have also distinguished themselves through various individual accomplishments in the wider society. In relating their experiences to Fog Olwig, they present themselves as individuals who have made their own choices in constructing their lives from their distinct vantage points. They have established their own ways of asserting themselves as human beings, albeit under a more general structure of constraints. Nevertheless, they present themselves as having grown up within a social setting that not only features mutual give and take but that also made them the individuals they are.

Parminder Bhachu's chapter investigates how fashion entrepreneurs in London have constructed new culturally mediated markets. This is accomplished by introducing racialized and politicized styles in a previously stigmatized economy of "ethnic" clothing that features the Punjabi suit or *salwaar kameez*. The careers of these design innovators depend upon their ability to balance the competing demands of distinctiveness with those of cultural belonging. They strive to create designs that are distinct from those offered by competitors while exercising care to respond to the stylistic expectations and social preferences of their customers. Bhachu's account explains how two British Asian designers have managed to reconcile these demands by enlisting their customers' involvement in co-producing distinctively designed *salwaar kameez*. Their success contrasts with the experience of an Indian-based elite designer who, though well known for a distinctive design signature, has focused more upon selling to the "West" than nurturing the individuality and style sensibilities of British Asian women.

Vered Amit's chapter explores the work practices and narratives of Canadian development consultants who in the course of their working lives move frequently between the global North and South. Asking whether, and if so how, claims of individuality can be articulated with larger systemic transformations, Amit probes the ways in which contemporary notions of "flexibility" are connected to the career choices and experiences of a varied range of mobile Canadian consultants. In view of the uncertainties related to these arrangements, how do organizations enlist professionals for this work? Amit outlines two organizational strategies of recruitment. In each case recruits are encouraged to conjoin a specific set of organizational imperatives with a sense of personal commitment. In contrasting the orientations of two sets of traveling consultants Amit shows that in so far as they are able to feel that they are choosing their working conditions, rather than bowing to structural imposition, they can claim as their own even institutional imperatives.

Julia Harrison's chapter interrogates the travels of middle class and upper middle class Canadian tourists as a means for claiming individuality. Claiming to be "not just any tourist", these men and women undertake trips that constitute journeys into the exploration of self. Travel for them becomes a confirmation and sometimes a confrontation with the matter of who "I am". Encounters with new aspects of individuality become an anticipated feature of every trip, for typically these travelers return home to well established routines. Yet within their immediate social circles only rarely does anyone wish to learn any of the details of a trip beyond the fact that it has been completed. Although initially frustrating for travel enthusiasts, the amassing of more and more untranslatable experiences comes to be seen as a form of accumulated "private capital". It serves to afford committed travelers a distinctive and valued identity with which to resume their everyday lives at home.

Deborah Reed-Danahay's chapter reflects upon the ways in which published life stories in rural France deal with individuality. How do these works contrive to reconcile a foregrounding of the self that is characteristic of first-person narrative with a desire to represent authentic, shared peasant backgrounds? The tension between being representative and being individual is readily apparent in these popular autobiographies. Since rural French discourse tends to disparage those who attempt to "distinguish" themselves, someone who singles out his or her individuality in writing or narrating a life history must, in Reed-Danahay's terms, "tread a delicate balance". If one accepts Pierre Bourdieu's theories of habitus and distinction, then the authors of these rural narratives might be said to have obtained through education a secondary habitus that permits them to write about the habitus of their childhood. Reed-Danahay concludes by asking whether this really means that one must be educated in order to become an individual.

Nigel Rapport's chapter provides a rich account of a distinctive fashioning of identity by a resident in the Northern English valley of Wanet. Although Trevor Jeffries took himself, his locality and his way of life most seriously, he was willing and able to satirize all of these through humorous performances in his village pub. In constructing a decidedly popular village persona, Trevor mounted what Rapport terms a "life-project". Defined existentially, this entails an individual giving his or her life a particular character, direction and force. Significantly, Trevor's humor was very much scripted for village insiders about various facets of local lives. Being centrally implicated in local activities and concerns, Trevor's pub performances earned him an appreciative audience. Nonetheless, as Rapport observes, this was very much Trevor's show. He was in control and it was consciously his act, his persona and his world that were presented.

Marie Nathalie LeBlanc's chapter traces the emergence since the mid 1990s of a group of young Muslim pilgrims in Côte d'Ivoire. Among West African Muslims it is expected that with age one's religious practice should adhere more closely to locally prescribed orthodoxy. Embarking upon the *Hajj* or yearly pilgrimage to *Makkah* serves as a crucial marker in this passage, but historically the *Hajj* was expected to be a once-in-a-lifetime event that was to be performed by elders. In recent years, however, becoming a pilgrim has become a condition for the expression of an Arabized Islamic identity among young middle class men and women. Arabizing youths reject the social rules and obligations perpetuated by elders, especially those involving family based marriage rules on the grounds that in Islam one is only required to marry a Muslim. While claims for an Arabized Islam do not bring absolute individualized freedom, they enable younger people to challenge notions of authority based on kinship and age.

In reflecting upon the experiences of those who have returned to Croatia from the diaspora following independence from the former Yugoslavia in 1991, Daphne Winland's chapter poignantly reminds us that claims for individuality are usually caught up in negotiations over the terms of collective belonging rather than of separation. As well as discussing the diasporic national imaginaries that inspired some to become returnees, Winland recounts the motivations of the Croatian government that initially courted them and of their subsequent reception and treatment by homeland Croats. Typically, returnees have experienced varying degrees of shock and disappointment at being configured as the "Other" in their encounters with homeland Croats. Increasingly returnees are marginalized by the state and its vision of the new Croatia, one that differs markedly from those conceived in the diaspora. Seeking to repair the personal embarrassment and costs incurred in opting to reintegrate themselves into the Croatian collectivity, rationales for having chosen to return are reinterpreted as matters of individual preference. Together these experiences lay bare the paradox of the dream of return with return itself.

All of the chapters in this volume portray the efforts of individuals to work through the structural and social parameters mediating their critical life choices. But the stances and decisions described in these contributions diverge considerably. In using the term "distinction" to refer to the objects and outcomes at stake in all of these varied ethnographic chapters, we are employing it in its most general sense of distinguishing one person from others rather than as a connotation of individual status and prestige. On a spectrum of potential opposition between the collective and the individual we find at one end the young Côte d'Ivorian pilgrims to Mecca described by Marie Nathalie LeBlanc and at the other end Karen Fog Olwig's account of the choices made by Carol and Samuel, the two young members of an extended family on Nevis. By identifying with a globalized Islamic *ummah*, the young Côte d'Ivorian pilgrims are directly challenging longstanding traditions of generational authority and asserting their right to make independent and individual choices about marriage. In contrast, Carol and Samuel view their extended generational and peer relations as affording recognition of and enabling their capacity, even at a tender age, to make distinctive personal choices about education, career paths, and even about who they will live with. Between these two poles, we find the efforts by four members of an extended Iyangar Brahman family to work cautiously, bit by bit, without openly challenging "the old ways", towards a different society, one which affords them greater control over their individual lives. Clearly the politics of distinction may be played out with respect to decidedly mundane social arrangements as well as more dramatic alternatives proffered by large-scale social and religious movements.

If Kalyani and the other members of her Iyangar family described by Mattison Mines extend their room for making choices by trying not to draw too much public attention to themselves, the cases described by Harrison, Amit and Rapport involve more open bids for social recognition of distinctive accomplishments, albeit with varying success. In the Northern English valley of Wanet, Trevor Jeffries succeeded in crafting a pub persona that was as idiosyncratic as it was popular, offering an individual vision of a collective village life that changed the normative expectations of those with whom he interacted regularly. The committed Canadian tourists featured in Harrison's account have traveled in a quest for self-understanding and affirmation that they hope will also impart to them a special cosmopolitan status. But their families and friends have little desire to know the details of their accomplishments as dedicated travelers. Similarly, the "international" development consultants with whom Amit's chapter is concerned assert authorship over their unusually peripatetic careers. But they are also aware that the success they have achieved in winning organizational recognition of their capacities as seasoned travelers constitutes a double-edged sword, potentially limiting their room to make choices between international and domestic projects.

The recognition achieved by two British Asian fashion designers has extended beyond the ethnic niche in which they first launched their careers. But, as Bhachu explains, their success has continued to draw on the assertion of a particular diasporic location and clothing tradition as much as on their capacity to distinctively reinterpret this style vernacular in collaboration with their customers. However, the protagonists in the two European situations described respectively by Winland and Reed-Danahay do not appear to have been as successful in reconciling collective and individual identities. In response to the disappointment and rejection attending their "return" to Croatia, Canadian "returnees" end up asserting the individuality of their paths within and sometimes out of Croatia, distancing themselves from the very nationalist categories with which they had originally sought to identify. By virtue of writing autobiographical accounts, the four narrators with whom Reed-Danahay is concerned are distancing themselves from the very rural Auvergne background that they are seeking to represent through these accounts.

In view of the enormous variation and ingenuity in the ways in which people make differing kinds of claims for diverse forms individuality, in their motivations for doing so, and in the consequences of their actions, it behooves anthropologists to treat this field of social engagement with the ethnographic curiosity and analytical rigour that it so clearly warrants.

REFERENCES

Abu-Lughod, L. (1991) 'Writing Against Culture'. In R.G. Fox (ed.) *Recapturing Anthropology: Working in the Present*. Santa Fe, NM: School of American Research Press, pp. 137–62.

Aman (1994) *Aman: The Story of a Somali Girl / by Aman*; as told to Virginia Lee Barnes and Janice Boddy. Toronto: Knopf.

Amit, V. (ed.) (2002) *Realizing Community: Concepts, Social Relationships and Sentiments*. London/New York: Routledge.

Amit-Talai, Vered (1996) 'Anthropology, Multiculturalism and the Culture Concept'. *Folk*, 38:125–33.

Amit, V. and Rapport, N. (2003) *The Trouble with Community: Anthropological Reflections on Movement, Identity and Collectivity*. London/Sterling, VA: Pluto.

Appadurai, A. (1996) *Modernity at Large: Cultural Dimensions of Globalization*. Minneapolis, MN/London: University of Minnesota Press.

Barth, F. (1966) *Models of Social Organization*. London: Royal Anthropological Institute Occasional Papers No. 23.

Barth, F. (ed.) (1969) *Ethnic Groups and Boundaries: The Social Organization of Cultural Difference*. Bergen: Universitetsforlaget.

Bourdieu, P. (1977) *Outline of a Theory of Practice*. Cambridge: Cambridge University Press.

Burridge, K. (1979) *Someone, No One: An Essay on Individuality*. Princeton, NJ: Princeton University Press.

Caputo, V. (2000) 'At "Home" and "Away": Reconfiguring the Field for Late Twentieth-Century Anthropology'. In V. Amit (ed.) *Constructing the Field: Ethnographic Fieldwork in the Contemporary World*. London/New York: Routledge, pp. 19–31.

Carrier, J.G. (1992) 'Occidentalism: The World Turned Upside-Down'. *American Ethnologist*, 19(2):195–212.

Carrithers, M., Collins, S. and Lukes, S. (eds) (1985) *The Category of the Person: Anthropology, Philosophy, History*. Cambridge/New York: Cambridge University Press.

Clifford, J. and Marcus, G. (eds) (1986) *Writing Culture: The Poetics and Politics of Ethnography*. Berkeley, CA/Los Angeles/London: University of California Press.

Cohen, A. (1969) *Custom and Politics in Urban Africa*. London: Routledge and Kegan Paul.

Cohen, A.P. (1994) *Self Consciousness: An Alternative Anthropology of Identity*. London: Routledge.

Cohen, A.P. and Rapport, N. (eds) (1995) *Questions of Consciousness*. London: Routledge.

Collins, P. (2006) 'The Practice of Discipline and the Discipline of Practice'. In N. Dyck (ed.) *Exploring Regimes of Discipline: The Dynamics of Restraint*. New York: Berghahn.

Cruikshank, J. (1990) *Life Lived Like a Story: Life Stories of Three Yukon Native Elders / by Julie Cruikshank in collaboration with Angela Sidney, Kitty Smith, and Annie Ned*. Lincoln, NE: University of Nebraska Press.

Dumont, L. (1986) *Essays on Individualism: Modern Ideology in Anthropological Perspective*. Chicago/London: University of Chicago Press.

Epstein, A.L. (1958) *Politics in an Urban African Community*. Manchester: Manchester University Press.
Fox, R.G. (1991a) 'Introduction: Working in the Present'. In Fox (ed.) *Recapturing Anthropology: Working in the Present*. Santa Fe, NM: School of American Research Press, pp. 1–16.
Fox, R.G. (1991b) 'For a Nearly New Culture History'. In Fox (ed.) *Recapturing Anthropology: Working in the Present*. Santa Fe, NM: School of American Research Press, pp. 93–113.
Giddens, A. (1976) *Modernity and Self-Identity: Self and Society in the Late Modern Age*. Cambridge: Polity.
Giddens, A. (1991) *New Rules of Sociological Method: A Positive Critique of Interpretative Sociologies*. London: Hutchinson.
Goodenough, W.H. (1973) *Culture, Language, and Society*. Reading, MA: Addison-Wesley.
Goodenough, W.H. (1976) 'Multiculturalism as the Normal Human Experience'. *Anthropology and Education Quarterly*, 7(4):4–6.
Gupta, A. and Ferguson, J. (eds) (1997) *Anthropological Locations: Boundaries and Grounds of a Field Science*. Berkeley, CA/Los Angeles/London: University of California Press.
Hannerz, U. (1969) *Soulside: Inquiries in Ghetto Culture and Community*. New York: Columbia University Press.
Hannerz, U. (1980) *Exploring the City: Inquiries Towards an Urban Anthropology*. New York: Columbia University Press.
Hannerz, U. (1990) *Cultural Complexity: Studies in the Social Organization of Meaning*. New York: Columbia University Press.
Karp, I. (1986) 'Agency and Social Theory: A Review of Anthony Giddens'. *American Ethnologist*, 13(1):131–7.
Marcus, G. and Fischer, M. (1986) *Anthropology as Cultural Critique: An Experimental Moment in the Human Sciences*. Chicago: University of Chicago Press.
Mines, M. (1994) *Public Faces, Private Voices: Community and Individuality in South India*. Berkeley, CA/Los Angeles/London: University of California Press.
Mitchell, J.C. (1956) *The Kalela Dance*. Rhodes-Livingstone Papers, No. 27. Manchester: Manchester University Press.
Moore, H.L. (1988) *Feminism and Anthropology*. Minneapolis, MN: University of Minnesota Press.
Morris, B. (1994) *Anthropology of the Self: The Individual in Cultural Perspective*. London/ Boulder, CO: Pluto.
Olwig, K.F. and Hastrup, K. (eds) (1997) *Siting Culture: The Shifting Anthropological Object*. London/New York: Routledge.
Ortner, S.B. (1995) 'The Case of the Disappearing Shamans, or No Individualism, No Relationalism'. *Ethos*, 23(3):355–90.
Ortner, S.B. and Whitehead, H. (eds) (1981) *Sexual Meanings: The Cultural Construction of Gender and Sexuality*. Cambridge/New York: Cambridge University Press.
Rapport, N.J. (2001) 'Anthropology of Personhood'. *International Encyclopedia of the Social and Behavioral Sciences*, pp. 11339–43.

Reed-Danahay, D. (2005) *Locating Bourdieu*. Bloomington and Indianapolis, IN: Indiana University Press.

Rosaldo, R. (1986) *Culture and Truth: The Remaking of Social Analysis*. Boston, MA: Beacon.

Shostak, M. (1981) *Nisa, the Life and Words off a !Kung Woman*. Cambridge, MA: Harvard University Press.

Williams, R. (1983) *Keywords: A Vocabulary of Culture and Society*. New York: Oxford University Press.

2
In the Aftermath of Death: Presenting Self, Individuality and Family in an Iyangar Family in Chennai, 1994[1]

Mattison Mines

On September 16 1993, Kalyani's husband, Narayan, died of complications stemming from a benign brain tumor. This chapter is about Kalyani, an Iyangar Brahman woman, age 38, and three of her closest kin who helped her through the crises of Narayan's illness and death: her mother, Lakshmi, Nalani, her elder sister, and Nalani's husband, Krishnan. My interest in presenting the narratives of these four is to explore how, in the aftermath of Narayan's affliction and death, each represents life and the experience of life among this intimate grouping of others and within the broader society. As a family, they have come together for protection and support and to plan their futures. These efforts are, of course, collective endeavors. But in each narrator's story the reader also observes the speaker's individuality, something of his or her personal character and sense of self, something of the issues that at the moment are the individual's particular concern. What interests me is the combined presence of these two perspectives, the collective and the individual, in the narratives, and what this dual sense – part interactive and argumentative, part internal, self-directed, and personal – reveals about the nature and location of self-awareness and agency in a contemporary, urban South Indian woman's life. I write, "a woman's life", because what the narratives reveal most of all is Kalyani's story.

The event of widowhood is, for an Iyangar woman, far more than a crisis of bereavement. The death of her husband unmoors a woman from social relations, transforming her and denying her positions of merit and value in her marriage house, among her kin, and in the greater society. Widowhood leaves her with relationships that are tenuous and, to a considerable extent, optional, a matter of the attitudes and choices of others. Nothing remains as it was in her life. Her circumstance, therefore, compels the widow to develop a new sense of self and to relocate herself among her relationships.

As emotions began to settle in the months following Narayan's death, in English I separately interviewed each of my four informants with the intent of using the narratives to tell the story of a modern, urban Iyangar family. But what I had not expected was the way in which the four, each talking about themselves, would, when the narratives were taken together, tell the story of Kalyani. The reader will see that I also figure in the narratives as the person being addressed. The speakers often introduce their thoughts by explaining Iyangar attitudes to me, an outsider to their society, or by explaining something of the turmoil they have been experiencing or something of particular issues they are facing. As a family friend, as well as an anthropologist who has known Krishnan, Nalani, and Lakshmi since 1979, my narrators are aware that they are subjects of my study and that they are explaining themselves and their society to me. Kalyani is the exception in that she and I had not met prior to this particular visit. During my previous stays in the city, she and her husband had lived elsewhere. Nalani and Kalyani also have a brother, whom I have met on different occasions over the years, but he and their father, Lakshmi's husband, are rarely principals in the narratives presented below, and I have chosen not to interview them. I omitted Lakshmi's husband because it is his disposition to keep his thoughts to himself, even among the family. Raised in a large, extended household, he learned early to keep his thoughts and feelings to himself as a way of avoiding household conflicts. Kalyani's brother is a peripheral figure in the narratives for a different reason. First, he has only recently returned to Chennai after having lived away for much of his adult life, and, second, his mother, Lakshmi, has long encouraged him to live independently, giving him a less central place in these particular narratives than he might otherwise have held. Having suffered as a young wife living in her husband's extended family, as a mother of a son in a patrilineal society, Lakshmi's aim has been to avoid subjecting her son and his wife to the demands patrilineal custom would allow her and her husband to make. In the narratives, it is Krishnan who has taken on some of the roles that might have been those of Lakshmi's son had he lived with them, but these are roles Krishnan chooses of his own volition.

I figure strongly, therefore, just outside of the reader's imagined field of vision: I am the addressee and listener. Yet, when I read through the four narratives and then juxtapose them, as I have below, I am struck by how quickly each narrator loses their reserve and is absorbed in their particular concerns and relationships. Although each is speaking to me separately, and there are a few things said that would not have been said in front of one or another of the others, for the most part, the feelings, attitudes, and sentiments expressed to me are well known to the others. Indeed, when the narratives are read together, what emerges is each speaker's engagement with others, especially with the other three of this set of four. Presenting themselves, they reveal their conversation and engagement with these others, their empathy, and sometimes their contention with them. The life story, then, is revealed as a kind of response in a form of conversation with the others of this close family set in which each presents his or her argument. Indeed, this is what I believe these four stories are: a kind of conversation or debate rendered to me by each speaker expressing and arguing their perspective. That these stories are a conversation, by which I denote a meaning laden, multidirectional interaction, reveals a feature central to the existential condition of self-awareness: that it is an awareness sustained in social relations, and in this particular situation self-awareness is located among these significant family members. Self-awareness, then, is not located solely within the mind of the individual human being separate from others but expresses the processes of interaction and debate among significant others as the individual interprets them (cf. Taylor 1991; see also Taylor 1989:509). This realization suggests that for the ethnographer who collects personal narratives or life story fragments, it is important to collect the narratives of those individuals who form the principal's intimate circle. In other words, a life history or life story fragment takes form within relationships and is only partial when it is told as autobiography. It is best told as a conversation or debate because awareness is located in conversation and argument with others. It is best told as poly-biography.

THE SOCIAL FIELD OF SELF-AWARENESS

Let me briefly outline four interrelated features that illustrate the advantage of the poly-biographical perspective. First consider the structure of individual awareness as it is expressed during an interview. Collecting personal narratives over the years I have noticed that when a person speaks about him or herself, an important feature of that telling involves the speaker's awareness of themselves as occupying a place in a graded social field of others that is differentiated by the degree of social proximity, or social closeness, these others occupy with respect to the speaker. Thus, during an interview, an informant seeking to describe him or herself might begin by addressing me, an American anthropologist and acquaintance, explaining to me Indian customs. Ours is a limited, relatively unimportant relationship, and they explain to me the social conditions governing their life, setting out for me what are the issues or problems for them. Thus, Kalyani, the young widow, explains Indian attitudes and the limits Iyangar society places on her in her particular circumstance. Her concern is how she will be judged and how she judges her relationships, what's allowed and what's not. Standards and rules are always specific to a particular circle of referents. Explaining Indian custom to me, Kalyani next describes how anonymous others, "the neighborhood", may estimate her. The neighborhood that matters is her caste community and unspecified kin, who observe her daily routines and are familiar enough to gossip. These relationships are constitutive of her sense of self. For, even though the narrator does not see these people observing her, taking notice of her, they are people before whom she can feel proud or embarrassed, victimized or assertive, rebellious or conforming, depending on what she has done or accomplished, what her status is, what her intentions are, and how she feels treated.

Employers and work colleagues may constitute a circle of referents who form an important feature of the speaker's self-awareness, but her sense of self among these is more limited, less complex, if still significant, compared to her sense of self among caste and kin. Yet closer to the speaker are household and family members, mother and father, husband and his kin, sisters and brothers, in-laws, and sons and daughters. Each is a relationship that has its own synchrony, emotional feel, rules, and standards and is central to self-awareness.

As my informant's audience, then, the reader will observe each speaker revealing their sense of self within a complex range of relationships – near to far – each constituted differently and governed by different rhythms, standards, and understandings. One aspect of self-awareness, then, is a sense of one's self at the center of a centripetal gradation, composed of those others who constitute one's social context, and, in addition to the above list, an individual may have relations with other circles of referents as well. But of course this sense of self within a graded field of relationships is just one feature of the speaker's sense of self.

A second feature of self-awareness is the discursive, multivocal manner in which the narrator thinks about his or her relationships with others. When we look closely at a speaker's explanation of their concerns, they will often reflect on their relationship with someone, briefly characterizing a moment of interaction with this person. The speaker might explain the other person's attitude towards them, how this person has spoken to them or has acted towards them. They might also explain how they responded and what they said and what the meaning of the interaction was for them. Yet again, the speaker may simply express an attitude that conveys a reaction to past interactions and experiences, and we recognize that the expressed attitude is a response to earlier interaction or argument. My informants think of relationships in terms of ongoing argument, although, I think, most are not fully aware of this feature of their thoughts. Here I am using the term "argument" not to denote open contention, but to stress that each party in the imagined interaction is understood to have their distinct point of view or agenda, and, consequent to these distinct views, the interaction process or dialogue is itself negotiated and open-ended or contended.

One need not appeal to psychology nor need one get "into" the minds of one's informants to recognize that self-consciousness is expressed in exchanges that constitute human sociality. Argument generates synchrony and discord in social relationships and expresses differences in judgment and motivation among those who share a social field. Self-awareness, therefore, is indeed sustained at least in part outside of oneself in the rhythms, harmonies, and disharmonies of colloquy, but because the actor necessarily participates, it cannot be conceptualized as external to the self nor as located within the logic of a cultural system.[2]

Bakhtin (1981:280ff.) has observed that, as in life, in such an imagined dialogic process, the speaker addresses another, shaping his or her presentation in expectation of a particular kind of response. The speaker, then, anticipates the reception of his or her action or speech and structures what they say or do to answer what the speaker believes the response of the other will be; at least to answer what the speaker imagines the response will be.

But speakers also conjecture future dialogues and interactions, sometimes combining in the imagination past dialogues with possible future action or intercourse. Reflecting in this manner allows the narrator to explore different ways of behaving without actually taking any action. In imagined interaction and dialogue with others, the speaker experiments with different decisions, with taking different attitudes, and with achieving different social positions, seeing how much latitude he or she has to choose, seeing what it would be like to live in another town or to pursue a different career, a different life. What difference would such choices make? To what degree are they constrained from making such choices, to what degree free, and what would others think? This, then, is a third feature of the speaker's sense of self. The narrator depicts him or herself as an actor, who assesses their situation, makes decisions, and not only does things affecting the direction of their own life, but also imagines how particular actions might alter their relationships within their social field.

It is, of course, a normal condition of life that each must choose how they shall act. And, equally obviously, we hold others responsible for their actions. It is no surprise, therefore, that actions taken are often preceded by considerable thought. Thus, in their internal debates, the speakers describe their goals and the process of argument through which they work out their goals. They make life plans and when they reveal their goals, often they rationalize their motivations as well.

This is the fourth aspect of self-awareness: that the individual makes life plans and is motivated to act in particular ways because he or she sets goals and makes plans to achieve those goals. This, of course, does not mean that individuals are autonomous actors. Individuals mostly act in relationship to others. Nor does this mean that individuals are rational actors, setting out goals and then methodically, step by step, carrying out the acts necessary to achieve them. Much human action is contingent, a matter of simply contending with the issues that circumstances bring. And when the narrators do make plans, the steps to achieve goals are often uncertain, more a matter of trial and error and of learning from experience than of sureness. And sometimes motivations are muddied by the emotions surrounding relationships so that the narrators themselves are uncertain why they act as they do. The narrators seem regularly to readjust their behavior. And, of course, no one knows what the consequences of particular decisions will be.

In sum, the four narrators of this upper middle class Iyangar family express their individual self-awareness in argument and debate. The issues at the heart of these dialogues focus on changing constructions of the household, relations among kin, the freedom of women to choose and to act as their own agents, and the emerging sense that responsibility for one's own life should be located in individual choices and self-reliance. The narrators see themselves as participating agents in this transition and as capable of leaving the old ways behind, even if they are not fully ready to do so.

DESCRIBING SELF AND FAMILY: FOUR NARRATIVES

In 1968, newly married to Nalani, Krishnan was a young, neophyte lawyer making only pocket money. In those early days of his marriage, he supported his new family with the rent he earned from the three other flats in the four-plex that was and is his residence. The four-plex had been built by his father and was among the first multiple-flat residences in the city. In 1982, when his father died, Krishnan inherited the four-plex, giving him discretion over the building. Then, in 1987, Lakshmi,[3] his wife's mother, suffered a heart attack, and he proposed she and her husband lease out their house and move into one of his flats. This way, he suggested, Nalani and he could better look after them. Similarly, in 1989, when Kalyani's husband endured his first brain tumor operation, Krishnan also invited them and their two young daughters to move into the complex, reasoning it would be easier for Nalani and himself to assist the ailing and their overtaxed spouses. In this manner, Krishnan has gathered his wife and her kin around him.

Here, then, is a modern household configuration: Krishnan surrounded by his affines rather than his agnates. He and Nalani, the pillars of both sides of the family, providing advice, practical assistance, and succor to the others. Elsewhere in the city this pattern is beginning to repeat itself among other families. These new configurations are innovations designed by their members to preserve modern, independent lifestyles while providing some of the benefits of the patrilineal joint family, but without its constraints and limitations. As Nalani tells me, nowadays people refuse to make the adjustments that make joint family living possible. I had known from earlier visits that Kalyani's marriage had been an unhappy one. Before moving to Madras she had lived with her husband in his parents' house where she had been severely abused by her parents-in-law, who sometimes punished her by locking her in a room for several days without food. Fearing that in her despair Kalyani might harm herself, Krishnan and Nalani confronted Narayan, Kalyani's husband, and told him he must move out of his parents' house or he and Nalani would initiate divorce proceedings. He moved out, but he begrudged being forced to do so.

Separating from his parents, Narayan transferred to Chennai, and, not long after, was there diagnosed with a brain tumor. He had his first operation to remove the tumor in 1989, and after a lengthy period of recovery he returned to work and to normal life. The tumor recurred in 1991, and again he underwent an operation and lengthy recovery. In January 1993, Narayan had his third operation and once more began the slow process of recovery. In late June, just when it seemed he would fully recover and be able to return to work, he suffered a bout of meningitis. Lakshmi says that after that he was a vegetable, unable to speak, feed himself, or recognize anyone. He died in late September at the age of 42. Kalyani was 38.

Nalani – the elder sister

In 1980, with both of her sons in school, Nalani decided to return to college to study law. Krishnan is a lawyer and both his father and Nalani's father and grandfather were lawyers, so it seemed a suitable choice, a way to expand her life after the housebound years of raising her young family. Since joining the bar, she has worked in her husband's law office in the Madras High Court. At the time of the interview Nalani was still experiencing the stress of the previous months. This stress had been further compounded when, shortly after my return, her mother Lakshmi suffered a second heart attack. Nalani was required to minister to her mother's needs, to arrange for her doctor and hospitalization, and subsequently to manage her home care. Adding to her stress, in January her eldest son (b. 1969), who was now living in the USA, indicated that he wanted her to arrange his marriage for the following December. Again, much of the burden fell on Nalani's shoulders. And she was irritated with her son because of his self-interested attitude towards women and because she believed he would blame her, should the woman she chose prove less than satisfactory. Her generation, she often told me, did not blame parents and elders when things did not turn out as hoped. She felt this was because, growing up in a joint family, she and the other children of the household had been left to their own devices. As a result, they developed a sense of being responsible for themselves. Today, parents put lots of pressure on children, and, today, children blame their parents when things don't work out. Also men discriminate against women, she told me. She had tried to teach her sons to be different.

Nalani tells me that when she was interviewed for admission to law college, the interviewers didn't even bother to ask about her professional interests but instead asked her about archaeology, a topic completely unrelated to the issue at hand. "I was not admitted on the first list, although I had first class degrees and an MA. So I went to my husband and said, 'Can you get me in?' He went to some judge, and I was on the second list". Nalani believes she would have been admitted on her own merits, if she had been a man.

Thinking about her son, Nalani tells me that she was married at 18, which was when Brahman women married at the time. She tells me that the attitude of her own two sons towards women is wrong. "I can't be blamed for it. I tried to bring them up with a different attitude toward girls. Varsha [the eldest] feels superior to girls and wants this, this, and this: tall, beautiful, fair, intelligent, but trained in household skills. He sees himself as a gift wrapped package: he thinks, 'I have a good salary potential and don't smoke, drink, or run around'", and, adds Nalani facetiously, "he won't beat his wife".

[The family is different today compared to when I was young.] Grandfather was a tyrant. When he came from court, we'd look out and move to another part of the house. Fifteen people with one bathroom, all going out [of the house] by 9.30 [AM]. It was never a problem.

It would be impossible today.

The younger accepted the authority of elders. Now we're more casual with kids, and kids give less respect. I never had any conversation with grandfather. I tried to avoid him. We kids stayed up on the first floor. Parents and Grandfather never went up. Parents would only come up to sleep. Now you can't tell kids what to do. They always want to know, "Why not?" and kids don't obey. But we did. We had little opportunity to go out. We were always stuck in the house. We were not allowed to play with others. We were never told to study; there was no pressure. Now it is different: there is lots of pressure to study.

Nalani tells me,

We're now in a transition period between the joint family and something new. Now people find it difficult to adjust in the joint family. Attitudes have changed and people have experienced living separately, and there is no support from servants ... By going to work, I've added to my problems. My husband and kids want cooked food. I have to run around and do all the errands, go to the electricity board, go to get the ration card ... Life has become more difficult for women.

I feel relaxed in the office. The office is a peaceful place compared to the house. I used to say, "Let the man relax at home. He's had a tough day at the office". But when I went to the office, I found it a peaceful, relaxing place.

Several months later in another interview, Nalani tells me about the satisfactions she gets from the law. After her marriage, she tells me, she had no ambitions and then in November 1969, Varsha, her first son, was born and in April 1971, her second son, Srinivasan. "So by the time I'd learned to tie a nappy, I knew I was pregnant [again]. Then came growing up and tying shoe laces". However, by 1979, she told me she felt that life was passing her by.

I thought the children were still small ... so I'd do something that would help my husband. So I joined law college. There were so many family commitments: Krishnan's nieces getting married, people coming to Madras for operations. So I thought I really couldn't manage a career. There were lots of family demands.

In 1983, Nalani enrolled as a lawyer, working in her husband's office.

After starting work, I didn't go full tilt. The kids were still small and many people were still visiting. Often I'd stay home. It's only in the past four or five years that I've been doing regular work.

Although I'm intelligent, it was only after I started as a lawyer that men started showing me respect. Sometimes I feel that I'm playing second fiddle [to Krishnan] plus I [must] subdue my temperament [because I] must treat him as [my] Senior and also follow his rules [for the office]. It's a delicate position being the Senior's wife. I have to be subdued. Even now I feel I have to restrain myself so as not to offend anyone in the office or outside. Some days I want to murder the clerk because he's so inefficient, but I can't because I'm Mrs Krishnan. But others can strangle him. Even sympathy ... Krishnan doesn't want to show favoritism. But I want to prove myself ... not that I'm his wife, but that I can accomplish something. I feel like I have to be invisible all the time. If I had joined elsewhere then I would have made my own achievements.

Nalani goes on to say that if she were abrasive, it would make things difficult. Consequently being unobtrusive "saves lots of trouble. If I show I'm angry, then I'm the boss's wife. [I behave like I do] also because Krishnan is like this". She tells me it is Krishnan's style to keep his own counsel and to avoid stirring envy. At first the judges were unaware that she was Krishnan's wife.

> Slowly I started working in court, so people got to know me as a lawyer [initially, then as Krishnan's wife]. At first colleagues were struck by the difference between my personality and Krishnan's reserve. But in the workplace I had to adjust to his complexes. Also the work built up so he needed more and more help. I worked carefully so as not to make any glaring mistakes and not to anger judges. Also when I joined, it really made a difference in the reputation of the firm. I'm not sure why ... but perhaps it was that there was so much work that he needed his wife to work. It took some time for people to come to see that I had come to stay and that I had come to do my own work and not to borrow from his reputation ... And that I didn't throw my weight around.

Nalani pauses, then starts to tell me about being the only woman among three men in the house. "I tried to show my kids that as a wife and mother that I did things out of choice. I never minced matters". She observes that she never had the joint family problems of her mother's sort (see Mines 1994:159–65).

One thought is triggering another. Again Nalani starts to tell me about how values in India are changing. I know she is concerned about choosing a bride for her son Varsha. Also Kalyani, who is living with their mother and father in the adjacent flat, isn't getting along with her mother. There is constant friction between the two, and, to complicate matters, Kalyani's eldest daughter (aged eleven), a good student until her father's death, is not doing well in school. I gather she has been misbehaving at home. It all has to do with Narayan, Nalani explains. Everyone has been unbalanced by his death. "Kalyani", she tells me,

> was a brilliant student and doesn't blame her mother for her [unhappy] marriage. Now kids would blame their parents. Once the kids [Nalani's sons] got angry at Krishnan. They wrote him, "Give us credit for some intelligence and honesty. At 22 [years] you did this, you did that ..." [that letter] left a mark on my memory. They blame. It angers me. I don't blame ... Varsha [Nalani's eldest] has now asked us to find a girl. So he's passed the buck.

Nalani feels if the marriage is arranged, then he might later blame her. "If he makes his own choice, then he takes responsibility for himself. But he says, 'No, it is too hard to make a choice knowing only a handful of girls and with no one to consult' ".

Later Nalani tells me,

I've been thinking for a long time: "Could I have lived my life differently?" Sometimes things happen too easily. I wonder if I missed out of some of life's experiences. [Really] the only other thing I thought about doing was teaching in college. But I don't think that would have been any better.

Earlier she had told me that she liked to do everything she did well. That she was often frustrated.

I have had a lot of trouble making ends meet [that is, having time for everything]. I involve myself in everything and am frustrated because I'm unable to cope ... My mother falling ill, Kalyani's husband, Narayan. I have to learn to let things slide. If I can't cook, I can send out to get something to eat. I'm having to let things go for the first time. If I go to court and I'm [just] sitting, then I feel frustrated because there are things at home that need to be done. Frustrated!

When Nalani talks about living her life differently, I remembered how once many years before, in 1979, she had ruminated with me about divorce and the social price a woman paid should she divorce. I now ask her if divorce was one of the things she thought about. She remembers the occasion some 15 years before and responds:

In 1979 my talk about divorce had to do with Kalyani who was having a hard time in her marriage. The whole family told Narayan that if he wanted to, he could walk out [of the marriage]. We told him that we weren't interested in a marriage that was all suffering. Also, at that time, a cousin, a doctor, had chosen to marry an American, [which caused a] big upheaval in the family. But Varsha [Nalani's son, now living in the States] says she's much nicer than the wife the family chose for another cousin.

Kalyani's parents-in-law were cruel to her. They wouldn't feed her. Narayan was always taking sides ... shouting at her. We found them cruel. [They] locked a small boy out on the terrace [without food or water]. Kalyani was quite terrified of the family.

Narayan became a general manager at 35; he was very capable. But Narayan didn't treat her [Kalyani] well. The whole family [Nalani's] saw the problem: Kalyani couldn't live with her in-laws. Narayan couldn't live without them. So we thought the earlier the two were separated, the better. [Our thinking was, she] should not be put in a position where she can't escape. She might commit suicide. The whole family felt that she should leave, even my father. And the family went to Narayan and told him. Surprise![4]

Kalyani is a real life heroine. Kalyani is a very enterprising, gutsy person. Mother feels guilty [for arranging the marriage] so she finds fault with Kalyani for not knowing how to tackle her husband. [And, after he left his parent's house,] Narayan also felt guilty that he didn't take care of his parents. He thought that he'd sided with his wife against his parents, so he had lots of guilt.

I lost five kilos during Narayan's last illness, and I haven't gotten it back. I feel that I get too involved. I feel that I don't take things as they come. I get too involved. It has been hard on my health and my mentality.

Krishnan – Kalyani's brother-in-law

Krishnan is one of my closest friends, a man whom I greatly respect. To Nalani's rapid-fire wit and quick humor, Krishnan brings a quiet reserve. Generous and considerate of others, in the High Court, which is where he has his practice and maintains an office, he is known among judges and lawyers for his integrity and for always being prepared. He is an effective advocate and a formidable opponent. Krishnan is proud of his reputation and has worked hard to develop it and to maintain it. In his office, he teaches his style and approach to law and the bench to his juniors. Although I often had discussions with Krishnan, the interview below occurred on May 18 1994, when we were talking about the sense of personal reward that comes from commitment to work and to kin.

Shortly before I arrived in Chennai, Krishnan had been elevated to Senior Counsel. In September 1993,

I was sitting in court waiting for a case, when X, a friend, said to me, "Come on Krishnan, we'll both become Senior Counsels". We had both joined the bar at the same time, but we had not had much interaction. Why should he pick on me? Nalani, too, doesn't know ... These are some of the things that give you mental satisfaction, that you've achieved something and it's recognized.

I told him "Let me think about it". I told Nalani, but I didn't very seriously consider it. Then the next week: "What are you doing? I got the papers with a judge proposing and a Senior Advocate seconding". He didn't give me any time. The papers are placed before the full complement of judges, and they must unanimously support an advocate.

So on the 15th morning [of September] I submitted my application.

Krishnan had thought that the next day [the 16th] was new moon day [*ammavashiya*], an auspicious day,

but on the 15th morning my friend called and said, "Stupid fool, the 15th is *ammavashiya*". [So I submitted my papers on the 15th.] On the 16th Kalyani's husband passed away – a serious blow for all. We were taken unawares.

From the 16th to the 29th there were ceremonies to be performed by a male [ideally a son], but Kalyani has only daughters and Narayan's people were not keen[5] about it because his brother has a crippled hand. So I took it on myself to do the ceremonies for 13 days.

As a result, Krishnan only returned to court on the 30th and that day learned that he had been elevated to Senior Advocate.

I hadn't even thought of being a Senior Advocate. Someone else had thought of it. It gives me satisfaction that our efforts have not been in vain. It is also why I have some faith in something beyond me.

After a death in the house, for one year we perform a [monthly] ceremony in the house. I had arranged for a Brahman. I fixed up an old Brahman to come to our house every month on the date fixed for Narayan, the first day after *ammavashya*. The Brahman would come, and I'd give the *bhishai* donation (coconut, rice, and vegetables), plus some rupees. He was coming regularly, then suddenly this man passed away. The next day was the ceremony day. Not all Brahmans will accept [an appointment to do this ceremony]. You won't believe it ... On the next day, an old Brahman came – at 7.30 AM. He asked Nalani's father whether this was the address. [He was looking for someone else and had come to the wrong address.] I gave *bhishai* and fixed him up for [the] subsequent months.

Who made him come? ... and on that day? He'd come to the wrong address. I feel these ceremonies are as important as the marriage rites. There is nothing degrading about it. I am only too happy to perform this. I don't want to have someone tell me or ask me to do this. On Narayan's death I took the responsibility. It was my decision. No one else wanted to do it, either. No one objected.

In 1989, when Narayan first fell ill and needed surgery, I asked them [Kalyani and Narayan] to shift from the flats opposite the Woodlands so that we could all be together and help. The first operation was in '89, the second in '91, and the third in '93.

Describing these events, Krishnan spoke with deep feeling. Choked by emotion, he was unable to speak. After a long pause, he changed the subject back to his experiences before the court.

Lakshmi – Kalyani's mother

My interview with Lakshmi occurred on May 27 1994. She tells me that when Narayan became ill, she moved in with Kalyani to give her "moral support. She was mentally run down". But then, a few weeks previous to our interview, she herself suffered a second heart attack.

After my son-in-law's death, I have not been keeping well. I worry about how Kalyani'll manage with two girls. It gives me a lot of mental strain when I think about that. Life has become unhappy now. [Narayan's] disease affected the whole family, and the children, though they can't express it verbally. At Narayan's birthday, she [Kalyani] was crying the whole day. It has affected Nalani also ... pulled her down. She's not healthy. So many things happen in life that you don't expect that upset daily life.

It was so difficult to get Kalyani to go to the office again. She had run and hid herself. Also we have customs ... [a widow is] not supposed to go to anyone's house for one year [after her husband's death]. [Kalyani] herself doesn't want to go out. She's afraid of the gossip. She just goes to the office and comes back. That's all. We were at each other's throats. She must get accustomed to making her own decisions and tackling her own problems. She has to be able to be alone and handle her own affairs. I feel that she should be strong enough to ignore old foolish customs. I'm forward thinking. I'm very forward in my views now. It's all foolish customs.

Men were so dominating. They made women live subdued lives and not remarry. Even now my husband's views are old fashioned. But he can't change because he was brought up like that. Even now he expects me to cook and take care of the household, even at this age. I ask him to go stay with our son for one month so I can get rest. But he says, "No". He doesn't want to. "If you think I'm a burden to you, I'll go to an old man's home". Men should realize that women are not servants ... except for this old man, who doesn't change and doesn't want to change.

Lakshmi tells me, "The best thing in my life was getting my first son-in-law [Krishnan], who is like a son to me. He is very fond of us. He is so nice to me and my family. I like him [like] my son ... ."

Lakshmi's thoughts turn to Narayan.

He was a nice person and died so young, and he had a top post in his office. And just to die like that – suddenly – it was a big blow to our family.

Kalyani's in-laws don't care. They don't help her in any way. How will she marry and educate two daughters? Everything she must do herself. I worry about that ... .

Son-in-law was stubborn. In certain ways, he had his own way. He was very clever and had a good name in the office. But he'd do what he wanted. For a highly educated man, he was very conservative. Most men in India are like that. Dominating. Some are adjusting. The view is still there that men should dominate women. He was a dominating type. When he got married, he said his parents were old and so won't live long ... so [he wanted] to do what they said. His grandmother is 98 and washing her own clothes! Now he's dead and they still live. They spoiled his life, also. He moved out because Kalyani and her mother-in-law didn't agree. So they were living separately. But they were not kind; they dominated and ill-treated her.

In the joint house, every day was unpleasant. Two or three times they brought her to me and left her. So I said I wouldn't bring her back to them. I feared Kalyani might do something desperate ... suicide or something. Everyone was afraid. I thought I would not send her back to live in a hell like this. So I thought: educate her and get her a good job, and then let her live separately ... .

But [instead] she went off without telling me. Still people think that once you marry you can't divorce and remarry. Most still think remarriage is not possible.

The in-laws have never given any presents to the grandchildren [i.e., Kalyani's two girls]. They have never visited; they show no interest in them now. When [Narayan] was in hospital and talking, she [his mother] visited. But when he stopped talking, she didn't come again. And when he died, they came only for one half hour. You never run across a person like her! A terrible person!

Even on the first day I met her, she had two faces to show. She spoke so nicely and relatives and friends called to say the son was a nice person with good habits – he didn't drink, smoke, or have bad habits – that he was coming up well in his office. I didn't know about the parents ... .

[Kalyani's] mother-in-law threatened her, locking her in a room or on a balcony for three or four days without food. She [Kalyani] had diarrhea for 15 days. They wouldn't take her to hospital even though there was a hospital free right across the road. She [Kalyani] couldn't even stand up. When [the mother-in-law] had a daughter-in-law, she got rid of her servants and made Kalyani do the work. Kalyani's skin was red ... just flesh. I was horrified. That was the time I refused to send her back. She was using some corrosive powder for cleaning. The mother-in-law also lost a daughter ... because of neglect and she gave her no medical aid. She did not shed even a tear. Ten days later she celebrated the father's birthday. Now, four months after her son's death, no one has bothered to come and see Kalyani ... no one has turned up yet. I can't understand how [she] can't like grandchildren. She's only after money.

Now I have given [my] jewels to her [Kalyani]. Even [my] daughter-in-law [son's wife] says to give as I like to Kalyani.

Lakshmi and her husband sold their house to a developer, who built an apartment building on the site. They now own three flats in the building. "I will give one flat to Nalani and the rest to Kalyani because there is no one to earn in her family but her. She's in a better situation now". It is apparent that Lakshmi is thinking about Kalyani's daughters and the great expenditure their marriages will require.

"When I had Kalyani, I was crying: 'Why a second girl?'" Nalani was her first child.

Father said that when Kalyani was grown, the costly marriages would have gone ... not to worry. But in fact marriages are more expensive. It is just a waste. Everyone talks about how it is [a waste], but when it comes to their own son's marriage, it's a different matter. When my son married, I myself didn't want a dowry. It burdens parents. The man should be able to support [the family]. My son said we shouldn't buy furniture or anything. But the girl's parents were in the cinema business and wanted things to be big. I don't know what they gave. So ... the result is our relationship is good. One daughter can put parents in debt.

Krishnan's father ... such nice people ... Character is what is important. "Money", he [Krishnan's father] said, "the old women will come and ask you to do something. Just ignore them". After this marriage [Nalani and Krishnan], I don't know how I managed to fix up Narayan.

Kalyani – widow

After Kalyani and Narayan had moved to Chennai, Kalyani taught in a private school for a while. But then, when her husband became ill, she was forced to resign. She started looking for work that would give her the flexibility that she needed. As luck would have it, she landed a part time job working as a copywriter for an advertising firm. It was quite small and did not have much work. Because it did not, Kalyani found the flexibility she needed and the opportunity to learn about the trade. When she was able to handle more work, she had the skills, as well. When an opportunity arose to move to a larger firm, Vibravision, she took it.

I wasn't willing to compromise on the children's care. I [didn't] want to entrust them to an *ayah* or put them in a crèche or something like that, because I don't know what values, what morals, they [might] have, and I [did] not want them to feel neglected. And some of our magazines here in fact are terribly angled against working women. They think they are out only to get money for cosmetics and have a gala time and to spend on, you know, saris and stuff like that, just for extravagance and not for anything else. They don't really think there is a need for women to work unless she needs some money and so you have, maybe, you have guilt feelings also, and you wouldn't want to neglect the children to go out to work. So, I wanted the cake, wanted to have the cake and eat it too. Fortunately for me, it has worked out, though I have to be patient and really struggled because I had no godfather, no one to introduce me to the business. I have to make my way out of my own merit and hard work. It is a lot of hard work, to learn a new profession, to be good at it. It takes a lot of effort ... I want to be the best.

[H]ere there are, you know, stereotypes, "this is how you should behave, this is what you should be, this is the only thing that is right for you, this is the only way your children should be brought up", you know. So I feel ... if it were possible to move to a more open society [I would] because I feel at times that I am being dragged back by people here ... strong types, who are holding you back and though you may be convinced of what you are going to do, it is not that I am going to do something rash or sensational or, what do you say, scandalous, but ... just maybe going out or maybe driving a car, maybe just wearing your *bindi*, or ... just looking smart, may raise a lot of eyebrows. People may just look on the surface and decide that you ... don't have feelings, or ... you ... are not behaving as a widow should behave. They have their own conceptions, and sometimes I find that my ideas are not the same. I changed faster than the world has around here ... Brahmans like we have lots of do's and don'ts, which they very firmly believe in, and they don't mind stuffing it down your throat ... it offends you, it hurts you, it upsets you. You feel, "Oh, God!, why do I have to take this? It's not necessary". Why can't people live and let live? They are so ready to pass judgment.

[The] problem is here there are a lot of taboos, you know, inauspicious and auspicious, portents of some things are good and [of] some things are bad. So, a widow comes outside ... it is bad. That [judgment] is valid here. It's valid in Bombay. It's valid in Calcutta. It's valid in Delhi. So what's the point of jumping from the frying pan into the fire, jumping into a new city, where language, the people, the culture may be different and feeling alien and also being made to feel cursed. It is not going to really make a difference in which city in India [I am].

Here I'd have family support. As you see, I live in [an] adjoining flat to my sister; brother is just around the corner; my parents live downstairs ... [H]aving two daughters also makes a difference, in the sense that it isn't safe really to send them out in the night ... Now I am forced to do all the jobs ... getting shopping or stuff like that, being responsible [for my daughters]. It really isn't safe here ... I don't know if we are hearing more about it nowadays or if it is that the world has become more perverted. Even small, young children aren't very safe any more, and I would hate to expose my children to any kind of perverts or any kind of unpleasantness that would ... scar them for life and be traumatic. So the fact that I do have two daughters and I do want to make sure that they are in no way endangered by the criminal elements or whatever, that also has a lot to do with my opting for a cushioned environment ... because if there is an emergency, I can always call on my brother, or brother-in-law, or my father – which I would find a problem in a strange city.

I ask her, does she ever think of getting married again? In reply she says,

No, I don't think so ... The first marriage as such was a big problem. Probably I wasn't equipped for it. [We were] still a joint family. The in-laws were terrible and half the time I didn't know what was going on. It's like a horror movie sometimes ... mm ... a lot of hassles ... Afterwards, the person [i.e., Narayan] fell ill, and I am not the person to ditch or shirk responsibilities. So I tried to cope the best way I could. But it has really been a terrible experience ... I think even if I do get remarried, which is a remote, a very remote possibility, it would probably endanger the future of my daughters. Being born ... in [a] Brahman family ... and their in-laws to be will, in addition to looking at the fact that they lost their father, think I am living in sin, even though married to another man and so ... maybe the daughters are slutty like the mother ... that's how it becomes true. It's just not done. So I don't think it would be worthwhile [unless] something really ... cataclysmic happens to make me change my mind. Even then there will be a whole lot of other people who will tell me not to do it, and it is going to be very tough. I don't know if I have the energy or the inclination or the enthusiasm any more ... The fact that we have not ... come down in the world significantly [after Narayan's death], it really has put a lot of backs up.

[Now, I tell myself] think of the plus points. You have a job, you have a career, you are not out in the streets, you have enough monetary backup. So you have to get on with life. It's very difficult. You do come across people who hurt you, maybe unintentionally. There are a lot of taboos, which you would rather keep away from. I still don't attend weddings. I don't go to the temple. I don't visit friends or relatives because for a year or so we are not supposed to, I believe. So I would rather not find out. I would rather not go there and ... face a snub. I don't feel it's necessary. Why should I? I have had enough hassles in life. So, why go there and wonder if they've turned away or maybe [I've] imagined [the] slight ... ah ... maybe they don't mean to hurt but they do hurt you all the same. So there are a lot of things I still can't do or rather that I don't want to do. So, OK, fine ... like wear flowers, I can probably wear flowers. I do love them. I love jasmines. Now it gives me a creepy feeling to look at them. I think from a state of hurt and shock, I have moved to a state of acceptance ... [L]ooking back on all the battles and in-laws and husband and death and two children and a lot of calamities ... too many, I think I have done okay, finally. Well, it has taken me a very long time to get there from 19 [when Kalyani married] to 38, but, then, the world isn't all that easy. At least I got somewhere.

There is a long pause. I can see that Kalyani has begun to cry softly.

NALANI AND KRISHNAN: REFLECTIONS ON BEING PILLARS OF THE FAMILY

On more than one occasion, Nalani has told me how family members come to Krishnan to seek his advice. Relatives from all over the state come to them, she explains, because over time they have learned they can come to Nalani and Krishnan with their problems and it will go no further. Also Krishnan is nonjudgmental in his demeanor.

Krishnan is slow to react, but careful in his advice. People know he works hard as a lawyer and is very loyal to the family. He never lets them down, and he doesn't let secrets go any further. The nephew that married the American – he called up and asked me to talk to his mother. He knew we wouldn't spoil things by talking to others. We tackle other people's problems. They figure things will stop with us and spread no further. Krishnan listens and doesn't comment. We're always here and everyone [in the family] knows they can depend on us. We're stable and mature ... Even little kids ask Krishnan, "Who gets to sleep under the fan?" As his wife, it is hard to know what he thinks. But for outsiders, they find him good [in his advice].

Krishnan gives an example:

My sister-in-law [Kalyani] and mother-in-law [Lakshmi] came here and asked us to draft mother-in-law's will, even though she knew we had an interest in what went to sister-in-law. But they knew that we wouldn't pass anything on.

I couldn't have avoided the role [of becoming the center of the family]. It was put on me. We had all lived together and grown affectionate together. Also I was in Madras and Madras is strategically placed.

Nalani, too, has a reputation for keeping her own counsel. She tells me she never talked about her in-laws to her own siblings. She says, when she first married, they were dying to know all about her father-in-law: how much he made, how he treated her, and so on. Also, she says, she never complained about her sisters-in-law, or about kin staying with them, even though it was hard. She says,

It would have made things difficult for me and for Krishnan, each in our own way. So I have never said anything about anyone (of the relatives) that can hurt anyone.

When Krishnan's father died, he left the Madras property to Krishnan. Krishnan thought this was not really fair to his brother. But no one fought. Everyone knew that if he or she complained about Krishnan getting the Madras property, then Krishnan would have thrown the property back at them. He would not have taken anything. There is no way to divide property equally. It is unusual for brothers not to fight about the division, but this has kept the family together. We have affection for one another. We never miss going for important [family] functions to Cuddalore and [other places]. We go when necessary.

Nalani tells me, "I feel the burden of caring for all these people. When it's a happy occasion, then I don't mind. But sickness and death, these really drain you".

CONCLUSIONS

What emotional intensity these final sentences have when read at the conclusion of the other narratives. When the narrative of a single informant is juxtaposed with those of significant others, it takes on intensity and meaning. These added voices also enable us to see the speakers changing their circumstances through dialogue, exchange, and debate. Seen from multiple perspectives, the life story is made three-dimensional. This three-dimensionality is an outgrowth of the poly-biographical technique and is its strength.

Consider the poly-biographical nature of the above narratives. The metaphor that comes to mind is of a human scale solar system. Each individual is his or her own being, but the group of four is held together by the strong forces of mutual social and emotional involvement, a gravitational pull that is unbreakable because each narrator's sense of self is an aspect of the synchrony, rhythm, and debate generated by their interaction. Remove any one of the four from the narrative of any of the remaining three, and it is plain to see that elision distorts the narrator's story, makes it disconnected, atomistic, and only partially intelligible to the observer. Among the four, Krishnan and Nalani are the mainstays of the family, providing support. But Kalyani is the central figure of concern that unites their thoughts. She gives the grouping its focus during this fateful year. Later, we can imagine, there will be other issues that generate the pull that holds these four together in colloquy and rhythm and another member of the group may be then the focus. Here, during this period, Narayan's death and the swirling aftermath, resettling the emotions of children, supporting Kalyani through her crisis, and, together – all of them, especially the women, rethinking the options allowed for a widow, but also for all women – these are their mutual concerns. We see them working together to change the status of women, to give women more options.

Yet within this rhythm of intercourse, each of the four narrators also has their independent story to tell, their own perspective, personal issues, and assessment of how things are and of how to address them. Simply enough, each has their own life to lead; each has their own identity, and each has relationships with other individuals not counted among these four, who are features of their separate self-awareness. And each has their character, upon which the narrators sometimes comment. Each has their individual sentiments, aspirations, grievances, anger, and manner of expressing love for the others and for the family as a group. It is easy to recognize each narrator's individuality in the tellings.

These two aspects of the self – part collective, part separate – are entwined features of being a person. Take the narratives together, and the fullness of relationships takes form and we begin to understand what is happening and, perhaps most important, we recognize what it is that the four are attempting. They seek to change things for women. The four are not rebels, but they plan a rebellion in order to make room for Kalyani and to give her a future. The processes of self-consciousness presented in the narratives are those of internal and actual interpersonal argument and exchange, which lead to the making of plans, affecting all of them. Thus, we see in the narratives the four aspects of self-awareness: the self sustained in a graded social field of relationships; awareness that takes form in argument; the use of real and imagined exchange and debate to think through alternative ways of behaving and to choose and set goals; and, finally, the narrators' sense that they are agents of their own lives and aware participants in social change.

But, of course, the individual's ability to choose and to affect society is always constrained. Normally, when a person fantasizes future action, their thoughts include awareness of social and existential limits. In Chennai, such existential definitives include an individual's sex, age, caste, social class, kin, and historical moment, aspects of being beyond the individual's control. Also existential are shared understandings or conceptual frameworks, technologies of the self, as Foucault has conceived them (Foucault 1983; see also Taylor 1989:509; Ortner 1991).

Social constraints are the outcome of human sociality. There are, in addition, laws, institutional structures, ethical and moral conventions and practices, public opinion, and etiquette. By defining the form choices should take, these facilitate human planning and action even while they limit choices (Giddens 1994; Elias 2000). Etiquette, public opinion, moral codes, and law are not necessarily concordant, we recognize. These are separate systems of meaning and may be complexly opposed in different circumstances.[6] The status of wife has certain rights before the law, for example, but the widow's status may have none, this status being defined by etiquette, moral codes, and public opinion. These limitations to human choice are also changeable things, of course. And the individual is often motivated to bring about changes, interested action being a source of politics in personal and in public life. Kalyani thinks of escaping the limits of society by moving to another city, but then dismisses the idea when she realizes that wherever she might live in India widowhood is considered inauspicious, and in Chennai her status as a widow is counterbalanced by the advantage of family support. In her narrative, Kalyani also weighs the influence of social rank and relative power in her interaction with others. Rank and power, too, are crucial features of choice because the socially powerful and high ranking may both be more constrained in some dimensions of their lives and also have available to them a greater range of choices. Also often overlooked is the fact that persons of high rank sustain their sense of self within social fields that are potentially much more extensive than those of lower ranking persons. Regardless, when either a low status person or a high status person acts in alliance with others, the organization of support multiplies the social effect of individual agency. This is how an individual within a set of relationships may initiate social change.

Social constraints come to mind when the actor conceives of behaving in ways that might test social limits. Planning her action, Kalyani assesses how others will judge her as a widow should she choose to behave in a range of different ways that she arrays before her imagination: wearing flowers and a pretty sari, driving a car, remarriage, even, during this first year of her widowhood, visiting friends and kin. But notice that the thought processes of dialogic interaction generate a high level of self-consciousness concerned with judging and planning actions. This observation stands in contrast to social theory that hypothesizes that the principles governing how to behave appropriately and meaningfully – Bourdieu's habitus or "feel for the game", is a prime example (e.g., 1990:79–80) – is knowledge that is largely internalized and out of normal awareness. Certainly, such lack of awareness is true of much human behavior – of acquired tastes that express one's education and class, for example. But, as a concept, habitus overdetermines human behavior and ignores the significant, everyday human practice of debating behavior, which is also an important feature of how humans live their lives (cf. Sewell 1999).

Consider the notion of habitus. For Bourdieu, habitus is what gives human practice its predictability and society its conformity. Consequently, Bourdieu's actor is much more a player whose success depends on his feel for the game and on his player's skills than he is a conscious thinker capable of weighing options through dialogue, leading to action that initiates social change. "'Habitus is not fatal', [says] Mr. Bourdieu. 'But unfortunately it can move only within very limited parameters'" (*New York Times* 2001, A15, A17). By contrast, Kalyani reflects that it is unlikely she will remarry because of how it might affect her daughters, but she chooses multiple ways of acting that are contrary to what she knows is expected of widows. Her success opens the way for others to follow.

Part of the problem with the game metaphor of social behavior is that it not only suggests daily social life is too fast moving and complex for thoughtful self-awareness, it also assumes that society is set or that society's grammar for action is set because it is internalized. But what these narratives reveal is a narrowly focused form of reasoning, a multivocal, multidimensional way of thinking that is characteristic of social relations and of argument in which relationships are in fact negotiated and open to change, even in the face of counter-efforts to prevent change.[7] One recognizes the human as an agonistic actor, one who has the potential to act not as a "rational actor", but nonetheless with reason and so consciously to participate in the processes of social change (Mines 1999).

Among the four, Lakshmi takes the most radical position when it comes to rebelling against the existing social order: she dismisses traditions that keep women down and argues that a woman should be educated, self-reliant, and ignore what others say. She feels that if one is strong, then one can ignore public criticisms. The changes she advocates are what others want too, she feels, and so why not throw off the shackles of customs that limit and control women? One also realizes that she feels she is partially responsible for Kalyani's troubles because it was she who arranged her marriage. She believes she should have investigated more carefully what Narayan and his parents were like.

Kalyani is much less sure about what she can do; she is still playing out different scenarios in her mind. "If I do this ... then this might happen". But in her actions she nonetheless defies several of what she senses are the expectations of conservative neighbors and kin. She tells us that, as a widow, she has put people's backs up because she has not come down in the world. Instead she is pursuing a career that she enjoys, a career that has the possibility of providing her with professional success, and one that she finds fulfilling. Also she is learning to drive a car, despite the gossip of neighbors. A few months after her interview, she did again attend an auspicious family function, her nephew Varsha's wedding, and she began again to wear jasmine flowers and fashionable saris. All these are acts that run counter to the norms surrounding widowhood conceived as inauspicious.

Nalani, who when speaking of others, speaks obliquely of her own concerns, is a key figure in encouraging her sister, in helping her to cope with her adjustments, and in assisting with the emotional support of her daughters. Of course, she also gives support to Lakshmi. Nalani reflects on her life and wonders if she might have done things differently. One senses that she does so to reassure herself that she has not just let her life take its own course. She wants her life to be of her own choosing. Later, when her son married, she used the wedding to involve Kalyani in what is an auspicious function from which widows are normally excluded. This iconoclastic act announced to kin and to friends that they and the bride's family had rejected the notion that Kalyani was made inauspicious by her widowhood. The wedding photographs show her a smiling participant in this most propitious of family events. We see, then, in these three women's narratives and actions a reworking and repositioning of a widow's place in society.

Krishnan, for all his quiet reserve, also plays a powerful role supporting the agency of these women. It is he who makes the creation of this new form of family a reality by inviting his affinal kin to live in the apartment complex that he owns. And it is he who takes over responsibility for Narayan's funeral and monthly memorial rituals. Both are actions that are unusual, if not unique, in patrilineal Tamil society. Funerals and memorial rituals are inauspicious and polluting functions. But, likening these rituals to marriage, Krishnan dismisses such cultural determinism. It gives him great satisfaction to assist in these ways, and Krishnan's actions express the special affection he feels for this, his extended affinal family. For Krishnan, the sense of affection gives meaning to relationships, and such a sense has an important place in his professional life as a lawyer as well. To be recognized as prepared and good at what he does, to be viewed with affection, pleases him and gives meaning to both his private and public life.

All four of the narratives reveal individuals who believe that to some extent how they lead their lives is their own choice. They see themselves as poised between an older, more conservative society and a more open one that allows them greater control over their individual lives. They believe that simply to reject the old ways would cause them great difficulty with others and in all likelihood would in the future also cause trouble for their children. They choose to be thoughtful in their actions, therefore. They pick mindfully calculated paths that move them towards the society that they imagine. They keep their intentions to themselves and strive without much public comment. As little by little they move towards the achievement of some of their goals, they are modest before others, and they try to show regard for others. They believe that modesty and keeping their own counsel enables them to avoid multiplying their difficulties. They seek to avoid envy. It is their style.

How, then, do these individuals participate as agents in the creation of their society and social change? These four narratives reveal that self-awareness is sustained in social relationships and is expressed when the speaker locates him or herself within relationships with others. These significant others include the larger society, which is sensed as the collective attitudes and values of the community in which the individual must live, friends and workplace colleagues, and kin, especially those kin who form one's most intimate society. The individual is able to see him or herself from the perspective of these others, but also is able to imagine him or herself as engaged in argument with these others. The self in argument and exchange is a dynamic understanding that is shaped by the issues, events, and goals that give form and meaning to the processes of the speaker's life. Consequently, the self is not a monologic awareness but a multivocal, argumentative exchange, sustained in colloquy and is most fully represented in poly-biography.

NOTES

1 The narratives on which this essay is based were collected in Chennai (Madras) City during 1993–94, with the support of a J. William Fulbright Research Fellowship. An earlier version of this material was presented at Oxford University on 4 June 1999, at a "Life Histories Workshop". The author wishes to thank the Department of Anthropology, University of Madras for its intellectual support during the period of fieldwork and J.P. Parry, D.A. Washbrook, and the workshop participants for their helpful comments.

2 Self-awareness expressed in the narratives below demonstrates the weakness of cultural explanations of social action, including those of such varied theorists as Clifford Geertz (1984), Marshall Sahlins (1985), McKim Marriott (1989) and E. Valentine Daniel (1984) among others, who locate awareness within a cultural logic. These thinkers contend that culture – which in various ways they reckon as a symbolic system integrated by its own logic – determines self-awareness and the logic of social action, and they locate the person conceptually within this cultural logic. Clearly, Obeyesekere (1992) is correct to judge Sahlins' (1985) views misguided because he ignores the dialogic nature of self-awareness. People converse, and because society is a process of human sociality, sometimes people do act in ways that change social synchrony, effecting social change (cf. Carrithers 1992; Taylor 1989). One need not embrace volunteerism to recognize that humans act in goal oriented ways that lead to social change, admittedly often as a result of unintended consequences.

3 I describe Lakshmi's life history up to about 1986 in Mines (1994:159–65).

4 Note how Nalani is describing the family arguments, debates, and exchanges to me.

5 Again note Krishnan is describing an interaction or dialogue that occurred between himself and Narayan's people.

6 Notice how heterogeneous and potentially contentious this social reality is compared to Geertz's interpretation of cultural systems as homogeneous (cf. Sewell 1999).
7 I am not suggesting that change is easy, but I am suggesting that no relationship is a constant. The implications of patriliny for relationships is a process of metamorphosis.

REFERENCES

Bakhtin, M.M. (1981) 'Discourse in the Novel'. In *The Dialogic Imagination: Four Essays by M.M. Bakhtin*, M. Holquist (ed.), C. Emerson and M. Holquist (trans.). Austin, TX: University of Texas Press.

Bourdieu, P. (1990) *In Other Words: Essays Towards a Reflexive Sociology*. Stanford, CA: Stanford University Press.

Carrithers, M. (1992) *Why Humans Have Cultures: Explaining Anthropology and Social Diversity*. Oxford/New York: Oxford University Press.

Daniel, E.V. (1984) *Fluid Signs: Being a Person the Tamil Way*. Berkeley, CA: University of California Press.

Elias, N. (2000) *The Civilizing Process: Sociogenetic and Psychogenetic Investigations*. Revised edition. Oxford: Blackwell.

Foucault, M. (1983) 'On the Genealogy of Ethics: An Overview of Work in Progress'. In H.L. Dreyfus and P. Rabinow (eds) *Michel Foucault: Beyond Structuralism and Hermeneutics*. Second edition. Chicago: University of Chicago Press.

Geertz, C. (1984) '"From the Natives' Point of View": On the Nature of Anthropological Understanding'. In R.A. Shweder and R.A. LeVine (eds) *Culture Theory: Essays on Mind, Self, and Emotion*. Cambridge: Cambridge University Press.

Giddens, A. (1994 [1979]) *Central Problems in Social Theory: Action, Structure and Contradiction in Social Analysis*. Berkeley, CA: University of California Press.

Marriott, McK. (1989) 'Constructing an Indian Ethnosociology', *Contributions to Indian Sociology* (n.s.), 23(1):1–39.

Mines, M. (1994) *Public Faces, Private Voices: Community and Individuality in South India*. Berkeley, CA: University of California Press.

Mines, M. (1999) 'Heterodox Lives: Agonistic Individuality and Agency in South Indian History'. In R. Guha and J.P. Parry (eds) *Institutions and Inequalities: Essays in Honour of Andre Beteille*. New Delhi: Oxford University Press.

New York Times (2001) 'Social Status Tends to Seal One's Fate, Says France's Master Thinker', by Emily Eakin, January 6.

Obeyesekere, G. (1992) *The Apotheosis of Captain Cook*. Princeton, NJ: Princeton University Press.

Ortner, S.B. (1991) *Narrativity in History, Culture, and Lives*. CSST Working Papers, No. 66. Ann Arbor, MI: University of Michigan.

Sahlins, M. (1985) 'Captain James Cook; or the Dying God'. In M. Sahlins, *Islands of History*. Chicago: University of Chicago Press.

Sewell, W. Jr (1999) 'Geertz, Cultural Systems, and History: From Synchrony to Transformation'. In S.B. Ortner (ed.) *The Fate of "Culture"*. Berkeley, CA: University of California Press.

Taylor, C. (1989) *Sources of the Self: The Making of the Modern Identity*. Cambridge, MA: Harvard University Press.

Taylor, C. (1991) 'The Dialogical Self'. In D.R. Hiley, J.F. Bohman and R. Shusterman (eds) *The Interpretive Turn: Philosophy, Science, Culture*. Ithaca, NY: Cornell University Press.

3
Growing up in the Caribbean: Individuality in the Making

Karen Fog Olwig

In a drawing in the weekly magazine, the *New Yorker*, the cartoonist Barbara Smaller depicts what is presumably a pregnant moment in the development of intergenerational relations in an American nuclear family. The image shows a father returning home from work, still clutching his briefcase under his arm. He has just walked past his small daughter who is sitting on the floor next to the sofa, where she appears to be so preoccupied with paper and crayons that she is entirely oblivious to her father's arrival. His wife, who is holding a teddy bear, greets him eagerly, however, and exclaims: "Our little girl is growing up – this very morning she told me she hates me" (Smaller 2000:56).

The *New Yorker* is well known for its many witty cartoons that portray the ins and outs of life in New York, a global trendsetter in contemporary urban, sophisticated life. A central theme in many of the images concerns the individual's cultivating of his or her particular sense of being and the various idiosyncratic, if not far-out, ways in which a sense of self is expressed in the postmodern fragmented world. Thus the cartoon described above shows the turning point in the young daughter's life, where she begins to assert her independence as a person by not just exploring her creative ability with crayons and paper, but also distancing herself from her mother, who symbolizes her early childhood dependence. At the same time, however, one gets the feeling that the daughter's display of independence is keenly anticipated and cherished by the mother, and, that it therefore very much conforms to the parents' expectations and wishes. The daughter, in other words, is displaying her autonomy according to culturally accepted norms. The daughter's expression of hatred towards her mother therefore is interpreted by the mother as the sign of a precocious and bright child who is turning into an individual in her own right.

This cartoon may serve as an apt, if rather ironic, illustration of a common notion of the way in which children are expected to develop their own individuality in some contemporary Western societies. This notion, according to the Norwegian anthropologist Marianne Gullestad, is one where children are expected to "find themselves" through a process of "resisting and reshaping the influence of their parents". It therefore "emphasizes separateness and discontinuity" between the generations (Gullestad 1997:215). As a result of this understanding of individuality, Gullestad argues, "[d]ifferences between generations are emphasized, both in the home and in the mass media" (ibid.:216). However, a conscious engagement with the world from the unique perspectival vantage point of a specific individual does not necessarily entail the demarcation of individual difference and distinction, qualities that are often seen to develop in opposition to the elder generation in Western societies. Rather, at a more general level, it concerns the development of an ability to realize, and win recognition of, the unique capacity one possesses as an individual to engage consciously with the world in socially and culturally recognized ways – whatever they may be.

In this chapter I discuss individuality through the analysis of two life stories related by two young people, a sister and a brother, who have grown up in a village on the Caribbean island of Nevis. I shall argue that within this setting the various contexts of life that young people negotiate, as they develop and assert their individuality, involve them in a variety of social relations that reflect their ability to contribute in socially responsible ways to the collectivity of the family and home, and to demonstrate their unique talents in extradomestic spheres of life. Within this ethnographic setting a sense of individuality therefore can be formed and asserted through constructive involvement in intergenerational family relations, as well as through individual achievement in the wider society.

TWO LIFE STORIES

In 1980 I visited, for the first time, the small Caribbean island of Nevis in connection with a research project on children's role in migration. Since then I have spent several extended periods of time on the island during various research projects, most of the time living in a single rural village. During these periods of fieldwork I developed a close relationship with a particular family, and on several visits to Nevis I have stayed with this family. When I began doing life story interviews with members of the family, as part of a larger research project on migration and dispersed Caribbean family networks, I therefore had known the family for close to 20 years.[1] The two young people, whose life stories I shall discuss below, I had seen at regular intervals since they were young children. Much of what they related therefore was not new to me. Their life stories, however, shed new light on the ways in which they, as young people, described the process of growing up and saw themselves as members of the family and the surrounding society. The life story interviews proved to be an especially good tool with which to investigate narrators' awareness of their particular engagement with, and place in, the world. Thus, through the very relating of a life story "we construct an orderly world, locate ourselves within it, and make ourselves meaningful and understandable to ourselves and others" (Rapport 1997:47). By relating life stories individuals therefore represent their individuality in narrative form.

Carol's story

Carol was 17 when I interviewed her in January 1997. She was the second youngest of seven children (six girls and one boy), and had grown up in the small house that her mother acquired, in the early 1980s, after leaving her husband, who was an alcoholic. He died a few years afterwards. I first met Carol when she was only a couple of years old. At that time she spent most of her time with her maternal grandparents in "The Pasture", a neighborhood at the other end of the village, because her mother had wage employment in nearby Charlestown, the main town on the island. When I started my interview with Carol by asking her to tell me her life story she presented a short and factual account:

> My life has been brief. I grew up, and as far as I could remember I lived here. But it has always been two homes: here and "The Pasture". So we shared time with people here and there. We used to visit our grandparents on Saturdays. When I was four years old I had an interest in school – I living so close to the school – so I went for visits there. The teacher invited me to the class, and unofficially I started school at four years old. I left primary school at 11, the usual age being 12. I went to 1A1 and went to the A-stream to fifth form. I did seven subjects for CXC and passed six. Then I went to the sixth form, and I am doing three subjects. I begin examinations in May.
>
> What I can remember is basically about school. Nothing exciting.

In some ways Carol's narrative is quite similar to the sort of life stories that one might expect young people in Western societies to relate. Carol notes that she has always lived in her childhood home, but that she also spent a great deal of time with her grandparents. She further explains that she has attended school from an early age and is preparing to take her final exams. She concludes that most of her recollections are about the school. This interpretation, however, fails to examine Carol's life story within the local context in which it was related. Thus while it may seem to be very ordinary from a Western point of view it is, in fact, far from ordinary given Carol's social and cultural background. Carol is the only one in the large group of siblings who ever reached as far in school. Even though her four older sisters, encouraged by their mother, had high ambitions about acquiring the best possible education, none of them were able to pass a sufficient number of exams, after fifth form, to continue in the academic sixth form college. Whenever I returned to Nevis, family members expressed disappointment that yet another child had not succeeded at passing enough subjects to become accepted in the sixth form college. Carol's narrative about her education, in other words, is an unusual success story that makes her stand out, not just in the family, but also in the local community where education constitutes the preferred and most respectable but also the most difficult way of improving one's status in society.

The school, the most ubiquitous and influential social institution of childhood, is often presented in the literature on Western childhood as a social institution created by adults for children and therefore as restricting children's freedom. Thus, many of the new studies of children and childhood have critically examined children's possibilities of creating their own spaces of social action in societies where children spend an increasing part of their childhood in institutionalized settings such as schools and day care programs (see, for example, Ehn 1983; Prout and James 1990; Ennew 1994; James 1998; Gulløv 1999; Anderson 2000; Olwig and Gulløv 2003). This is not how Carol describes it. She emphasizes that she has enjoyed school and that this is the reason why she has done so well in school. Furthermore, she relates that she chose, herself, to begin in school by simply showing up at the age of four, a whole year before she was supposed to begin, and somehow convincing the teacher to invite her into the classroom. In the interview that followed her own presentation of her life story Carol explained that she had begun school so young because she did not want to be left behind, when the older siblings left. Later, she grew to like the school because she learned to master the work:

> It [the school] has taken up most of my life. I have been in school for 13 of my 17 years. I always liked school, I don't know why. The teachers are nice. When I think back I guess that I liked to have a place to go as the others, so I went to the school. And when you started school, it began to grow on you and you realized the importance of the things. Lately there have been times when I could have done with a few more breaks, but otherwise it has been ok. I like the idea of the work, being around the people. It is something familiar and I especially like it when I could do something well.

Carol, in other words, did not describe the school as an external, adult defined structure to which she had to accommodate. She rather presented it as an opportunity that she took advantage of, when she found it interesting, even though she did not fall within the proper age range of this age segregated social institution.

Although the school loomed large in Carol's life, family and neighborhood were also important, and as in the case of the school, Carol described this arena of life as one in which she was able to engage as an individual in her own right. Whereas the school had emphasized individual achievement in peer groups, the family had encouraged the assumption of responsibility across the generations. When I asked Carol whether she had any particular role in the home, she explained:

> Linda [one of her sisters] is away, and I sort of take care of her son. Sandra [another sister] has her own children, and my mother is working. We all help. I am the one in the position to do it. Even when his mother was here, he used to be here, and I would bathe and feed him. It is not difficult. He is big now. He could do some, but it is easier to do it for him. I mend his clothes and clean him. Benjamin [Linda's son] was always with us, so he is used to being here. There is not much change with Linda being away. He would like his mother back, but he is not too much affected.

According to Carol's account, she had cared for her nephew since she was 13 years old. Assuming responsibility for looking after a young child would seem to be a rather daunting task for a schoolgirl. In a Caribbean context, however, there is nothing unusual in an older child looking after a younger one. Carol therefore did not describe her care for the nephew as an especially demanding or challenging task, but rather as something that was natural, given the child's need for care and her being there to care for him. Her oldest sisters, she explained, had looked after her, when she was small, because their mother held two jobs to support the family and therefore was out of the home a great deal:

There were a lot of us – six[2] – so the older ones cared for the younger ones. They might tell you to do what you didn't think you should do, but then you had to do it, because they told you to, they being older.

This suggests that older children, who are willing to undertake responsibility in relation to younger children, possess a position of respect and authority among the children. Indeed, the very assumption of a position of responsibility towards a younger child creates a generation-like relationship between two children, where the older child assumes adult-like responsibility towards the young child, with the obligations and duties toward a minor that this entails. The younger child becomes dependent upon the older child and is required to show the respect and obedience due to the care provider. Becoming a provider of care therefore presents not just a burden, but also an opportunity to gain a position of authority in the family. This is apparent in Carol's account of her role as caretaker of her nephew. She did not describe her care for her nephew as a burden that placed unpleasant restrictions on her life. While she does not explicitly say so, it is quite apparent that by taking upon herself to care for her nephew she established a position of authority vis-à-vis her nephew that she would not have had if she had just remained the little sister at the bottom of the hierarchy of siblings.

In my interview with Carol she explained that she had also created her own relationships outside the home, both with relatives and neighbors. As was the case in the domestic relations, an important foundation for these relationships was the extending of help to others:

[You prefer living in this home?]

It works out fine for me. When a neighbor's husband died she asked me to stay with her for the night. I did that for a while to keep her company during the night, for about a year. When the husband was sick, and she was alone in the home, I always used to visit. After a while I just stopped sleeping there. This was when I was in primary school. She lived just the second house from home. So I was still at home anyway, and it didn't bother me.

In this description of the neighbor, who needed help, she depicted herself as the one who initiated the relationship by visiting the neighbor, when the neighbor's husband was ill. Despite the fact that she could not have been more than ten to eleven years old when the husband died, she had no qualms about spending the night with the widow, seeing it just as an extension of her visits in the home. And when this sleeping arrangement did not seem to be necessary any longer she quite simply stopped going to the neighbor at nights.

Throughout the interview, Carol represented herself as an individual who became involved with her surroundings from her individual vantage point. She had done so by exploring the opportunities available to her, whether in the form of a societal institution external to home and family where she was able to develop her aptitude for learning, or in the form of intergenerational relationships with family members and friends in the local community where she demonstrated her capacity to engage in socially responsible relations with others. Her way of maneuvering within these two fields of relations is characteristic of many girls in the Caribbean, because the school as well as the home and family constitute social arenas where girls, and women more generally, may assert and negotiate positions of authority in socially approved ways (Wilson 1973). The situation is somewhat different for boys. The following life story interview with Carol's only brother, Samuel, points to some of the spheres of social action that are of importance to boys. These spheres are also informed by generational and age specific relations, although in somewhat different ways.

Samuel's story

When I asked Samuel to tell me his life story he presented the following account:

> Twenty-four years ago Samuel Burdon was born on October 2. I started out rough, and I am still rough. But as I get experienced to the world I make it.
>
> From an early age I played soccer, football. I played for the national team for two years, and recently – soccer gives no income, if you go in you get nothing out of it – I chose cricket. It is a more West Indian sport. And there are opportunities to meet different people. I started three years ago, and I am already on the national team for Nevis. I started [on the team] two years ago. I was very ok in my performance. But not high, because I needed more exposure from the captain and the management. My first success was on St Croix. I had to prove myself, and I picked up five wickets for 13 runs.

I still play cricket, it is exciting and interesting. I keep myself physical, I played in the local cup matches before I went on the national team. I play for [the village]. We won one year, and we are always among the first three. [The village] has generated a lot of great players.

I was offered a contract for South Africa. It didn't work, but I am going to England in January 1997. I have always wished to enjoy myself, meet people in the game of cricket.

The family means somewhat to me. Without the family I was not to get this far in cricket. Ruth Johnson raised me from nothing to what I am. She was loving and caring, she would take out her heart and give it to you. From birth I had a bond to her.

I always speak more of grandmother than of my birth mother. I can't speak of it other than that. I care for her, but really though I give grandmother full credit, I must respect my birth mother.

In his narrative, Samuel described his life as centered on various sports. He related how he began playing sports as a young kid, participated in the local tournaments, played on the national team and was hoping to enter the international stage as a professional player. His life, in other words, had revolved around an activity that took place outside the home, first informally when he began to play with other children in the village, but then in more organized sports. Indeed, sports became so important to him that it took the place of school. Thus when I asked him about school he stated that he never finished secondary school, explaining, "I used to [like school], but then I thought about how far I could get in sports. And that was my first priority". In Samuel's account, sports had brought him into contact with the larger world and smoothed his somewhat rough character.

Samuel's life story, however, acknowledges another important influence in his life, that of Ruth Johnson, his grandmother with whom he had a close relationship. He described this relationship as one based on natural affinity existing since his birth. It becomes apparent, however, that the tie to his grandmother was one that he had cultivated himself at the expense of his tie to his mother and sisters:

[Who did you grow up with?]

I grew up with my mother for about two years. I used to live with my mother, but I spent more time with grandmother. I would sneak in and gradually move my pants and shirts into the [grandmother's] house. She wanted me to go back, because she thought that it would cause segregation between mother and grandmother.

[Did it?]

Yes. I kissed up grandmother, and she comforted my mother. But I am not close to my mother, so I don't feel that close to her. Most of the time you must follow your feeling, and I felt close to grandmother, and so I chose to be with her. What also brought me closer was the fact that my mother left me for a couple of years when she went to the Virgin Islands. I don't remember this, it is about 17 years ago, I was about seven. She came and went, maybe once a year.

In living [with the grandmother] I would be comfortable, and seeing that I was the only boy child [in the mother's house] might be the reason for my coming, because there were four other guys here and none at home. There was nobody to play soccer and cricket with. I started to play soccer for the village when I was 11.

[...]

[Did you just move into the house on your own?]

At first grandmother wanted me out, but then she accepted me, because there was this bond between her and me. And the other guys encouraged me to stay.

In his move out of his mother's house, Samuel evoked generational as well as age specific and gender specific relations. He realized that he really ought to stay with his mother, but emphasized that he had become close to his grandmother, because he had stayed with her for a couple of years when his mother was abroad. It was therefore to be expected, he felt, that he showed her so much affection and wanted to stay with her. He could also understand, however, that his grandmother wished to send him back to his mother because she did not wish to interfere in the mother–son relationship. In order to avoid this return, Samuel played on the fact that he was an only boy in his mother's house, and that he had a need to play with other boys his age. By appealing to both generational and age based relations, he therefore managed to stay in his grandmother's house.

Life in the grandmother's home was not only one of play with the other boys. Boys, especially, were expected to care for the animals and they were also encouraged to have some of their own:

I should say that when I grew up I had plenty of animals. So it was not just play. Grandfather loved animals, and he encouraged me to come home from school and look after the animals before I played. The animals must feel love. I had goats, sheep, fowl, pigs and donkey – jackass.

The care for animals seems to have provided an important context for the development of intergenerational relationships with men. Thus Samuel only referred to his grandfather in connection with his animals. Furthermore, he noted that he developed a good relationship with his father because they had a mutual interest in animals. It is significant that Samuel, the only son, is the only one of the siblings who mentioned his father favorably: [What relation did you have to your father?] "I had a good relation. He is the one who gave me my first goat".

Men, however, seem to have played a relatively marginal role in the intergenerational relationships within the family. Samuel, as noted, emphasized the importance of his grandmother with whom he had a very affectionate relationship. Another central person is the aunt who was, in effect, in charge of the daily running of his grandparents' home:

> [My aunt] Claudette, I always respected her. I got lots of licks to prevent me from bad company. She wanted you to always be at home occupied in the yard, but that wouldn't have helped me in sports. So it would have been bad if I had to stay in the home. I would only be good in the kitchen. She was outstanding in the kitchen. She was also very fondable, and she played netball, she was on the village team in netball. She realized how I felt and gave me more free time. Sunday mornings she came to the pasture with a whip to make sure that I went to church. She had me running around in the pasture to avoid going to church. And as soon as it was over I was out in the field. And she wanted me to stay to eat lunch before going out again to play. But I feed myself on sports. I have a lot of energy. She was always home, she was the home girl. Even when grandfather was sick she was home. Just recently she went out, she went abroad. We had a close bond.

One might expect that Samuel's description of his aunt as someone who beat him, made him help in the kitchen, forced him to go to church and then prevented him from playing before he had eaten his Sunday dinner would be an angry man's bitter account of the mistreatment he had received as a child. This is not the case at all, quite the contrary. Samuel begins the account by emphasizing how much he respected his aunt, goes on to state in the middle that she really was a "fondable" person and ends up by concluding that they had "a close bond" until she left. He thus makes clear that he was shaped as a person through the close relationship he developed with his aunt who assumed responsibility for his wellbeing. It is by the same logic that Samuel accounts for the fact that his mother is relatively unimportant to him. Indeed, he does not say anything negative about his mother, but merely notes that she went away for several years, with the result that he was cared for by his grandmother who, he states, "raised me from nothing to what I am". Therefore he developed a close relationship with her.

In his life story Samuel, like Carol, portrayed himself as a social actor, who had constructed his own life. As a young boy he decided to live with his grandmother rather than his mother, and he chose to use sports as a central area of personal development and learning. In his development as a person he had played on intergenerational as well as age specific relations. Thus he emphasized the significance of peer relations with boys his age who were good playmates in sports. But he also acknowledged the significance of intergenerational relations with his aunt, father and grandparents that taught him the importance of commitment, responsibility and respect. Both sets of relations, he felt, had been equally important to his development as the person he had become.

CONCLUSION

The two young people who grew up in a rural community on a small Caribbean island presented themselves in quite different ways in their life stories. Carol pointed to the significance of the school, her mother's home and the immediate neighborhood. Her seven-year older brother emphasized his grandmother's home, the surrounding pasture and bushlands and sports clubs. These differences are, to a certain extent, gender specific. Thus in the Caribbean the household, with its domestic activities, is defined as an important sphere for women to develop and demonstrate the gender specific capacities that confer respect on them in society. Open public spaces, such as the bush, the pasture and the road, on the other hand, have been described as an arena for male pursuits that give them reputation within the local community (Wilson 1973; Abrahams 1983; Olwig 1993). Nevertheless, there is great variety in the extent to which children choose to identify with these gender specific spheres of life. Thus Carol's and Samuel's younger sister was not concerned about making herself useful in the home or doing well in school, but preferred, like Samuel, to play and do sports outside the home. One of their male cousins, who lived in his grandmother's home for a while, had little interest in sports, but devoted all his energy to raising his own animals. He had developed this passion for animals largely because his grandfather took him along to the bush every day to help care for the animals.

The young people established their own ways of asserting themselves as human beings, but under a more general structure of constraints, such as expected gender roles, labor needs in the household and societal institutions, such as the school and the church. They tended not to dwell on this structural framework of life, or to describe it as imposing severe constraints, however, but rather chose to present themselves as social actors who lived their lives, drawing on, circumventing or, at least, somehow coping with these institutions. This does not mean that they were not subjected to a great many constraints, but rather that they did not see these as having posed great obstacles to their development as human beings. On the contrary, they preferred to see constraints – and the ways in which they learned to deal with them – as important elements in the shaping of their character. Samuel therefore did not express any resentment at his aunt who whipped him into going to church. On the contrary, he interpreted her behavior as concern for his wellbeing that resulted in a smoothing of his rough character. He also, however, saw his success at circumventing undesirable adult requirements without creating too much of a fuss, such as Sunday lunch with the family or life with five sisters in his mother's home, as achievements that reflected just as well on him as a person. Carol described herself as having eagerly sought out relationships with others that must have required a fair amount of time and effort on her part.

I suggest that the main reason why Carol and Samuel did not view obligations and duties towards others as constraints is that they did not see themselves in opposition to imposing others. Rather they presented themselves as having grown up in a field of relations of mutual give and take that had made them the individuals they were. Thus Carol described herself as an individual through the relation as a caregiver she developed with her younger nephew, as a companion for a neighbor, and as a good student recognized by the teachers and liked by her peers. Samuel presented himself through the close relation he developed with his grandmother and aunt who, he explained, cared for him and showed an interest in his welfare and made him the person he was, but he also described how he developed his special skills as a sportsman in the company of his friends. It was through their engagement as social actors in these fields of relations, and through the sense of relatedness (cf. Carsten 2000) towards people that emerged through this engagement, that they became aware of their individuality. These fields consisted of both intergenerational and intragenerational ties. The intergenerational ties built on notions of gratitude and respect towards the older generation that had reared them, and responsibility toward the younger ones who need their help. The intragenerational ties, on the other hand, entailed peer relations of young people their own age with whom they could develop their intellectual and creative talents.

The notion that children develop their individuality by becoming involved as social actors in intergenerational as well as peer relations, expressed in Carol's and Samuel's life stories, is quite different from the idea that children need to find themselves by opposing the elder generation, that comes across in the *New Yorker* cartoon by Barbara Smaller. The little girl shown in the cartoon is portrayed as demarcating herself by distancing herself from her parents, whereas the Caribbean youths described their childhood as one of exploring, and incorporating in their own life project, the various relations and opportunities that presented themselves, given their specific life circumstances. This suggests that Caribbean individuals are seen as defining themselves through their involvement with others, who both shape them and are shaped by them. This is in contrast to Gullestad's suggestion that Western children are perceived as needing to "find themselves" as unique persons, an idea that suggests that their individuality already exists, but that they can be prevented from uncovering it, if others place too many obstacles in their way.

In the new sociology and anthropology of childhood there has been a great deal of interest in the ways in which children in modern, industrialized countries are subjected to control and close monitoring by adults. An important aspect of this control, as noted earlier, is the confinement of children to adult created spaces for children, such as the home and the school. Indeed, James, Jenks and Prout suggest that "children either occupy designated spaces, that is they are placed, as in nurseries or schools, or they are conspicuous by their inappropriate or precocious invasion of adult territory" (1998:37). The strong interest in structures of control in Western studies of children and childhood may be elicited by the fact that children in Western societies are, indeed, subjected to increasing regimes of discipline. It may also, however, be related to particular notions of individuality, implicit in much of this literature, that emphasize the need for children to express, and realize, themselves on their own terms if they are to develop into individuals in their own right. From this point of view, adult structures of authority and control will therefore be seen as a threat to children. This emphasis on the importance of children developing as individuals on their own is ironic in light of the fact that children are, by definition, enmeshed in complex fields of intergenerational relations. James, Jenks and Prout have noted (1998:66) that the "relational dimension of childhood" is often forgotten and that it is important to remember that "the child is a child only in relation to its adult counterpart, identified both through its difference from adults in general and through kinship links with pairs of particular adults ... And that relationship of difference and particularity is, in essence, generational" (ibid.:66). It would therefore seem that children develop a consciousness of themselves as unique human beings through relations with different adults as well as with similar peers. This suggests that researchers might do well to focus on the nature of these varying relations, and the complex ways in which children learn to navigate them.

NOTES

1 The life story research pertaining to Nevis is presented in Olwig 1999, 2002, and 2005.
2 The youngest sister was not yet born during Carol's early childhood.

REFERENCES

Abrahams, R.D. (1983) *The Man-of-Words in the West Indies*. Baltimore, MD: Johns Hopkins University Press.

Anderson, S. (2000) *I en klasse for sig*. Copenhagen: Gyldendal, Socialpædagogiske Bibliotek.

Carsten, J. (2000) *Cultures of Relatedness: New Approaches to the Study of Kinship*. Cambridge: Cambridge University Press.

Ehn, B. (1983) *Ska vi leka tiger? Daghemsliv ur kulturell synsvinkel*. Malmö: Liber.

Ennew, J. (1994) 'Time for Children or Time for Adults?' In J. Qvortrup et al. (eds) *Childhood Matters: Social Theory, Practice and Politics*. Aldershot: Avebury, pp. 125–43.

Gullestad, M. (1997) 'From Being of Use to Finding Oneself: Dilemmas of Value Transmission between the Generations in Norway.' In M. Gullestad and M. Segalen (eds) *Family and Kinship in Europe*. London: Pinter, pp. 202–18.

Gulløv, E. (1999) *Betydningsdannelse blandt børn*. Copenhagen: Gyldendal, Socialpædagogiske Bibliotek.

James, A. (1998) 'Imagining Children at Home and in the Family: Spacial and Temporary Markers of Childhood Identities'. In N. Rapport and A. Dawson (eds) *Migrants of Identity – Perceptions of Home in a World in Movement.* Oxford: Berg, pp. 139–60.

James, A., Jenks, C. and Prout, A. (1998) *Theorizing Childhood.* Cambridge: Polity.

Olwig, K.F. (1993) *Global Culture, Island Identity: Continuity and Change in the Afro-Caribbean Community of Nevis.* London: Harwood Academic Publishers.

Olwig, K.F. (1999) 'Narratives of the Children Left Behind: Home and Identity in Globalised Caribbean Families'. *Journal of Ethnic and Migration Studies*, 25(2):267–84.

Olwig, K.F. (2002) 'A Wedding in the Family: Home Making in a Global Kin Network'. *Global Communities*, 2(3):205–18.

Olwig, K.F. (2005) 'Narratives of Home: Visions of "Betterment" and Belonging in a Dispersed Family'. In J. Besson and K.F. Olwig (eds) *Caribbean Narratives of Belonging: Fields of Relations, Sites of Identity.* London: Macmillan, pp. 189–205.

Olwig, K.F. and Gulløv, E. (2003) 'Towards an Anthropology of Children and Place'. In Olwig and Gulløv (eds) *Children's Places: Cross-Cultural Perspectives*. London: Routledge, pp. 1–19.

Prout, A. and James, A. (1990) 'A New Paradigm for the Sociology of Childhood? Provenance, Promise and Problems'. In A. James and A. Prout (eds) *Constructing and Reconstructing Childhood: Contemporary Issues in the Sociological Study of Children*. London: Falmer, pp. 7–34.

Rapport, N. (1997) *Transcendent Individual.* London: Routledge.

Smaller, B. (2000) Cartoon. *New Yorker*, May 22.

Wilson, P. (1973) *Crab Antics: The Social Anthropology of English-Speaking Negro Societies of the Caribbean*. New Haven, CT: Yale University Press.

4
Distinction and Co-construction: Diaspora Asian Fashion Entrepreneurs in London[1]

Parminder Bhachu

In this chapter, I want to examine the ways in which fashion entrepreneurs in London have created new culturally mediated markets through the assertion of racialized and politicized diasporic styles in a formerly stigmatized economy of "ethnic clothes" – in particular the Punjabi suit or *salwaar kameez*. Since the 1990s, this economy has moved into mainstream arenas and has been reimagined and recoded. From the margins, the work of these fashion entrepreneurs has given expression to highly distinctive and customized styles. The creation of their individuality and distinction is based on constant improvisation and co-construction, the defining modus operandi of diasporic lives and products, which in turn gives them an innovative edge in contemporary global markets.[2] Their design inventions in fashion markets are generated on their own terms through their own classificatory systems.

I will contrast these diasporic strategies with those employed by designers located in India, who want to "make it in the West" and who seek to recontextualize their heritages through the adaptation of contemporary design vocabularies for both national and transnational markets. Powerful state institutions and finance support the work of these fashion professionals. These designers also occupy elite positions of enormous cultural capital and classificatory command in their home locations in the subcontinent. Their projects are in accord with the Indian government's desire to increase their current $39 million share of the global apparel market to $225 within a decade (Sengupta 2003, 2005). The India based fashion professionals are responding to a national desire to increase the world market share of India designed clothes through reworking and reimagining India's highly developed heritage of embroideries and craft skills.

Accordingly, in the following sections I examine some of the dynamics of London based diasporic fashion entrepreneurs who responded to the local scene from the margins in the situations of weak power in which they live, politic, and improvise versus Indian elites who are ambassadors of national sites and who recontextualize their national heritages for transnational audiences much less successfully than radically innovative local diasporics. But firstly it will be necessary to provide some background on the Punjabi suit economy and its movement into mainstream markets in London as well as the role of diasporic designers in creating these micro-markets of fashion and style.

LONDON'S DIASPORIC SUIT ECONOMY

Punjabi suits represented clothes worn during the 1960s and 1970s in London by immigrant women originating in the Punjab region of North India and Pakistan. These clothes were also worn by multiply migrant women who had come to the United Kingdom via East Africa, the "twice migrant" communities (Bhachu 1985, 1993, 1996) who had left India almost a hundred years before migration to Britain. As a result, these clothes were negatively coded given their identification with low status working class immigrants. These were the women associated with the wave of labor migration recruited from British colonies to fill labor shortages in the United Kingdom after the Second World War. As a result of this colonial association, these immigrants for the most part arrived in the United Kingdom with British citizenship and passports already in hand.

The clothes of these immigrants identified a general threat: the arrival of the colonized in the heart of the land of the colonizers. The negative coding of the Punjabi suit worn by women had parallels to the stigmas applied to the turbans worn by their male counterparts. During the 1950s and 1960s, Sikhs engaged in a number of struggles around the turban: struggles to be allowed to wear the turban as bus conductors, on motor bikes (instead of crash helmets), in the public spaces of banks and post offices, as well as for their sons to be allowed to wear turbans in private schools.[3] Many Sikhs cut their hair and gave up their turbans. However, in the late 1970s and 1980s they donned their turbans again as community infrastructures and religious institutions developed further and a critical mass of turban wearing people was established, buttressing ethnic and sartorial confidences. The story of the Punjabi suit and its revitalization has many similarities with this struggle.

The heroines of my tale are the older immigrant women who kept the suit economy alive by continuing to adhere to and reproduce suit styles they had worn and stitched for years. They persisted in maintaining their cultural and sartorial frames despite the racial slurs and the frequent taunts directed at this apparel. They were told they were "Pakis" wearing nightsuits and pyjamas, despite the fact that many were not from Pakistan, others had never been to India and many others still had been born and/or raised in Britain. The older women in classically styled suits provided their British raised and British born daughters with a cultural framework that legitimized suit wearing. In many cases they stitched these suits collaboratively with their daughters, taking account both of their personal fashion idiosyncrasies as well as the more general fashion trends of the time.

My own mother persuaded me to wear a suit during the overtly racist 1970s when there were few stylish young Punjabi women in my London circuits wearing "young fashionable suits". When I was in my late teens and early twenties, my mother responded to my own styles and design codes and lovingly stitched suits for me by a collaborative co-construction in which we were both integrally involved. She also taught me to cut and sew suits for myself, a craft in which I achieved proficiency by the time I was in my mid twenties. Thus, she gave me a sartorial template of cultural confidence through clothes denigrated in the public realms of that time, a design template that was intended to give me ethnic pride on my terms. By so doing, she also gave me the confidence to be ethnically and racially myself on my own terms regardless of the terrain in which I found myself, in all the many sites where I have lived in as a multiple migrant and in which I have worn the suit. I am a "thrice migrant" who is now a product of four continents.

My own suit wearing story is but one of many similar narratives of astute mothers who socialized their second generation daughters into wearing trendy fashion conscious suits with pride against the racial and sartorial odds of the time. Their daughters further developed their own British subcultural and subclass styles, images and fashion trends both in the domestic domain and later in commercial markets. In the discussion below, I will discuss the cases of two London diasporic design entrepreneurs, both from similar multiply migrant backgrounds, who responded by initiating their own styles when they could not find suits they liked in the available marketplace. They responded to their own particular cultural and racial moment and created clothes they liked for themselves which in turn found a market niche amongst other London based Asian women like themselves. These were organic markets that developed out of an aesthetic of racialization and ethnicization in the local landscapes of London whilst also drawing on an improvisational diasporic inheritance of *sina-prona*,[4] the highly developed and established cultures of the stitch, craft, and domestic skills that characterized their mothers' and grandmothers' lives in previous sites of settlement. These British Asian second generation daughters who were raised in London have spearheaded the commercial economies of the suit using global communications as well as cheap manufacturing sites in India and Pakistan. In the 1980s, they were able to create commercial micro-markets on their own terms, drawing on their personal and distinctive interpretations of the suit. But they also developed these markets through dialogic micro-design conversations with their customers. These niche markets encode struggles that were going on in the margins for many years before they had a commercial face. Subsequently, during the 1990s, these designers were able to translate their ethnic niche success into the garment mainstream, a process that has advanced even further in the new millennium when the clothes they design are worn regularly both by high fashion icons as well as women from diverse backgrounds on the street. This reimagination of the suit has parallels with other Asianizing trends in Britain including the enormous popularity of Indian food, *pashmina* shawls, *bhangra* music and so on (see Bhachu 2004 for further details).

The two designers I am concerned with in this chapter were both born in Kenya and raised in London. One of these is Geeta Sarin, who pioneered the suit trend in London and now in her mid 50s; she arrived in Britain as a teenager. She shares the same multiply migrant trajectory as the younger Bubby Mahil, who came to London as a two year old and who is now in her late 30s. Both these designers represent the improvisational, dialogic diasporic aesthetics par excellence. They are thus in synch with the defining characteristics of new capitalist processes, the hallmark of new global economies, which emphasize customization and co-construction of products to respond to the authentic voices of customers.

I will compare the strategies employed by Geeta and Bubby with the design and commercial narrative of Ritu Kumar, a renowned and commercially successful revivalist Indian designer who has been considered "the doyenne of Indian fashion for 40 years" (Sengupta 2005) and a "couturier to the stars", counting among her clients women of the Indian aristocracy such as Sonia Gandhi as well as fashion icons such as the late Princess Diana and her friend Jemima Goldsmith Khan.[5] While the enterprises of diasporic design entrepreneurs such as Geeta and Bubby flourished, Ritu Kumar's London Mayfair shop closed three years after it opened in 1996, a fate shared by similar subcontinental high status elite shops like Libas and Yazz, that sold high craft/high art India and Pakistan produced fashions. I would suggest that the failure of these shops to flourish reflected their static nature. These were top-down clothes fabricated without direct input from clients. As such, the design orientation of Ritu was in marked contrast to that of her London counterparts who understood their local markets intimately and paid heed to the voices of their clients, which they mingled and articulated with their own ideas.

A PIONEERING DIASPORIC DESIGNER: GEETA SARIN

Geeta Sarin was amongst the first to open a London boutique for British Asians, which she called Rivaaz. She spearheaded the designer suit movement whilst also rendering ready made Asian clothes more easily available in Britain. As well as her Wembley shop in North West London, she developed an alternative market – the first Asian mail order catalogues of Indian clothes. She is a pioneer and a groundbreaker in this economy.

She started her business in 1981 as a design consultant working out of her husband's offices: he ran the magazine *Image* and she had her studio alongside. She had previously attended a prestigious London fashion school and had completed a three year diploma program. She also had the benefit of working with some well known European designers but this experience did not provide her with any control over her designs or a signature of her own, even when she had been responsible for the major design work on these clothes. She therefore felt exploited and wanted to be her own agent with her own design identity. However, Geeta's training really began much earlier when, as a young girl, she constantly read the fashion pages of magazines and took a close interest in fashionable clothes generally. Her sewing background gave her an expertise and a deeper understanding of clothes. She says her mother

> ... was an excellent seamstress and in Kenya, all the girls were supposed to know something about stitching or tailoring. My mother and other women in

the joint household constantly emphasized that all the girls should know sewing, stitching and cooking, apart from anything else. This is how I learnt. Also I had a bit of talent and I always loved good clothes.

Geeta represents the professional end of the *sina-prona* diasporic sewing cultures (Bhachu 2004), which are defined by their improvisational and individualized dialogic design and craft sensibilities. Later on when she worked as a fashion journalist for her husband's magazine, she interviewed leading mainstream fashion designers such as Zandra Rhodes. At this stage, she also designed suits using her fashion school expertise to produce cutting edge designs. As a fashion conscious woman from a sewing background, she noticed a deficiency in the market, as ready made Asian clothes were just becoming available in Britain but were neither stylish nor of good quality. Shops selling fabrics and other general household goods like linens, haberdashery items, suitcases and so on would also have a few ready made clothes hung up on racks. They were shoddily made, badly cut and manufactured without any understanding of the clothes codes of British Asian women as these had developed in the context of various subcultural locations. Someone had simply been to India and bought some suits and put them in the shop.

Geeta was able to identify a potential market niche from what she could observe at the Indian social functions she attended:

There were beautiful young Asian women who were wearing ready made *salwaar-kameez* but they were not the right cuts or the right colors ... I could see that there was a definite need for the younger generation. Obviously they had no choice but to tell mum, "Alright fine, you are making me a *salwaar-kameez*, I will wear it because this particular function requires me to wear a *salwaar-kameez*" ... So I went straight into it but my cuts were very Western.

Geeta's first two shops in Wembley – she moved from smaller premises to the current larger ones in 1984 – established her in the market. Having established a customer base (about 80 per cent Asians and 20 per cent Europeans), and having operated in Wembley for over a decade, Geeta wanted to move into mainstream markets. Her goal, she says, was "to sell Indian clothes to Europeans, period". Of course, her customer base remained primarily Asian but she also has a transformative commercial and cultural agenda of selling her Asian styled clothes to Europeans. Geeta offers fusion elements in her clothes and it is this aspect that is attractive both to niche diaspora markets as well as to the transnationally based Indians and Pakistanis who are also her clients.

Dialogic individualized designs

As I noted earlier, Geeta started Rivaaz not as a shop at first but as a design consultancy. People would visit her and she would design an outfit together with a client, then she would get it made in India. She built up these workroom connections on various trips to the subcontinent. Her initial design consultancy emerged out of her fashion training and fashion journalism. This design concept then became a retail outlet as a result of the demand and interest from her clients. She said she always negotiated designs with her clients:

> ... always, the whole concept started from designing and it then became a retailing outlet because my clothes were so popular. I got the contact through demand. People desperately wanted suits. It was a demand and supply kind of situation where the demand started picking up and Rivaaz was the first to start with and people got to know me ... .

Since those times in the early 1980s, Geeta's business has flourished and has become an established niche market in which she has a long and well proven record. She currently works almost exclusively on referrals. It is also easier now to create these individually negotiated clothes because of the availability of more rapid communications to the manufacturing site in India: design instructions can simply be faxed. Geeta states that people have become more aware of the fact that these garments are easily available in London and that she can supply them according to the client's taste, each individually tailored. Her modus operandi even now remains a "guided dialogue" between herself and her clients. She is there herself in her shops to deal with customers directly, negotiating patterns with them through a process she herself describes as "the engineering of an outfit".

Although many people do buy the stylish off-the-peg clothes displayed in her shop, most of her business involves the production of individually cut and tailored suits for both men and women. She says 80 per cent of her business is made to measure, 20 per cent of it is contracted and made according to her cuts and designs.

> You pick a *Lucknow kurta*, a *Lucknow kurta* is a *Lucknow kurta*. It's *kurta* with no shape. The same thing, if I was to define it, which is what I have done, and given

it my own style and idea, which is here [she shows me a *kurta*], it's a little bit more tapered. It has more shape and it's better cut. These are my designs from my paper cuttings and fabrics and I contract it out to young designers to do it. The cut makes a lot of difference.

The emphasis on the "cut" is what gives Rivaaz clothes their diasporic edge, a reinterpreted "Westernness". The shape and the silhouette indicate their British Asian registers and mark out their distinctiveness even when the clothes may initially look similar to those available in other exclusive designer boutiques.

So how is the potency of the cut achieved? I asked her about the process of negotiating the sketch, the design template of lines on paper that constitute the drawing, which is later faxed to India for production. The ideas within this design format often come from many sources, her own inputs, the client's suggestions and desires as well as fashion magazines. Geeta functions as a design consultant as well as a guide, molding the ideas from all of these sources through her sketching. Indeed it is the use of the sketch as an instrument of negotiation that allows her to be more democratic in her designs. She says,

Ritu and Rohit Bal [two famous India based designers who had and have shops in London] and other Indian designers sell you what they made and designed. They do not make individually tailored clothes. Mine is very one to one. It's very individually done right from the beginning.

It is now possible to get this British conceived, India manufactured suit in London within as short a period as four days because Geeta has a manufacturing unit in India that can quickly churn out these clothes. This production unit has worked for Geeta for over 20 years. It is now primed for her design processes and instructions. In order to complete urgent orders, she can speed up manufacturing of her designs in India by doubling the money she pays tailors and workers to work overtime. As a result, she can have suits made for clients within as little as two days. As she explains:

I had a suit made in two days – 48 hours – menswear. Womenswear, ladies' wear, it depends on how intricate the work is. Plain suits with no embroidery, I can churn out 20 a day. Minimum lead time is three to four weeks. In the peak season I take six to eight weeks because the workload is so much and the intensity of the heat in India is so much ... .

Encoding racialization in designs

As I have noted elsewhere (Bhachu 2005), Geeta emphasizes the importance of her cultural background and racial experiences for her own design sensibilities. She notes that when the British ruled India, they exported most of the finest Indian crafts and attacked the most highly skilled craftsmen:

> We still let them keep doing this to us here and in India. Why are we ashamed of our culture? My inspiration is cultural. Absolutely. Most Indians from India living abroad were ashamed of their background. I have seen that wealthy Indian elites would wear only [European] designer clothes and shoes like Louis Vuitton, Versace, Cardin, a whole bunch of other designer names. Now there are people who can afford to buy designer clothes but also wear the *salwaar-kameez* and with confidence and pride. They can afford both European designer clothes and also wear our own clothes.

Geeta is adamant that she has:

> ... stuck to my roots. I stuck to my cultural heritage. I have never been ashamed of it. I have not moved away from my cultural background. People like us are making their mark now. People don't bother with all these others who were ashamed of their cultures. These are the people who are behind. They were culturally ashamed and never spoke their language to their children, who were so confused, they didn't know where they were coming [from] and where they were going.

When she first started designing and producing clothes, she had not imagined that her suits would be worn by leading fashion icons. She had wanted to provide well designed clothes for Asians like herself, who were interested in fashion and wanted to dress well. Geeta talks about the derogatory way in which the *salwaar-kameez* suit had been viewed in England as a "Paki" dress. However, her strategy in developing her style was to negate this racism and to emphasize cultural pride in the face of destructive British Imperialism:

> The *salwaar-kameez* used to be a Paki dress. We were told that all the time. Today, every high street store has outfits that are and look like a long *kameez* with *kaajs* on the side and trousers, sometimes straight cut ones. The *salwaar-kameez* has come a long way. There was a lot of racism. Gone are the days when people used to say "you smell of curry". They are eating curry all the time. Every

time I go to the supermarket, I see chicken tikka masala, or some onion bhaji or some curry something or the other in their trolleys.

Geeta Sarin's articulation of how and why she defined her own style comes from her ability to sustain herself on the strengths of her diaspora heritage, honed by the East African experience in Kenya as well as by her subsequent experiences in Britain. Her interpretation of her clothes and her enterprise is explicitly couched in terms of maintaining cultural pride in the face of negative comments from both local whites and upper class Indians, who often express disdain for Asian immigrants and second generation Asians' taste in clothes. Her recoded designs of Indian clothes are inserted into the European and international markets, thereby using the market not just as a straightforward mechanism of exchange but also as a means of negotiating a distinctive diasporic style.

A SECOND GENERATION DIASPORIC IMPROVISOR: BUBBY MAHIL

"Young Asians and Europeans don't want something that is totally Asian: they want something with an Asian element", opines Bubs Mahil, who designs Indianwear for the British Prime Minister Tony Blair's wife Cherie. (Bhasi 2003)

Like Geeta Sarin, Bubby epitomizes the racialized and politicized diaspora aesthetics that animate the hybridized suit economies in Britain particularly well. She is the designer of Cherie Booth's high profile suits that have been well covered in the media. She designed many of the outfits worn by Aishwaryai Rai, the central heroine of *Bride and Prejudice*, a production by diasporic film director Gurinder Chadha, and she has designed costumes for a Harry Potter film. Bubby extended the diaspora *sina-prona* sewing culture to fashion an identity for herself that is acutely reflective of her particular context and biography. Younger than Geeta Sarin, Bubby reworks traditional designs more radically, involving a greater fusion of different elements. The *salwaar-kameez* features in her work but is not central to it. Like Geeta, Bubby is also a pioneer in the fashion field.

Bubby came to London when she was three years old. Both her parents were born and raised in Kenya. She went to school in East London. She started a BTech Diploma in fashion but left after a year and half, because she was already knowledgeable about fashion and a proficient seamstress, having learnt to sew at home from a young age. By this stage, many of her friends and others in her social and neighborhood circuits wanted to acquire the clothes she was producing. For the first three years, she carried out all the stitching herself. She would buy the fabrics, make the outfits and sell them at suit parties she organized in other people's houses. She used to make between 15 to 20 suits for these parties, all products of her own sewing labor. She was supremely successful and became busy so fast that she decided to open up a shop.

A cultural battle transforms into an influential commercial site

Bubby's genius is that she has developed a fusion style that is reflective of her context and which also captures the youth consumer styles of her time. This encoding of the complex cultural textures in clothes is continuously responsive to local and global fashion trends as well as the individual idiosyncrasies of her customers. She constantly improvises and co-constructs and therefore captures the new and what is not yet spoken in a dialogue with her customers. The resulting design is not fixed in advance and brought over from an outside site by an outside agency. She is not "just bringing India to Britain", she says, but is rather developing new styles which reflect her continuously changing hybrid contexts. Hence she achieves a voice through the clothes and asserts her own version of her ethnicity and culture. Her fusion style is the product of her experience of growing up in an often hostile, racist environment. She politicized her friends' casually racist comments and decided to respond to them defiantly. As she explains:

> I know it sounds really stupid, but in those days, I mean, if you were walking down the road I didn't have any Indian friends, all my friends were English, if you were walking down the road going down somewhere and you would see an Indian girl wearing the *salwaar-kameez*, my friends would automatically say "Paki", just because they were wearing a *salwaar-kameez*. That is when it offended me and I thought, "Why am I ashamed of wearing what we do?" That is our culture, that I have got to do it in such a way that they accept it as well.

This was the backdrop to Bubby's desire to make suits that combined different elements to create new silhouettes and designs and also define a style for herself. In reacting to the racist anti-*salwaar*-suit domain in which she grew up, she was able to channel her cultural anger into developing a new fusion style that created a distinct commercial space. She remembers two designs as particularly crucial in the development of her style. The first was a wedding dress for a white girl friend. Bubby was 18 or 19 years old at that time.

> It was something that was very Eastern and Western as well. It was a really good mix. It was only when I made it for [her friend] that I realized it can be accepted. She loved it, she really did. And I realized how much the Western market appreciates our embroideries and our fabrics, although designs and shapes they do not really go for.

She had the embroidery completed in India because she had gone there for a trip. She made what looked like a *lengha,* an ankle length skirt cut on the bias, with a hip length top. It was a mix between a European white wedding dress, a *lengha* and a *chuni,* the long scarf. She refers to this as the 'mix', hybrid forms that characterize much cultural production in diaspora settings.

Her second breakthrough design was a dress she made for herself: a ruched chiffon lined, high waisted frock with *choost*-pyjama, long parallel trousers that form folds at the ankle. She made this outfit in the late 1970s when she was in her late teens, and was preparing to attend a cousin's wedding. She had been out with her sister "hunting for suits to wear" everywhere but could not find anything. In the end,

> what I made was *churi-dhar* pyjama and, you know, the frock-style you get with a bodice. I bought chiffon and put the chiffon over the top and ruched it all up and it just looked so nice. Now it sounds awful but at the time it really did look lovely. It was all one color.

Her sewing skills helped her negotiate a style for herself that reflected her subcultural context and asserted her design sensibilities. Her confidence soared as she created more of these syncretic styles. She is determined to adhere to her own style.

> Because of things I experienced when I was young, which I was ashamed of, I do not want to lose it now. Wearing *salwaar-kameez* and the way everybody always used to look at us and our dress, you know, I just do not want to lose that.

Collaborative sketching

Bubby's innovative working style, similar to that of her design and commercial "cousin" Geeta Sarin, contributes to the vitality of the finished garments. A design is negotiated with a customer, later elaborated by Bubby, and faxed to India where the outfit is made and then sent back to Britain within three weeks. This is why Bubby is constantly on the phone to her Indian manufacturers whilst she is in the shop, during and after shop hours. She is checking on deadlines, getting the latest on the manufacturing status of various garments and giving instructions. At all times of the day, regular couriers arrive bringing packages and assistants scurry off to collect packages from customer clearance at airports. The intensity of the phone calls, the frequent faxing and extensive use of courier services really bring home to the observer the use of technology to compress markets.

Yet it is the simple pencil sketch that comprises the first stage in this sophisticated global process of production. It is through the sketch that she negotiates designs with her customer. She says she has always done this, right from the beginning. I witnessed this dialogue of co-construction and found it absolutely fascinating. It captured many of the processes of globalization and time-space compression. These design dialogues, micro-interactions in micro-markets led by women for women, represented the high point of my fieldwork in this area. Bubby can *never imagine* not negotiating a design, she says, even ten years down the road when she will be better established.

The process of the design dialogue and sketch was clearly demonstrated in the incident of a tall, plump woman who came into the shop. This woman knew Bubby quite well socially and purchased clothes from her regularly. She had access to Indian markets as she frequently visited India with her businessman Indian husband, but she still preferred to buy from Bubby most of the time. I watched Bubby draw a simple sketch as the client described the type of neckline she wanted, the shape and the collar, the embroidery and the extent of it, using some of the styles already in the shop. She decided on the *lungi* suit with a short just-below-the-hips *kameez*. Bubby convinced her that a *lungi* suit with a straight, ankle-length skirt rather than a sarong would be flattering for a plump person, given her height, especially with a shorter top. A rough sketch was drawn by Bubby as they discussed the various possibilities and finalized the style, fabric and embroidery.

Later Bubby elaborated the sketch into a fully fledged drawing with instructions for all the various details, elaborating the conversation with the outline sketch. She faxed the drawing to India that day. She also subsequently talked the sketch through by phone to India to clarify the instructions, and made several other calls to check on the progress of the outfit. Within three weeks, the outfit was ready for the customer to pick up at Bubby's shop.

Distinction through politicized designs

Bubby uses her diaspora sewing background to craft a style that is reflective of her context. She uses the technical skill pools of cultural reproduction developed elsewhere in her family's earlier phases of migration to create a style that represents her hybrid experiences. She has kept alive the skills she started off with, using that experience to negotiate designs with customers. She combines different elements to produce something that makes sense to her customers because it is grounded in the subcultural tastes and norms she shares with them. This process reflects the ways in which diaspora cultures are created through constant negotiation and transformation in new spaces, suturing displacement and rupture through innovative recontextualization.

New design lexicons are thus negotiated through transnationalized local spaces. These connections and transformations are what have made Bubby commercially successful in diaspora markets. Bubby has developed an almost subaltern voice through style, expressed in the fusion clothes she designs. The suit previously had no positive public registers in a mainstream public domain. Bubby has used the market not just as a mechanism of exchange but also as a way of negotiating a new identity, and at the same time, of shifting the consumer landscapes of Britain. For this identity is given further, new inflections when such members of the white British elite such as Prime Minister Tony Blair's wife, Cherie Booth, wear Bubby's clothes. As a result, Bubby's commercial space has influenced the sartorial style of the powerful elite in Britain. Entrepreneurs like Bubby have opened commercial spaces that are now part of the common landscapes of white and black and all British women. Bubby's design process, like that of Geeta Sarin, is at once local and global. Bubby is using global communications technology to create a British Asian mediated transnational space through localized design dialogues. The resulting market is the politicized site of important cultural battles that alter mainstream sartorial consumer and cultural economies, whilst also colluding with capitalist processes. The syncretic clothes forms that Bubby produces are far more complex in content than, as she says, "just picking up India and bringing it to Britain".

SELLING INDIA TO THE "WEST": RITU KUMAR

"Indianness" was also very much the theme for Ritu Kumar, the doyen of Indian fashion. "Everything works as long as we, as Indians, sell it as Indian and not try to sell it as something else", said Kumar, among the most respected Indian designers, after showing off slinky tops replete with Hindu iconography. (Sengupta 2003)

I grew up in a culture where to wear Indian was chic, but Indian, aesthetically top of the bracket Indian ... There has always been a very chic aesthetic India with its balance of colour .... (Interview, Zee TV, May 1996)

Ritu opened her London Mayfair shop in 1996, thus extending to twelve, at the time, the chain of shops she had already established in major cities in India. In 2003, her shops expanded to16 nationwide outlets in India. She had already been commercially successful and renowned in Indian markets, described as the "grand lady of revivalist ethnic fashion" and as the "high priestess of traditional *zardozi*"[6] (*Galaxzee*, May–June 1996). Ritu Kumar has helped to revive many declining Indian embroidery and craft traditions. She is highly articulate and commands design discourses amongst many other vocabularies of arts and crafts. She is an executive member of the Delhi Crafts Council. She is acquainted with leading Indian artists and craftspeople as well as the influential and powerful decision makers in the state sanctioned arts and crafts institutions and handloom industries. She is the author of books including a publication entitled *Costumes and Textiles of Royal India*, which was launched by Christie's in 1999. She trained in museology in the United States before embarking on a career devoted to a revival of traditional arts and crafts in India. The annual turnover from her Indian domestic enterprises alone is estimated at 10 billion crore rupees, higher than any other Indian designer (*Outlook*, 20 April 1998:63). Having been supremely successful in India, she subsequently wanted to extend this success internationally. Her London shop, however, closed only three years after opening.

The arts and crafts agenda was the hallmark of the London shop. There was a gallery of contemporary Indian art, ARKS, on the floor below the shop. Its aim, as stated in the press release, was that of "a bold new project to present the best of contemporary Indian art to collectors in Britain". The point that I want to emphasize here is the congruency between Ritu's merchandise and the agenda of the gallery, which was to change the perception of India, to present a new picture of the "East", in the form of a contemporized dynamic Indian aesthetic in art and design. It showcased contemporary India in crafted art clothes and lifestyle products as well as through contemporary Indian art. This commercial art space was thus intended to have an educational role, along with being an area of economic exchange. The contemporary art gallery reminded people that this was an art space, hence the commodities sold within the perimeters of the space were reflective of that art. Ritu clothes are highly crafted art clothes, suits that have a defined design aesthetic that is strongly controlled through Ritu's definitive design signature. I was told a number of times by discriminating consumers of such creations that they could recognize a Ritu design immediately.

Ritu viewed her London shop as

> ... very much a window to the East, and in particular a window to India. What I always thought was there was a reflection of India in various ways, one was from the Indian film industry, which was very strong ... The second is you would get some merchandise that is available already in different shops, even in Mayfair. But there was a certain thing missing there. There wasn't one *defined design identity* that was coming in with the merchandise. It was assorted merchandise. Accompanying it, what I wanted so very much was to have a reflection of contemporary Indian art. (Interview, Zee TV, May 1996)

Ritu considered that she was selling "top of the range" India, an India that reflects "ancient traditions of Indian craftsmanship" rather than kitsch. Her highly crafted clothes were initially designed for elite Indians but these chic products were then transferred to an international market, primarily for a white elite market in Britain and only secondarily to wealthy Indians resident in the UK. Ritu emphasized that she wanted to stress India's dynamic modernity as played out through a revived "contemporariness" located in an international arena. She stated this was "not folklorish India, it's not ethnic India, it's contemporary India" (interview with Zee TV, May 1996). Ritu wanted to educate exclusive "Western" markets about classic chic India and its sophisticated contemporary design economies regulated by influential professionals like herself.

I asked her how she understood the market and customer profile in London and whether there were differences between what she was selling in India and in London. She answered:

> We haven't changed. We are coming with our own identity. More than perceiving markets, I think there is an education process that there is an alternative. We are not slotting ourselves into what the market needs ... We are saying this is what we are, this is what India is, we will not change. How we are perceived in the market we do not know.

Her posture of commercial disinterest in the market was asserted even though she is a famous and successful market leader in India, far more successful than any of the other competing Indian designers who barely reach half her annual turnover. Even though the explicit agenda of her joint enterprise with the ARKS gallery was intended to educate the "West" about the sophisticated high chic and arts and crafts aesthetics of India, she was not shy of using this sphere for commercial as well as cultural exchange. Her sophisticated website and entry into hi-tech cyber marketing are a testament to her commercial savvyness.

Ritu's effort to represent her country's heritage in the development of new international markets for her own merchandise has benefited from the support of government sponsorship. This is a position of privilege in comparison to diaspora designers, who have had to develop their own markets and commerce without any state or institutional help. Diaspora designers from marginal immigrant locations do not represent a codified aesthetic in their clothes merchandise. They interpret an individual experience, an experience of migration that is about displacement and replacement. Indian fashion entrepreneurs are very differently located, in terms of class, experiences of the nation and their design intentions in the marketplace.

Ritu's commitment to the revival of arts and crafts tradition is couched in a nationalist and anti-imperialist discourse that serves to obscure the market interests which this supremely class conscious commercial sphere caters for. Her more tacit but no less crucial agenda was to sell to the "West", which Ritu associated with the wealthy elite whites and transnational South Asian elites, but not locally based Indian immigrants living in and produced by racialized contexts. In my interview with her, Ritu stated:

> But what comes out of the country and what represents India to a lot of people who live abroad, especially to the Indian who has kind of lost touch with

India ... For them unfortunately, it's still a limited gypsy clothing culture. And I think they are looking for something to identify with and there's a great deal of confusion there outside the country as to who people are; particularly, I see it through the clothing.

Ritu is not alone in her views since these kinds of negative attitudes about British Asians are pervasive amongst many subcontinental elites. Those Indians who occupy an elite class position in India try to dissociate themselves from British Indians whose very different class and racial location threatens their own privileged placement as Indians. So it is hardly surprising if they refuse to acknowledge the local British Asian scene. A diasporic Asian intellectual also suggested that:

They do not want to be seen as people of color and are not going to be denigrated immigrants, as British Asians. There is a very racialized consciousness among South Asians from India. They do not want to be identified as people of color, racialized subjects in very racialized countries. So by keeping to their India label and being transnational psychologically and otherwise, they do not have to fall into racialized hierarchies.

INDIVIDUALIZATION THROUGH RACIALIZED HYBRIDIZATION VS DISTINCTION THROUGH NATIONAL PURITIES

All three of these fashion entrepreneurs are making strong political statements through their commercial practices and commodities and all of them engage a discourse of cultural pride. The experience of racist taunts and stereotyping spurred Bubby to create a defiant hybrid style that is both true to its context and responsive to the sartorial mores of her youthful subcultures. Geeta Sarin responded to English racism by asserting pride "in our culture". In Ritu's case however, her design agendas emerged as a response to imperialism as well as through her own transformative personal experiences of being educated in the West, experiences which prompted her to learn about her own cultural background and the arts and crafts of her country. It is an agenda that is also integrally linked with the Indian nationalist movement whose influential members spearheaded the revivalist initiative. Ritu's design aesthetics revolve around a past-oriented discourse of revitalizing an ancient nation's craft skills and design vocabularies. According to the publicity material released for the 1996 launch of her shop in London, Ritu was offering a "unique style reflecting the ancient traditions of Indian craftsmanship in a contemporary vocabulary". Thus Ritu was represented as performing a kind of ambassadorial function for India.

In contrast, diasporic fashion entrepreneurs like Bubby and Geeta are engaged in future- and present-oriented dialogues that are in a way anti-nationalist. They are not trying to preserve or even revitalize a national heritage or ancient past. Rather they are negotiating an emergent national space. True to their biographical experiences, migration trajectory and racialized cultural locations, their designs are a celebration of syncretic forms which they assert in the market. Since they are already located in the West they are not trying to capture "Western" markets. Rather they are constituting these economies from the inside, creating markets for their designs by "doing their own thing" in the communities within which they live and have been part of since their childhoods. Designers like Geeta and Bubby have the skills to capture the new and the moment. Their power has been acquired from their struggles to represent themselves on their own terms, to create the new licenses of participation that emerge from a new sacred, a sacred that captures the not yet spoken, and that creates new fusions which are eloquent in their continuous contextualization and recontextualization. These are the racialized and politicized sensibilities that are reflected in the negotiated aesthetics of co-construction and dialogic designing in which they collaborate with their customers in London fashion markets. This is a location that is sharply distinct from that of the Indian and Pakistani elites who are new to dissonant situations, especially outside their national strongholds.

CONCLUSION

The sixth government sponsored *Lakme* India fashion show took place in Delhi in April 2005 (Sengupta 2005). Leading Indian designers like Ritu Kumar were the stars of these platforms that had been instituted to enable India based designers to "make it in the West" and thus capture a larger share of global apparel markets (ibid.). However, in attempting to establish international markets for their exclusive products, these designers were not able to assert their individuality on their own terms. They had to filter their design signatures through the agendas defined by European and American personnel and commercial agencies. American and European buyers can exercise enormous classificatory pressure in commissioning fashion collections for import, demanding that Indian styles conform to the design distinctions already incorporated into their Western repertoires. In selling to the "West" on the terms of the West, India based designers are in fact surrendering to a form of neocolonialism in design and style economies. This is the price Indian designers have to pay if they want to "make it in the West".

In contrast, diasporic Londoners are already located in the "West" as insiders. They are not submitting to pressures to conform to the design desires and requirements of outsider agencies. Instead they are seeking to fashion and sell designs on their own terms in domains they have helped to produce and which they know intimately. The notion of "making it in the West" is an irrelevant frame for these racialized locals whose efforts to represent themselves and their creations as distinctively and innovatively British Asian cannot be separated from the very particular Western location in which they have developed.

India based designers, buttressed by powerful government sponsorships and financial clout, through premier institutions like the Fashion and Design Council of India (FDCI), create contemporary styles through retrospective distinctions. That is to say, the distinctions they reproduce, preserve, and rehabilitate have already been explicitly significant in their native landscapes for centuries. As Basil Bernstein states:

> Retrospective identities are shaped by national, cultural, grand narratives of the past ... What is foregrounded ... is the collective social base as revealed by the recontextualized grand narrative of the past ... What is at stake here is stabilizing the past and projecting it into the future. (2000:67)

In contrast, the markets and current success of their diasporic London counterparts developed through their own response to the local moment and to their own desire for the type of clothes they wanted to wear in the present. Their "prospective" individualities, to adapt Basil Bernstein's phrase, "are essentially future orientated" (Bernstein 2000:76). "They rest as with retrospective identities upon narratives but these narrative resources ground the identity not in the past but in the future" (ibid.).

Elite subcontinental design professionals like Ritu Kumar command prodigious cultural capital and political clout in India but they cannot easily translate these national licensing privileges into the fluid landscapes of global markets. In their efforts to placate the American and European gatekeepers of these larger markets they end up lending their design dictionaries to foreign agencies that can raid them, fracture them, and diminish their fundamental significances.

However, British Asian design innovators are seeking to claim their own distinctive styles by rearticulating the aesthetics negotiated by previous generations during earlier phases of settlement in the UK, in the process asserting a powerful sense of belonging. This shared belonging is easily read and decoded by others familiar with the various elements which have been the source codes of this aesthetic background, the clothes, cooking styles, combinational musical forms, hybrid languages such as Swahilized Punjabi, and so on. These commonly held diasporic subcultures are thus the ground upon which these flourishing co-constructed design enterprises have been developed.

Yet there is a careful balance as well as tension in the co-constructed improvisational designs these designers are negotiating with their savvy customers. They are negotiating variations on the contours of the Punjabi suit or *salwaar-kameez*. These contours are clearly recognized, whether they are as radically reinterpreted as in Bubby Mahil's designs, or less so, as in the case of Geeta Sarin's clothes. Thus, in co-constructing their designs with their customers, these designers are recontextualizing the core elements of the *salwaar-kameez* that emerge from a shared social context. The designers as well as the clients thus draw their individualistic styles from the negotiation of a style sensibility and silhouette that is shared. The success of their design enterprises reflects this common source of belonging, which animates their highly individualized designs. This balancing act on the part of diasporic designers encodes this tension of accepting the desires of stylish customers who are attuned to the nuances of their shared diasporic subcultural niche, whilst still endeavoring to create innovative silhouettes that reflect their own unique design signatures as style professionals. In this chapter I have therefore sought to outline two contrasting styles of individuality and distinction. On the one hand, we have a British Asian style comprising an improvisational *sina-prona* ethos, negotiative stitching and an assertion of individual creativity by designers whose work developed on the social margins. In this context, claims for distinction rest paradoxically on the collaborative interpretation of a shared sartorial vernacular. On the other hand, we have a style identified with Indian elites who occupy powerful national positions as opinion forming design experts that they want to convert into transnational commerce. Here claims for distinction rest on the assertion of a privileged expertise in representing and interpreting a historic national tradition. Both sets of style innovators are asserting and claiming individuality and distinction through different strategies that are authentic to their locations, biographical experiences, cultural heritages and political locations. These different claims to individuality are in the end strong reflections of the powerful socialization all these entrepreneurial actors have been subject to, in one case through highly mobile social structures that have traversed borders, and in the other case, through longstanding and deeply rooted structures. These are the complex modalities of distinction that diasporic and elite designers produce dynamically through their divergent design strategies and source codes.

NOTES

1 A more detailed and comprehensive version of the material in this chapter appears in my book *Dangerous Designs: Asian Women Fashion the Diaspora Economies* (Bhachu 2004). A shorter treatment of some of the material considered in this chapter also appears in my essay, 'Diaspora Politics through Style: Racialized and Politicized Fashion in Global Markets' (Bhachu 2005).

2 Contemporary global markets emphasize the customization of products as a vehicle for the expression of individual identities in reflexive landscapes where sign values matter more than the labor process. Products are geared to define individuality without the backing of grand narratives of the past, often emerging from disembedded aesthetics (Giddens 1991) being tailored to take account of individual desires for distinction in the present. Lash and Urry state, "what is produced are not material objects, but signs ..."(1994:15), and they go onto note that "the production of the design component comprises an increasing component of goods. The specific labour process is becoming less important in contribution to value-added and the 'design process' is progressively more central" (ibid.:58).

On similar ground, Jim Gee has argued that "[t]he new capitalism ... is about customization: the design of products and service perfectly dovetailed to the needs, desires, and identities of individuals on the basis of their differences. These differences may be rooted in their sub-group affiliations or in their unique individuality" (1996:43).

3 The struggle over school uniforms crystallized during the 1980s in the famous Mandla vs Lee case, which was sparked off by the refusal of the headmaster of a private Catholic school, Mr Dowell-Lee, to give an East African Sikh boy, Gurinder Mandla, permission to wear a turban as part of his school uniform. The Sikhs successfully got themselves defined as a "race", which increased their right to define their identities as separate people and whose right to don their religious symbols were recognized

legally. Gurinder Mandla as a consequence wore a turban in the public domains of a public school.

4 The sources of diasporic improvisation are embedded in the culture of *sina-prona*, which consists of stitching and beading through improvisational patterning. It is a metaphor for the many skills that constitute the making of a home, the high level of domestic expertise that was pooled and elaborated especially in frontier contexts. *Sina-prona* reproduced the infrastructure of pioneer communities in contexts in which there were no or few service professionals. These skills established and reproduced a developed grounded aesthetic that predisposes second generation diasporic designers towards the possibility of co-construction and improvisation (see Bhachu 2004 for further details of these cultural and commercial economies).

Similar diasporic *sina-prona* economies are found amongst Caribbean women in England and Jamaica who were innovative "designer-makers" as Carol Tulloch calls them. They used the "freehand dressmaking" methods and churned out highly individualistic designs by sewing freehand using their own highly developed sewing expertise and imagination (Tulloch 1999:111–28). Also, L.M. Montgomery (1994 [1925]), in her novel *Anne of Green Gables*, set on Prince Edward Island in Canada, describes an economy of Anglo-Saxon diasporics. In the novel Mrs Rachel Lynde "ran a sewing circle" and made the heroine, Anne, a puff-sleeve dress in the "very latest fashion", going against the wishes of Anne's stern adoptive mother who wanted her to have a simpler dress which took less material.

5 The former wife of the famous Pakistani cricketer Imran Khan and daughter of James Goldsmith, who was one of the wealthiest men in Britain.

6 *Zardozi* is the embroidery of the royal courts of India, produced with pure gold and silver thread and also in lurex, a cheaper substitute used later in a less glamorous aesthetic than that pure form developed in the Mughal courts. This beautiful embroidery is used on many wedding clothes and in other exclusive clothes worn by both men and women.

REFERENCES

Bernstein, B. (2000) *Pedagogy and Symbolic Control and Identity: Theory, Research, Critique*. Revised edition. Oxford: Rowman and Littlefield.

Bhachu, P. (1985) *Twice Migrants: East African Sikh Settlers in Britain*. London/New York: Tavistock.

Bhachu, P. (1993) 'Twice versus Direct Migrants'. In I. Light and P. Bhachu (eds) *Immigration and Entrepreneurship: Culture, Capital and Ethnic Networks*. Rutgers, NJ: Transactions, pp. 163–84.

Bhachu, P. (1996) 'Multiple Migrants and Multiple Diasporas'. In P. Singh and S. Singh Thandi (eds) *Globalization and the Region: Explorations in Punjabi Identity*. Coventry: APS, pp. 342–56.

Bhachu, P. (2004) *Dangerous Designs: Asian Women Fashion the Diaspora Economies*. London/New York: Routledge.

Bhachu, P. (2005) 'Diaspora Politics Through Style: Racialized and Politicized Fashion in Global Markets'. In C. Alexander and C. Knowles (eds) *Making*

Race Matter: Bodies, Space and Identity. Basingstoke: Palgrave Macmillan, pp. 42–59.
Bhasi, I. (2003) 'British-Asian Designers: Ready to Bear'. *India Today*, September 22, "Designs on the World" section, 30–8.
Gee, J.P. (1996) 'Fast Capitalism: Theory and Practice'. In J.P. Gee, G. Hull and C. Llankkshear (eds) *The New Work Order: Behind the Language of the New Capitalism*. Boulder, CO: Westview, pp. 24–44.
Giddens, A. (1991) *Modernity and Self Identity: Self and Society in the Modern Age*. Palo Alto, CA: Stanford University Press.
Kumar, R. (1999) *Costumes and Textiles of Royal India*. London: Christie's.
Lash, S. and Urry, J. (1994) *Economy of Signs and Space*. London/Newbury Park, CA: Sage.
Montgomery, L.M. (1994 [1925]) *Anne of Green Gables*. London: Puffin.
Sengupta, H. (2003) '4th Lakme India Fashion Week "translates heritage into clothes"'. *News India-Times*, August 1:28.
Sengupta, H. (2005) '6th Lakme India Fashion Week "An Alternative to Western Fashion?" Have You Even Thought of the World Emulating India?'. *News India-Times*, May 6:21.
Tulloch, C. (1999) 'There's No Place Like Home: Dressmaking and Creativity in the Jamaican Community of the 1940s and 1960s'. In B. Burman (ed.) *The Culture of Sewing*. London/New York: Berg, pp. 111–28.

5
Claiming Individuality through "Flexibility": Career Choices and Constraints among Traveling Consultants

Vered Amit

Can claims of individuality be persuasively articulated with systemic transformations? In this chapter, I want to explore the divergent ways in which prevailing politico-economic formulations of "flexibility" are implicated in the career choices of a diverse range of mobile Canadian consultants and their sense of authorship over the attendant outcomes.

In his book *The Corrosion of Character*, Richard Sennett outlined the transformations in the organization of work and time that have been entailed in the shift towards "flexible capitalism", a transition exemplified by the motto "No long term" (1998:22). Rather than their parents' experience of a career measured by incremental progress through the hierarchy of one or two organizations, young Americans entering the job market at the start of the twenty-first century are likely to have to change employment numerous times in the course of their work lives. At the same time, corporations have outsourced many of the tasks they once performed to smaller organizations or to individuals employed on a freelance contractual basis. Accompanying this onus towards contractual and episodic work has been a flattening out of institutional hierarchies with an emphasis placed on organizational networks that are constantly being recomposed and redefined.

Sennett noted that under the terms of this "new" capitalism, uncertainty was no longer a concomitant of extraordinary events, but was now conceived as a normal part of everyday practices. And this orientation could leach out from the domain of work, in the process reconstituting domestic, friendship and neighborhood relations as well. Mobility between jobs might also necessitate mobility of residence, thus requiring multiple recompositions of personal networks. And the flattened hierarchies, risk taking and volatilities identified with paradigms of flexible capitalism were not likely to be happy models for stable family life.

> The conditions of time in the new capitalism have created a conflict between character and experience, the experience of disjointed time threatening the ability of people to form their characters into sustained narratives. (Sennett 1998:31)

In this chapter, I will be concerned with the practices and narratives of development consultants who, in the course of their work, move frequently and repeatedly between the global North and South. In many respects, the everyday circumstances of these peripatetic professionals could well serve as exemplars of the processes described above. Yet the authorship claimed by most of these consultants for their involvement in these practices diverges quite notably from the fear of losing control expressed by the figures featuring in Sennett's account. The transnational consultants on whom this chapter focuses are more likely to account for the episodic and fragmentary nature of their lives as a challenging but exciting lifestyle suited to their own distinctive personalities, cross-cultural curiosity and desire for exploration. Theirs are narratives of disjunction embraced as largely voluntary journeys of adventure and self-discovery. It may therefore be that even more important in the capacity to develop coherent narratives of identity than the effects of constant mobility, is the degree to which people feel that they are able to exercise a determining choice over this course, i.e., the extent to which they feel ownership over the conditions of their life stories.

NECESSARY MOBILITIES

In certain respects, it is hardly surprising that the practices of the transnational consultants being considered in this chapter should reflect recent capitalist transformations. After all, my research project on itinerant consulting was initially launched in an effort to explore the ways in which the global restructuring of production, labor and marketing can impel a spiraling interpolation of mobility and livelihood. The onus within flexible capitalism towards outsourcing, "network-like arrangements" and flattened hierarchies (Sennett 1998) has been associated with an explosive growth of highly specialized consultancy services, variously identified as "producer" (Sassen 1994) or "symbolic-analytic" (Reich 1991) services. These include the independent legal, financial, advertising, technical and accounting services which are being used by corporations to manage and control their scattered holdings and networks (Sassen 1994).

Consultants working across this enormously varied span of issues and specializations have in common increasingly peripatetic lives. As a matter of course, they must be able to adapt to a succession of different organizations for which, each in turn, they are providing temporary consultancy support. Their "place" of work is therefore serial, subjected to a constant recasting in terms of locale, social relationships and theatres of interaction. In embarking on this project, I reasoned that this pattern of successive contracts would increasingly be framed in extralocal and transnational terms given the extension of institutional activities and affiliation across space. Accordingly, I assumed that consultants would face greater pressures to undertake long distance travel and border crossings over the course of their various projects.

Initially I attempted to include a wide range of peripatetic consultants in this research and my preliminary assumptions about the "pressure" towards mobility and travel involved in this kind of work seemed to echo the reflections of some of the professionals I interviewed.[1] In the late 1990s, Paul set up a small independent training consultancy that specialized in assisting companies with transitions to new organizational and technological systems. The company had offices in Vancouver as well as in two locales across the Canadian/American border in Washington State. Although he had an apartment in Vancouver, "home" for Paul was now a house in the British Columbian Gulf Islands he was usually only able to visit on weekends. On my first interview with him in February 1998, Paul explained that a major new project had allowed him to curtail some of his traveling to the United States and spend more time in the Lower Mainland (Greater Vancouver) of British Columbia.

> I consider myself from the North American continent and I have a personal preference to be based in Vancouver. And this particular project [based in Vancouver] has allowed me to significantly do that. I really didn't have much of a Vancouver office. I used my apartment and I just went to the States. And my American office is way bigger and has way more employees than in Canada. This project has turned that around.

Paul was hoping that eventually developments in communications technology would allow him to direct his business from afar thereby reducing the amount of travel he had to undertake. Some months later at a second interview, the project in Greater Vancouver had ended and Paul was preparing to ratchet up his traveling again.

It's just ending so I'm beginning to increase travel. I've been down to ... we have an office in Everett still and we have a second office now in Bellingham so those are just south of Vancouver so I've begun traveling to those more regularly. I expect to be traveling for sales purposes to the Midwest soon and I'm also getting back into going to some professional conferences that I've basically not been able to go to for the last couple of years. So the project was extremely engrossing in time. It was a newspaper start-up and newspapers publish at nights and they manage in the day so I was there 24 hours a day, seven days a week. So it became very all encompassing. So that's ending and we're going down over the next two months and look for new business, for a couple of reasons. There's two parts to that and that is I have a history, relationships with companies in the States but the second thing is I'm like, unfortunately, a lot of people, fairly pessimistic about BC.

In 1998 when I first met them in Seattle, Richard and Monica, a married couple, were both working within the overlapping consulting sectors of information technology and information management. Like a number of their peers and friends in this area, they had relocated from Canada to the United States with Richard moving between branches of the same company and Monica taking up a position with a new employer. As Monica explained:

... the market base in Canada, including Toronto, is just very, very small compared to the US. And from a consulting point of view, if you want to do the work that makes an impact, if you want to do the work that's sort of recognized more worldwide, you have to be in a big centre and that would be a New York or a San Francisco. Seattle is actually considered small in the States but compared to Vancouver, it's much larger in terms of the business.

And given the nature of their work, they expected that at times they would probably have to travel beyond their home base towards more dispersed clients. As Monica explained, "All consulting requires some travel". When I first interviewed them, Richard had just returned from two weeks in Halifax and was now heading off for a two month stint in Los Angeles with likely weekend commutes back to Seattle. It was an assignment he was not looking forward to because of the inevitable disruption his absences would cause to their home life and he was hoping to persuade his employer to let him be more stationary in future assignments.

> ... I don't mind going off and traveling a couple of weeks or so but a stint where I'm going to have to go for, like this upcoming one, two months, it's a little too much really. And it really wasn't what I was expecting. I don't enjoy it. It's disruptive to our own lifestyle. We like to do things a lot together and we like to find out things together and when I'm away or she's away, the weekends are just sort of spent catching your breath and not really beginning to enjoy life and enjoying getting to know each other better and stuff like that. So yeah, I'm not enjoying it.

Meanwhile Monica, who had previously completed a similar stint of travel to a client in Boise, considered herself lucky to have a local work assignment in Seattle for several months. Richard and Monica explained to me that a willingness to move frequently between jobs, and to travel away to clients when required to, was a necessary entailment for rapid career advancement within consulting. As Richard explained: "So there's that trade in balance of either a stable lifestyle and less rewards or a nonstable lifestyle and more rewards". On another occasion when I asked Monica whether consulting companies would allow some choice about the amount of travel they required of their employees, she noted:

> They do. I think the companies do try to be sympathetic but on the other hand, if the choice is, well you know, you can take the less interesting work locally or you can travel, then they're sort of putting you in a difficult position, I think, because you sacrifice either your personal life or you sacrifice your career. So it becomes not much of a choice. It kind of, [laughs] either way you go, you're going to lose somewhere.

And with echoes of Sennett's account of repeated work shifts as the new "normal", regardless of the amount of travel involved in their future work assignments, both Monica and Richard fully expected their career would continue to feature mobility in the form of regular moves between companies, a form of flexibility that had already prompted two major relocations on their part, first across Canada and then from Canada to the United States. Monica said:

> I don't think that any consultant really takes it for granted that you're going to have a 20 year career path and stay with a certain company. So even if they go

somewhere else and don't want to travel, they might stay with that company for a few years and go to a different company. I think they're pretty much ready to change all the time.

PERSONAL FLEXIBILITY

But contrast Monica and Richard's version of travel and mobility as a structurally inescapable if not particularly desirable necessity with the following accounts of work related travel:

Michael: I'm a true Type A. I'm on the go constantly. I love to travel. I love working in other cultures. I don't like ruts. I will get to a certain point working here [in Vancouver] where what's the next fix? It's like the entrepreneur. The thrill isn't in the acquisition so much as it is in the chase, in getting there. And I guess for me it's the journey. It's getting from here to there and then getting immersed in these different projects. And it's the learning experience too. It's been really educational. Far more educational than I would have gotten if I was sitting working on domestic projects.

Marina: You know, for me, working overseas has been a discovery of myself, of my competences, my qualities, my faults. It's been a self discovery. And in my nature, I've always pushed myself, not necessarily because I love doing it but because I have this nature, because I felt I had to challenge myself. I'm older now and I really don't feel like challenging myself any more. I've done that. I've proved everything I had to prove to myself.

Christine: ... whenever I travel ... always, almost always, have personal objectives rather than professional objectives ... .

Vered: So what are the kinds of personal motivations that entice you to take on a project?

Christine: It's my therapy. It's me discovering me.

Vered: So, it's learning different facets of yourself?

Christine: Yeah, and it's amazing. And it's also helping ... every culture, every civilization's got something that you like and that you dislike and it's very interesting to be put in a situation where, "Oh, I didn't realize I was racist. Okay. Interesting. How come I'm a racist all of a sudden? What's creating that?" To me, it's really "Wow!". Discovering about myself. It's a therapy. But much more tailored to who I am. I'm very active, two speeds, friends usually say on or off. That's it. Nothing in between. So I can't picture myself sitting down and thinking about who I am or where I'm going, where I came from. But through these experiences, that's it. That's it. You realize that bang! Something flashes across your mind and so why am I thinking of that or whatever. So personally I think it's [work related traveling] a very, very rewarding, growing experience. Very rewarding.

Ian: It's, I mean, I've found it to be a fascinating pastime. I've seen some incredible countryside, met some wonderful people, felt terribly sorry for a lot of other people who I am sure would be wonderful if they didn't have to fight everyday to get a scrap of food on their table. But I think I've learned more than I have left behind, which perhaps is a bit selfish, but I've seen a lot of ugly, I suppose.

Tanya: It's sometimes very hard, and I haven't traveled for three months and I'm getting antsy because I see the same people every day [laughs]. I find that the opportunities and the challenges of doing international work usually overall outweigh the disadvantages. On a day to day basis, at various points in time, the stress can be, or the loneliness, or the fragmentation can be momentarily overbearing. So there are points when it gets pretty difficult. But in my own experience, just overall, the advantages outweigh that. Overall.

Vered: So what are the advantages?

Tanya: The advantages are the professional challenges of trying to understand how to ... most of these contracts that I do, in one form or another, could be called technical assistance. So how do you intervene in a constructive way in a situation? It's the problem solving, it's the problem definition, it's the problem solving, it's the excitement of learning about another country, another culture. It's the opportunities that [are] more limited than you would think, to indulge in a bit of tourism, if you will, being in foreign countries. It's a combination, I guess, of professional and personal stimulation.

These reflections all come from a set of Canadian based consultants who had based their career on international projects.[2] Tanya is a specialist in urban and environmental management. Ian is an economic planner focusing on large hydroelectric and energy studies. Christine and Marina are both engineers with particular expertise in hydroelectric development. Michael works on environmental aspects of infrastructure projects in the power and energy sector as well as in transportation development, including road rehabilitation and new road structures. At the times these comments were made, they were respectively based in Ontario, Quebec and British Columbia and had all been employed by large private Canadian engineering firms. Both Christine and Tanya subsequently shifted into independent consulting albeit largely working on projects with the same sorts of firms. At the time of the interview, Marina had left international work and was working in the same field but on local Canadian projects.

As my project developed, I shifted my attention from the relatively broad-brush approach with which I had started towards a focus on consultants who like Christine, Marina, Michael, Ian and Tanya had largely worked on development projects outside Canada. Many of these specialists worked on various aspects of power and energy development, an orientation that reflected Canadian firms' expertise in this field. However, others advised on training, communication, resettlement, social and environmental impact assessment. Like Monica, Richard and Paul, they worked on a succession of projects for a variety of clients and with a constantly changing array of colleagues. And across the diverse spectrum of sectors in which all these consultants worked, there was a correlation between an expanding ambit of markets and the institutional demand for mobile expertise. For example, the expansion of Canadian engineering firms into power and energy projects abroad reflected at least in part the diminishing opportunities for large scale hydroelectric development projects in North America.

But the parameters and structuring of mobility diverged quite markedly between different sectors of consultancy. As Marina explained:

> I see a lot of people traveling but they're traveling in North America and Europe. I mean the type of traveling I did, I don't think a lot of people do. I mean I lived in an area where dog was the main meat, rat and bat. So I had bat quite frequently, a lot of dog and I saved the rat for the day that I was really starving. That kind of travel, I don't think people do. They still don't. So I see a lot of people doing consulting but I think that the type of consulting that I did with [an engineering consulting company that Marina had worked for], yes, I would go to Calgary [from Vancouver] for three days and I'd come back. I'd go down to Seattle, I'd go down to San Francisco, back and forth, maybe two days for six weeks. That was not the kind of consulting that I [usually] did. I did consulting in Burkina Faso where I would live in the convent or I would live in a grass hut where there were numerous diseases that I was susceptible to catching, etc., etc. There are different kinds of overseas work. I think there has been a lot more, people are more mobile and they travel more. But they travel more within more familiar environments.

While many of the development consultants interviewed for this project did not usually operate in conditions as taxing as those described by Marina, their work entailed regular long distance travel from the global North to the global South. In turn, they, their colleagues and employers/clients had purposefully classified these roving professionals as specializing in "international" projects. Their occupational round did not involve travel incidentally – i.e., as a necessary extension of their clientele catchments area – but was integrally organized around this movement and carefully distinguished from the situation of their more locally based colleagues.

In sharp contrast to the qualified acceptance by Monica, Richard and Paul, the development consultants interviewed for this project emphasized that they had eagerly sought out opportunities for international occupational travel. And far from such travel simply being a general structural requirement of consulting, in many cases, it had been necessary to exert some effort to make oneself eligible for such travel opportunities. With an MA in Resource and Environmental Management, Michael had acquired first short term summer and then full time employment as a provincial government biologist in British Columbia. After working in this capacity for nearly five years, he knew he wanted to be able to do some traveling. He applied to the Canadian International Development Agency (CIDA) and was told that:

> I had good credentials because I was in water management, environmental management. However, because I hadn't done any international work and they'd had some bad experiences with people they'd sent overseas for extended contracts that hadn't overseas experience culturally, etc., they had elected not to take on junior professionals for overseas work.

But on the advice of the people at CIDA, he then applied and was hired by CUSO.[3] When he returned to Canada, he was hired by the same engineering company that at one time or another had also employed Tanya, Christine and Ian. He was hired as an environmental coordinator on the strength particularly of the work he had conducted for CUSO in Ghana but it still took a number of years before he was finally given a company assignment overseas.

> So in the late '80s, I first got involved in working in Nepal doing environmental assessments on hydro upgrading studies and once I established a reputation with certain key managers that do a lot of international work, I guess my currency as a consultant within the company was established and I was in demand for working overseas.

When she embarked on her professional engineering career, Christine joined a Quebec based firm in which many people traveled to overseas assignments. "I was dying to travel but of course it doesn't come right away". It took four years before she was given an opportunity for her first professional journey abroad, assisting a senior colleague to present a report to overseas clients in the Ivory Coast. Even then, had it not been for the persistence of this colleague, someone who had served as her "mentor" in the company, she might not have been given this opportunity in the face of concern among others in the firm that she was too young to be given this responsibility.

In contrast to the ambivalent necessity of movement featured in Sennett's analysis or in the explanations of Richard and Monica, a sense of determined authorship and personal preference was more commonly attributed to occupational travel in the accounts offered by the peripatetic development consultants interviewed for this project. They had sought out professional opportunities for long distance travel and enjoyed the challenges, excitement and discoveries it offered. Indeed excitement was an important theme that in one form or another reappeared in a number of these accounts.

After adopting a child, Marina had sought out a domestic engineering job with a British Columbian firm so that she could look after her daughter. Although her new job provided much needed stability she found working in this environment much less stimulating than her previous work with consulting companies:

> So a lot of people who work at [her Vancouver employer] are not exactly ... um, they're not necessarily as dynamic as other individuals although they're tremendously competent. It just means that people who work overseas are not looking necessarily for security. They're looking for the thrill of that experience. So I think if I set up my own consulting firm, I would be looking for the thrill of a project, of realizing that project.

When I asked Keith, an independent consultant based in Montreal who had been working on international projects for nearly three decades, what it was about assignments requiring travel abroad that kept drawing him back, he explained:

> Well, there aren't the same opportunities here. I mean it's partly the excitement because if you're working on a job here in Quebec or in Canada, you're part of a large team and it will be 9 to 5 work and there won't be any

> excitement to it, there won't be any intensity. And I think to a large extent, that's part of it, plus the lure of going to different places and seeing new parts of the world. And then my next job is in Mongolia which I've never been to, but I'm excited about the idea of going there.

As Marina had noted, this search for excitement was seen as distinguishing these "international" consultants from their more sedentary colleagues, people who might have relevant technical expertise to offer but who as Tanya put it, "love their barbecues", i.e., they don't want to be away from their homes, families or friends. As Tanya explained, the people who are on their second or subsequent international assignments have

> self selected in a lot of ways because the people who get sent out on a first assignment and don't like it, won't accept another one. And just as you know who they are, they know who they are most of the time right from the get go.

Daniel, a senior project manager, who had at one time worked with Tanya in a Montreal based engineering firm, noted that

> we have a large group of engineers who were born in Laval [a suburb of Montreal], they married the girl from Laval, they went to school in Laval and they have kids in Laval, they now have a house in Laval and they work in Laval.

According to Daniel, it was hard enough for these individuals to drive down the expressway to Montreal, let alone fly off for work in places like Burkina Faso or Benin. So finding someone like Tanya who really wanted to go abroad was a major factor in considering which people to assign to an international project. And it wasn't especially easy to find them.

"I mean I had somebody go out to China on a four week assignment and two days into the assignment, he was calling his wife and saying 'Get me out of here. I've got to have a plane ticket'", Tanya recounted. Given the expense and logistical efforts invested in sending consultants from the North to the South, firms especially wanted to avoid just this kind of situation. According to Tanya:

> You don't have the time, you don't have the luxury of dealing with people who can't function. It's far from a perfect situation in most developing countries. They are developing countries and you're putting up with a lot of things that

you wouldn't want to live with here in Montreal or here in Canada. But you've got to be able to do that. You've got to be flexible, in your living conditions, you've got to be able to accept all kinds of things.

Tanya went on to recount how a technician she knew to have completed excellent work in Canada was subsequently unable to handle the deficiency of particular sorts of baseline comparative data when she worked on a comparable project in China:

And she could not deal with that. She could not improvise around that in any reasonable, professional manner. She couldn't build the new systems. She was absolutely right that we should have been doing a characterization program but we didn't have the time or the money to do it so we had to make some assumptions. And she had a whole lot of difficulty doing that. And she said when she was finished: "International work is not for me".

There are several convergences operating here between institutional and individual interests. On the one hand, organizations exporting experts from the North to the South have an interest in ensuring that the people they recruit for these tasks will be able to "hit the ground running". But as Tanya's anecdotes are meant to illustrate, this kind of capacity is not necessarily ensured by technical credentials alone. So organizations concerned to minimize their own risks and costs look for people who are interested in but also have a previous track record of being able to work in Southern locales. On the other hand, professionals with this kind of profile emphasize the distinctiveness of the personal characteristics that orient them towards this kind of work: intensity, a desire for excitement, for new stimulations, a wish to avoid the staleness and predictability of regular 9 to 5 routines, curiosity about other cultures, places and traditions, an ongoing journey of self discovery, and so on.

Yet these characteristics could just as readily have featured in a description of the flexibilities demanded as systemic requirements of the "new capitalism" with which Richard Sennett was concerned. Among such features outlined by Sennett are an aversion to the repetitive staleness of regular 9 to 5 routines, an embrace of transient associations rather than long term connections, a commitment to teamwork "in which the team moves from task to task and the personnel of the team changes in the process", and an expectation that individuals will be able to adapt their work patterns and expectations to the changing circumstances and personnel of successive projects

(Sennett 1998:24), all orientations which were likely to be identified as their own individual capacities and predilections by consultants such as Tanya. So similar paradigms of work are respectively portrayed on the one hand, as a systemic feature of global twenty-first century capitalist practices and, on the other hand, as the expressions of very distinctive personal orientations towards unusually peripatetic careers.

COHERENCE AND INSTABILITY

In considering the normalization of instability apparently underpinning this paradigm of work, the key question preoccupying Sennett concerned its effects on identity and social location:

> How can a human being develop a narrative of identity and life history in a society composed of episodes and fragments? The conditions of the new economy feed instead on experience which drifts in time, from place to place, from job to job. If I could state Rico's dilemma more largely, short-term capitalism threatens to corrode his character, particularly those qualities of character which bind human beings to one another and furnish each with a sense of sustainable self. (Sennett 1998:26–7)

Yet this is in striking contrast to the often highly self-conscious and reflexive accounts offered by many of the international consultants interviewed for my own project, narratives of purposeful journeys towards and through traveling careers frequently characterized by invocations of self-selection, self-discovery and ongoing learning (see earlier quotes from Michael, Marina, Christine, Ian and Tanya). So does this case study of mobile professionals imply that Richard Sennett overestimated the corrosive effects of pervasive instability? I would say, "not exactly". Moreover, I would suggest that the highly particular parameters within which these professionals work emphasize the limits within which uncertainty is likely to be embraced and normalized.

Let me return therefore to the ambivalence that featured among the consultants with whom I started my project, professionals whose work, as Marina noted above, was largely circumscribed within the familiar ambits of North America and Europe. For these consultants, their travel to a dispersed set of clients or projects was part of a more general shift in the organization of work and markets. Rather than marking them out as distinctive, they assumed that more and more people in a wide range of occupations would face similar pressures to accept various forms of mobility. Hence they viewed their own movements as pragmatic and necessary adaptations to these new structural conditions, circumstances in which various forms of uncertainty were indeed perceived as the new "normal".

But as I noted above, this ambivalence contrasts with the excitement about travel that more often characterized the accounts of development consultants who journeyed further afield to the global South. It also contrasts with the distinction this latter set of professionals drew between their own willing engagement in work abroad and the more stable, localized orientations and involvements of most of their colleagues, friends and even families. These consultants came and went to a wide range of locations while many of those around them stayed put. Their families, neighbors or friends stayed "at home".

Ian was still based in Toronto, the city where he had been born. He explained:

> The curious isolating thing is, even when we are back here, is that we'll go out with friends that we've known for 35, 40 years. And as soon as you start talking about overseas, you can quite often see them glaze over, because they don't have the background to understand what you are really talking about. I mean they show interest and they'll sit through a few slides, but you don't get the sense of commitment that you get from other people who have been overseas a lot. And they can counter with their own bizarre stories and it's a different sense when you are with that group.

Ian's extended family often seemed to find it difficult to understand his extended traveling:

> As I said, they don't tend to travel much themselves, so they don't understand it or what joy there might be in it. I know I'll come back and my mother-in-law will say something like "That's that, isn't it?". As if you know, you've done this, now let's get back to normal. She doesn't seem to realize that this is normal for me.

As Daniel and Tanya described above, most of the employees in the large corporations for which many of these professionals had at one time or another worked did not venture far. And many of the people with whom these specialists interacted in their work at various locales, the "counterpart" consultants[4] or the representatives of the agency charged with executing the project and so on, were thoroughly implicated in localized domestic and work involvements. International consultants are, by definition, temporary sojourners at their dispersed work sites but many of their associates *live* in these locales. Thus the accentuated transnational mobility of these traveling "experts" is located amid multiple associations and connections that are by comparison relatively stable and localized. Indeed, although, like Monica and Richard, some of these development specialists had changed jobs a number of times and some, like Paul, had experience of working as independent consultants, others had been employed by the same corporation for many years, decades long in the case of several.

Like Richard Sennett's interlocutor, Rico, the consultants with whom my research began viewed their own movements between jobs, or in the course of their jobs, as taking place within an increasingly more unstable and mobile world. But the development consultants on whom my project came to focus viewed their own far more extended travel as a distinctive and accomplished way of life within otherwise largely routinized and localized worlds. The distinction in these two sets of consultants' interpretations of context has much to do, I would suggest, with the divergence between their respective evaluations of their own mobility, i.e., the ambivalence of the one and the enthusiasm of the other. If the restructuring of work and markets requires increased "flexibility" to succeed, then it is hard to view one's own adaptability to this circumstance as altogether or even primarily of one's own choice and making. Even Monica, who, prior to the burst of the technology bubble at the turn of the twenty-first century, assumed that her then much sought after expertise in information technology guaranteed special job security, as safe as "banking", (see Amit 2002 for a fuller account of this) wasn't as sanguine about the unpalatable "choices" vested in the very structure of contemporary consulting. Hence it is not surprising to see these professionals reprise the fear of losing control, in smaller or larger ways, that featured prominently in Sennett's account. If the world at large is becoming less stable, then it's difficult to be sure of command. But for Tanya and her peers in long distance development consulting, itinerancy was a choice and special individual capacity and for the most part, there were stable bases to come back to from yet another round of traveling. Indeed, because the world was *not* marching to the beat of this same drum this made it easier to construct an ongoing narrative of purposeful self-discovery through preferred modes of peripatetic work.

In short, I would note that the implications of flexibility (uncertainty, mobility, etc.) for people's capacity to create satisfying and coherent narratives of self vary in tandem with their appreciation of its particularity. I can better control – or at least feel more in control of – my own particularistic flexibility than I can command a comprehensive and systemic demand for flexibility from everyone. The former is *my* story, the latter is the general story of the day.

SOME PROVISOS

So are the differences between the two sets of consultants with which I am concerned primarily a matter of divergent outlooks or of actual distinctions in the extent to which they are able to exercise agency over the course and outcomes of their career flexibility? It's here that the story becomes more complicated and contradictory. First, there is considerable evidence to suggest that in spite of popular claims, the restructuring identified with flexibility has been anything but comprehensive:

> However, most labor remains inscribed within the circle of Fordism. Simple statistics are hard to come by, but a good estimate of the modern jobs described ... is that at least two thirds are repetitive in ways which Adam Smith would recognize as akin to those in his pin factory. (Sennett 1998:44)

And if the structure of a good deal of work has not changed markedly, so too the extent to which people's acceptance of mobility and instability has actually shifted may also be relatively limited. Indeed the conditions of "international" work discussed above suggest that employers are well aware that the number of highly specialized professionals who can actually be relied on to undertake work that repeatedly takes them far from home to unfamiliar situations is restricted. A lot of people want to "stay close to their barbecues", as Tanya wryly observed. So despite their divergent interpretations, both sets of consultants with whom I have been concerned in this chapter may have been closer in the particularity of their mobility than they might otherwise have been aware of or willing to acknowledge.

Similarly, as it turned out, both types of situations also featured constraints on the capacity of these mobile professionals to direct the entailments of their own mobility. As it turned out, "flexibility" could not in itself ensure security in the face of the aftermath of the

greater rewards – training, more interesting assignments, advancement – in exchange for "flexibility". The other actively tries to recruit people who have already expressed some degree of interest in a highly peripatetic career. In both cases, people are encouraged to articulate a particular set of institutional imperatives with a sense of personal investment. I have tried to show that the more idiosyncratic these preferences appear to be, the more easily people will be able to integrate them into a coherent narrative of self-development. The more that these choices appear to be made obligatory by broader structural contingencies, the greater the sense of qualification and ambivalence that can attend them, comprising pragmatic adaptation to an uncertain world as opposed to a self-motivated mobility through stable contexts. The same experience of fragmentation, attenuated social relationships and episodic activities can therefore be divergently viewed as the basis of a narrative of adventurous self-discovery or as the source of anxiety over future dislocations and fear over losing control. In other words, the issue is not necessarily the experience of fragmentation per se but the degree to which people can view these effects as largely determined, or not, by their own choices.

But either stratagem can knock up against the basic contradiction between institutional and personal interests, a tension that is not unique to but is especially accentuated within the paradigm of flexibility. At the end of the day, the mandate of "flexibility" is not to improve the personal development of workers, at whatever level of skill. It is to arrogate to institutions an enhanced capacity to assign persons to particular slots as convenient or profitable. The individuality that in some sense is encouraged by consulting is therefore ironically associated with institutional objectification: the right curriculum vitae for a particular ephemeral slot as opposed to a long term association and familiarity with a particular individual. It's preferable to fill that slot with enthusiastic adherents. Indeed, as the case of development consultants moving between the global North and South has illustrated, to a certain extent informed willingness may be part of the requirements to reliably fill that slot. But there are many more people willing to carry out localized assignments in the North so readiness for this kind of domestic work may not be as rare or as sought after a capacity.

A sense of individual agency can therefore be institutionally valorized when it converges with managerial imperatives and constrained or even rejected when it does not. When the desires of "experts" do not easily articulate with a valued organizational slot, no amount of expertise or flexibility or self-motivation is likely to assure these professionals an institutional respect for their individual aspirations and choices. It is in those circumstances that the uncertainties of the "new" capitalism are likely to be at their starkest and most corrosive. A conflict between character and experience is therefore not a straightforward outcome of flexibility in and of itself but of the extent to which this orientation – or for that matter, any dominant paradigm – is experienced as a structural imposition or as a personal choice.

ACKNOWLEDGEMENTS

I would like to thank Noel Dyck for his careful reading of and suggestions for this chapter. The responsibility for any infelicities or errors remains mine alone.

NOTES

1 These interviews were supported by a pilot project from the Concordia General Research Fund. In order to ensure confidentiality, aliases have been used in place of the actual names of the people involved.
2 This research was supported by a grant from the Social Sciences and Humanities Research Council of Canada. In order to ensure confidentiality, aliases have been used in place of the actual names of the people involved.
3 CUSO was originally founded as the Canadian University Services Overseas. It has since dropped the university affiliation from its title and is now simply known as CUSO.
4 Most of the large agencies, such as the World Bank, which fund many of the projects on which these consultants are employed now require that this work include some provision for a transfer of knowledge. As a result, most of these projects now include among their personnel local consultants who can be referred to as "counterpart" consultants.

REFERENCES

Amit, V. (2002) 'The Moving "Expert": A Study of Mobile Professionals in the Cayman Islands and North America'. In K.F. Olwig and N.N. Sørensen (eds) *Work and Migration: Life and Livelihood in a Globalizing World*. London/New York: Routledge.

Reich, R. (1991) *The Work of Nations*. New York: Knopf.

Sassen, S. (1994) *Cities in a World Economy*. Thousand Oaks, CA: Pine Forge.

Sennett, R. (1998) *The Corrosion of Character: The Personal Consequences of Work in the New Capitalism*. New York/London: Norton.

6
A Personalized Journey: Tourism and Individuality

Julia Harrison

It is well acknowledged that touristic travel is as much about "Us" as it is about the "Other" in Viet Nam, Peru, Poland or Morocco (Thurot and Thurot 1983; see also MacCannell 1976). While this "Us" can be seen to move *en masse*, at least statistically, touristic travel is for many about being something quite apart from that *masse*. Many who travel for pleasure are really saying that they want to be seen as individuals; they want to be seen as something unique (Cohen 1989; Jacobsen 2000; Prebsen, Larsen and Abelsen 2003).

In this chapter I argue that the travels of 33 middle/upper middle class Canadian tourists reveal one way that these people claimed individuality. When they traveled they did not see themselves as being just any tourist, not one of thousands who might have gone before them (Jacobsen 2000). Their travels comprised a journey in the exploration of self. No matter whether it comprised a packaged bus tour or an independent adventure guided by serendipity, each experience was valued as something decidedly personal. These journeys of exploration are shaped by the trajectory of personal "travel careers" engaging the shifting dynamics of particular physical/mental selves at different points in their lives. I highlight how significant collective self-determinants such as class and national identity are shaped and refined by these travel experiences. I conclude by acknowledging that no matter how it is understood, the journey of the exploration of self through touristic travel always willingly or unwillingly involves inviting other selves along for the ride.

One couple I interviewed traveled independently through South and South East Asia for about seven months in the mid 1990s. When Elaine and Benjamin left India, they were relieved. They had found increasingly uncomfortable the crowded streets, trains and buses, had become progressively more irritated with the bewildering system of train schedules (and unannounced, last minute changes in same); and they were unnerved by their periodic treatment by locals as something bizarre and exotic. They were most anxious to claim their personal space when they arrived at their next destination. This need was, they admitted, "hard to shake", an admission which made them "confront who they were" and acknowledge their "sense of privilege" about its requirement.

But just who were they? Gadamer argued that "the self we are does not possess itself" but rather just "happens", subject to the accidents and the fragments of history (Gadamer 1976:55; see also Sennett 1998:147). A private self, so constructed, particularly in this period of late capitalism, Asad would claim, stirs self-reflexive anxiety (2003:155). I argue that the touristic travels of a group of Canadian tourists such as Elaine and Benjamin were important fragments of their personal histories that allowed their "selves to happen". I suggest that their ongoing decision to commit time, money and energy to travel was something particularly consequential to their personal identity, what Giddens (1991:112) calls a "fateful moment".

Travel narratives can be key episodes, rich in complex symbolism, in the trajectory of individual lives (Edensor 1998:70; Noy 2004). As will become obvious below, the story of one trip, with its highs, its lows, its chance or its more structured encounters for tourists such as Elaine and Benjamin was not necessarily a central moment in their lives, as it might have been for the youthful backpackers Noy (2004) interviewed. But rather the cumulative experience and reflection on multiple touristic trips became critical mechanisms by which these tourists came to know themselves as individuals. I do not claim that these were the only personal narratives that were pivotal to understanding themselves. Obviously all the tourists with whom I spoke comprised more than just the experience of their travels, even if, as Olivia claimed, "my entire life is shaped by travel". They all had careers/businesses and families of one kind or another and personal narratives that extended beyond their travels. It was these lives into which their travel stories were integrated. Their travel histories were, however, as Nash (1996) suggested, important experiences of personal transition. They understood these experiences as something much enhanced, if not very distinct and distanced, from the reality of everyday lives (Urry 1990).[1]

Those who were the subjects of my research understood themselves first and foremost, without much self-reflexivity, thanks to their socialization and situatedness in the particular cultural context and habitus of their family, their social context and the state (see Gadamer 1975:245; Bourdieu 1977). Perceptions of personhood, class, race, gender and citizenship, no matter how implicit, are central to this understanding. At some point along the way, as the accidents and explorations of our personal lives and larger historical context unfold, we begin a more reflexive process of individualized self-examination. For my research subjects, much of these private selves were engaged and explored through their touristic travels. I argue that for these tourists, travel is, at least in part, about what Betz (1992) has called a "modern quest for self-understanding", a confirmation, and at times a confrontation with the matter of who "I am". Yet in keeping with the desire for continued exploration of new places through their physical travels, metaphorical "new places" of their individuality were part of the discovery of every trip, no matter its structure or destination.

To see oneself as an individual does not imply that one has to stand alone. Collective backdrops to one's personal reality are vital to who one is. I have discussed elsewhere how travel is a search for a myriad connections across a wide spectrum of linkages, creating a complex series of networks in which the self is situated (Harrison 2003). Here I further reflect on how these travels shape notions of self that are grounded in particular understandings of one's class and national identity and citizenship. I recognize the selectivity of these three, and that racial and gender identity are two further frames that could be added here.[2]

WHO ARE THESE TOURISTS?

I draw my comments here from interviews conducted with 33 Canadian middle/upper middle class tourists. I dubbed them "travel enthusiasts" as they were firmly committed to their touristic travels. They invested significant portions of their annual income, large amounts of psychological and emotional energies, as well as personal time, in their travels. For all of them, it was their main "hobby". Traveling regularly was a central part of their lives. Their ages ranged at the time of my interviews from 30 to 75. Most had been actively traveling for at least ten years, some for much longer.

Almost all of those I interviewed were working or had worked in some form of professional or managerial job. Their occupational fields included business, law, graphic design, urban planning, teaching, nursing, and engineering. They were small business owners and corporate executives, middle managers in the federal civil service, a director of an NGO (non-governmental organization), computer technicians and systems analysts. Some had very stable employment histories, while others chose to work only on contract or in short term positions to allow them the flexibility to travel. All were either Canadian citizens or landed immigrants.

About one third were retired. About half were in long term stable marriages; some were divorced, often from partners who did not share their love of travel. Some, though married, frequently traveled alone as their partners did not enjoy traveling to the degree that they did. A few had chosen never to marry; still others imagined they might do so one day, ideally to someone who also had a passion for travel. Those who had children did not, as a rule, travel with them, often because their children were adults themselves or at least older adolescents. The annual incomes of the "travel enthusiasts" ranged from about 20,000 to well over 180,000 Canadian dollars. Most had some postsecondary education, several having two or three degrees. Some who had not formally pursued their education at university or college levels described themselves as "well read and interested in the world".

No one kind of travel experience characterized the trips these people took. They traveled to almost every corner of the globe, finding their destinations in urban centers, national parks and game reserves, beach resorts, and remote villages. Some took package tours, others traveled completely independently, while yet others would do both of these things. Some went with carefully planned itineraries; others shunned any such structuring. Being away from home for more than six or seven weeks was an absolute must for some; others felt that three weeks away from home was their limit. Some went away only once a year; others at least three times a year. Travel was concentrated in one country or region for some; others wanted to visit as many places in the world as they could at least once in their lifetime, even if some stops were only for a few hours. Connecting with family and friends, seeing "world famous" sites, having a rest, physically challenging themselves, or visiting a place viewed as being "exotic" were all reasons these people said they traveled.

These travel enthusiasts were not the youthful backpackers discussed by Noy (2004) and Richards and Wilson (2004). It is important to note this distinction, as travel for this more youthful group has been called an experience of significant "self-change" (Noy 2004). Although part of the mass tourism experience, backpacker travel tends to be somewhat distinctive due to the highly developed networks of interpersonal communication that exist for this group. In addition, "global nomads", as Richards and Wilson call them, are all approximately the same age and thus at a parallel moment in their life history. Many, when they set off on their travels, have just completed some form of postsecondary education (or are in the process of doing so), have yet to join the workforce full time, begin a family, acquire property or, most critically, the mortgage that goes along with said property. Most are embarking on their first independent travel experience, something that distinguishes them significantly from those whom I interviewed. Their youthful age and limited life experience affords these backpackers a somewhat different attitude as to how their selves might grow and change through a travel experience. A further factor distinguishes the travel enthusiasts from the backpackers: travel enthusiasts always returned home and picked up on a well established life. Thus, I would argue that the travel enthusiasts' trips were not the pivotal transition points between major life stages that these can be for backpackers, but rather can be characterized as important moments in a well established life trajectory. But this positioning, as I suggest below, did not mean that the travel enthusiasts' trips were trivial experiences.

I interviewed these individuals (sometimes alone or as couples) on and off over a period of five years. For many I did two lengthy taped interviews, for others only one. These interviews were free flowing, often lasting for several hours. Conversations included a discussion of when they started to travel and why; the general scope of their travels; and the structure of their trips. The latter discussions usually ended up concentrating on one or two particularly memorable experiences as examples, due to the large number and different kinds of trips taken by these people. I continued to have contact with many through their postcards, annual letters, travel journals (which they sent me to read), telephone and face to face conversations and latterly, by email. All taped materials were transcribed and thematically analysed using a qualitative data analysis program. I integrated my field notes and other collected materials into this qualitative analysis.[3]

EXPLORING RATHER THAN FINDING SELF

There is much in contemporary academic writing that analyses the relationship of the local to the global, and vice versa. The last decade of the twentieth century generated wide ranging discussion, driven largely by the rhetoric of economics and politics, of how we would live, and come to understand who we are, in a globalized and deterritorialized world. Our identities were to be shaped by Clifford's (1992) "traveling cultures", as our mobile selves moved through time and space. In these discussions, the future of local identities and national citizenships was much in question. We were, it seemed, all to become global citizens, with our identities attached to no one fixed place. Yet at the half way point in the first decade of the twenty-first century, these assumptions are increasingly subject to critique and in some cases, outright rejection (Saul 2005).

Few would deny the significant impacts of globalization on local and national economies, the expansion of the reach of multinational corporations, and the potential interpersonal connectivity that characterizes the Internet. But the reaffirmation of borders and border crossings since September 11, 2001, the ongoing flaring of nationalist and fundamentalist religious conflicts at various points around the globe, and the recent rejection by French and Dutch citizens of the proposed European Union constitution, are just a small sampling that affirms what Saul (2005) and Amselle (2002) have argued, and what anthropologists have always known: namely, that any community is more than its economy. It would seem that most in the world want some form of localized identity.

The millions of tourists who travel purely for pleasure in ever increasing numbers constitute a privileged group whose members have willingly participated in the global flows of the last 50 years. The World Tourism Organization reports that tourism arrivals worldwide reached an all time high of 760 million in 2004.[4] The vast majority of those who make up this "globalized population" possess a secure localized identity, a point I will return to at the end of the chapter.

Unlike Asad (2003:155), I do not begin from the position that these travel enthusiasts overtly agonized that their private selves were under threat, riddled with anxiety and tension. In fact, they could generally be classified as well adjusted individuals who had succeeded in some significant measure to construct comfortable middle/upper middle class lives. They were not directly grappling with what Sennett (1998) terms the problems of constructing a "coherent narrative of self", something that he claims makes the "construction of character" difficult. In fact, they might be looking for some disruption to the consistent and predictable narratives of their daily lives at home. A couple of examples serve to demonstrate this point. Gwen, a working professional like many others mentioned in this chapter, married with teenage children, took an unprecedented leave of absence to travel to India for several months on her own. For her friends and family this was a most unexpected and rather incomprehensible decision. She simply had a pressing urge to do this. Similarly, Fred noted of himself that for over 40 years he had had the same wife, worked for the same company, and only moved his house three times. Such predictability was not mirrored in some of the spontaneous decisions he and his partner Susan made about their travels, such as the Christmas they left for a three week trip to Russia on a few days' notice – an action they relished as being quite out of character for them.

The travel enthusiasts did see their travels, as Munt (1994:108) suggests, as something that would increase their sense of worldliness, their adaptability, and their sensitivity to differences in people and places. Travel might enhance their character – even though none appeared to have been anxious about any obvious failings in this regard before they started to travel. That they all had the self-confidence to set out on their travels repeatedly would make this statement self-evident to them. Anomie, or "nothingness" – as one of Noy's (2004:87) backpackers said her world would be without travel – were not words the travel enthusiasts would have used to describe their sense of self or their world if they had not become committed travelers.

There are at least three situational perspectives from which one might examine how travel shapes notions of individuality among these travel enthusiasts. One is that of the locals or those van den Berghe (1994) calls the "tourees", who are at a minimum likely to be indifferent about what touristic travel does for these Canadian tourists' sense of self. A second group is those at home: friends, family, and more generically those who occupy similar sectors of the social spheres of these tourists at home. There are some analytical insights that I as an outside researcher might add about this perspective based upon what the travel enthusiasts told me. It is important to note that my insights may not always agree with what these tourists might say about themselves. Finally, there is what the tourists say about themselves and their own sense of what their travels reveal about them as individuals. Elsrud (2001:599) reminds us that these latter two categories need to be considered with equal validity.

Journalist Lawrence Osbourne, writing about an arduous trekking trip planned for a remote community in the highlands of the Indonesian province of Papua, commented, "We had not come to study an alien culture but to be changed ourselves" (2005:139). His musing highlights a common assumption about why people travel as tourists. In contrast, my research indicates that those I interviewed were neither looking for nor expecting a "transformation of self". Rather, as I have argued elsewhere, they were looking more for an exploration, and ultimately an affirmation of their "authentic self" (Harrison 2003). My thinking coheres with Wang's (2000: 56–60) notion of touristic "existential authenticity". Tourists, while away from home, feel that they are "much more authentic" than when at home (see also Uriely 2005:207).

I introduce the notion of the authentic self into the discussion of the "authentic Other" that MacCannell (1976) suggested tourists seek. He posited that the late twentieth century tourist – a metaphor he claimed for "modern man" – was someone alienated from the modern world in which he [sic] lived. Tourists, he argued, were certain that there was something out there more real and substantive than their lives. And it would be embodied in a more authentic "Other" who lives a life less mediated by technology and the alienation of the Western industrialized urban world. Citizens-cum-tourists of the late twentieth century, and now twenty-first century, thus go out and gaze – even if only fleetingly – upon this imagined purer, more real world to affirm its existence, and its relationship to their own (MacCannell 1976; Urry 1990).

While the academy has extensively discussed notions of the authentic and tourism since MacCannell introduced the idea some 30 years ago, promotional travel literature and guidebooks resolutely promote the idea that this "authentic, purer reality" exists out there for the tourist to encounter (Bruner 1991; Scarles 2004). With this conditioning (and other influences too numerous to discuss here), even if those who are gazed upon reflect little of this imaginary reality, some tourists often fail to note this discrepancy (MacCannell 1992). Feifer's (1985) and Urry's (1990) "posttourists" – a category in which I would include most of those with whom I spoke – are well aware of the constructed fantasies that tourist brochures suggest are out there to be seen, and readily recognize that what they have experienced in their encounters with imaginary "Others" was liberally coated with irony.[5]

Elsewhere I have argued that the tourists I interviewed did not feel alienated from the world in which they lived (Harrison 2003). They could clearly see the virtues of their world, and were content to return home at the end of their travels, even if it was only to begin to plan their next trip away. Osbourne (2005:140) actually reports that upon their return to "civilization", while finding difficult the readjustment to the "noise and weirdness" of the Western world, his fellow travelers – who could well be classed as travel enthusiasts – did not report any dramatic, transformative personal changes. They did speculate that those whom they "visited" in the distant reaches of the Papua jungle would likely be changed as a consequence of such visits and those of other tourists, a point made by anthropologist Edward Bruner (1991), who argued that in the touristic encounter the local is more dramatically altered than the tourist ever is.

While not radically transformative, the travels undertaken by the travel enthusiasts did have a significant personal impact. Travel allowed them, as Jennifer and Louise suggested, an opportunity for "soul searching" and "introspection". Elaine characterized her original move away from home as an opportunity to find out new things about her self. She continued to assume this posture in all subsequent travels she undertook. Travel allowed these tourists to find out new things about themselves, to understand the complexities of who they were. Robert put this most eloquently:

> To have the opportunity to, even accidentally, bump into parts of yourself that you didn't know that you have. In a sense, it's like having a limb go to sleep and then discovering it anew. By traveling to places I have an opportunity to discover parts of myself because of the way that I respond to something foreign. Living in Toronto which, of course, is where I was born and raised, I take too much of my surroundings for granted and as a result don't feel or sense the abrasion or the contact with myself that I do in foreign places by being for extended periods of time in cultures or places that are not native to me. I discover attitudes and assumptions that I carry and which would remain unknown to me in familiar surroundings. I have the opportunity to learn about myself in a way that is not only beneficial but incredibly enjoyable. I think I would likely do the same thing in prison. I've heard that spending extended periods of time in solitary confinement, one starts to encounter parts of oneself and I think that probably the result is similar, but it's a much nicer way to do it.

Travel facilitated an increased confidence in who these tourists understood themselves to be. It expanded their sense of themselves while acknowledging who they were not, nurturing a more nuanced acceptance of their particular character and self. As such, their touristic experiences served to self-reflexively stimulate, and thus engage, any anxieties about the "private self" of the late capitalist milieu with which Asad has suggested we are plagued. Such engagement had both expanding and limiting impacts on their actions while away from home.

Confidently and calmly addressing basic yet vital needs, such as finding satisfying food and comfortable, affordable, and safe lodging was read as a marker of personal capability and honed intuition. Simple things such as feeling rested after a night on a rooftop as there was literally no room at the inn in Marrakesh boosted self-esteem. After this experience Elaine acknowledged she was more rugged and adaptable than she had thought. Beth found that her psyche had to be paced in response to the bodily disorientation of jet lag. Her psychological self needed more time to make the same journey through space and time than air travel allowed. She was a "slow starter" in each new destination. For Michael, testing yet not overstepping his personal physical stamina while hiking in Greece or cycling in Viet Nam, or for Albert successfully reaching Everest Base Camp in Nepal, were parallel affirmations at a psychological and physical level. More subtle moments such as being able to appreciate the fairytale romance of a dinner at an elegant restaurant on the banks of the Danube, or being moved to tears when first setting eyes on a famous work of art at the Louvre, created moments for Bruce and Frances where the depth of the self was acknowledged and valued.

On a darker, more restrictive side, operating within the limits of one's fears, paranoias, and insecurities was also part of the travel experience. Non-negotiable thresholds for these tourists included acceptance by Rachel of the fact that the masses of people in the streets of China terrified her; by Olivia of being unnerved in Africa because of her irrational fear of contracting HIV/AIDS; by Michael of his fear of exploration of a foreign city after dark; and by Judith and Henry of their reluctance to abandon certain levels of sanitation and comfort in the "tourist zones" of some cities they visited. Elaine and Benjamin's need for personal space (mentioned earlier) offers another example. Facing realities such as these set limits around whom these tourists saw themselves to be, or who they might become.

Travel enthusiasts can be said to have travel careers mirroring the stages of "apprentice", "professional", and eventually, what might be called, "retiree" or "elder". In the "apprentice" stage several of these tourists participated in large group tours such as bus tours or cruises. Emboldened by this experience, they then ventured off more independently, as they became savvy about what they wanted to experience, and gained more confidence in their abilities to cope in foreign places. In the later stages of their travel careers some returned to group travel, but now in smaller groups, while others became focused on pursuing a specific type of holiday. The latter was at times a finely honed choice designed to be flexible and adaptable to an aging, and possibly slightly less energetic, body. Some opted for trips with a greater degree of intellectual stimulation where "experts" accompanied them, ensuring that every new travel experience built on, but did not duplicate, the rich body of knowledge many of them had gathered through their previous travels.

From the very first trip for some, and certainly as they traveled more, these tourists exercised a significant degree of discrimination in selecting and crafting their trips. Details about where they would go, why they were going, how they would get there and then move around while there, how long they would stay in any one place, and what type of accommodation they would choose, were just some of the details they addressed. This list became more carefully thought through the more some of them traveled and the more discerning they became. For others, the more they traveled the more they let serendipity guide them, as they gained ever increasing confidence in their ability to cope well in new situations. Their thresholds for risk, no matter how they defined them, were enhanced.

Notably, some of these travel enthusiasts could adapt themselves and their expectations to very different travel experiences at any stage in their career. Several could go on a guided bus tour, take an independent trip in a rented car, stay at a beach resort, and then go on a hiking/cycling holiday all in one year. Possessing the wisdom to know which form of travel they desired at any particular moment was central to satisfying their individualized tastes, moods and expectations. As they moved through their travel careers they expressed an increasing certainty in their ability to determine – independent of promotional materials and guidebooks – whether a particular trip or destination would be likely to suit them. Many became experts in a rather sophisticated form of discourse analysis. As they came to know their traveling selves better, they could strategically situate themselves and their mindset for a wide range of travel experiences.

I returned to speak with some of these people several years after I first met them. For some who had now passed middle age, they expressed a sadness that they were no longer able to undertake trips that were as physically demanding or excursions guided as much by chance as careful planning as they had once done. Their capacity for risk taking had diminished as their energy levels decreased, and their more vulnerable bodies put limits on where, how and for what duration they might travel. With much invested in their identities as well traveled individuals, this could prove to be a difficult period of adjustment. Leslie had predicted these days would come. She knew that one day she would take her meticulously crafted and proudly displayed photograph albums of her travels with her to the "old folks' home". She wanted them with her as mnemonic aids. She also said they might as well be burned up with her for they would mean nothing to anyone else.

The destination, duration, and type of the travel experience these tourists could still enjoy became a personal barometer of a self in transition. However, while the capacity of their physical and mental selves to absorb the shocks and adjustment to new places diminished, the resilience of the remembered self drew on what I suggest below is a wealth of hidden, very personalized capital they amassed through their travel careers.

FINDING ONESELF IN THE COLLECTIVE

I want to turn briefly to how the touristic travels of those I interviewed can be interpreted as a vehicle to claim attachment to particular social groupings such as class and national identity that distinguish one from the "great unwashed".

Reaching upward

A well traveled, learned acquaintance of mine, knowing of my interest in tourism, claimed he wanted to see himself as a traveler. He reluctantly admitted, however, that he was, in fact, that which he disdained – merely a tourist. If a traveler is seen to be someone who travels independently without a predetermined schedule and who remains open to engagement with the local communities, thereby meeting "real" people, then a tourist is generally perceived to be someone content with a more distanced experience, satisfied with staged performances of place and local cultures, willing to travel *en masse* and on a structured timetable. The former is implicitly assumed to be a sophisticated and superior experience. This distinction hints at notions of class differences that I argue were part of the process of claiming individuality.

Setting oneself apart from the masses by acquiring a reputation as someone well traveled can be read as an effort to claim, or at least affirm, a particular class position. Such desires, of course, imply an intention to position oneself on an upwardly mobile track in the social rankings, and to stave off any possibility that one might slip down the ladder. Ehrenreich (1990:11) argues that the middle class is perpetually concerned about falling back down the social scale, thus members of this category do not assume their position with any complacency. These rather precariously placed persons need continually to accumulate at least cultural, and ideally economic, capital to prevent any descent. The travel enthusiasts are examples of what Bourdieu (1977), and specifically Munt (1994), describe as the "new middle class": those who although not necessarily rich in economic capital seek to distinguish themselves through their discriminating consumption practices, exemplifying Bourdieu's "taste cultures".[6] Travel of the kind, scope and degree undertaken by the travel enthusiasts over their travel careers, is a defining – if not refining – commodity of taste and is thus indicative of class position.

Despite the incredible expansion of the global tourism infrastructure in the post-World War II era, those who can afford to access it are not as ubiquitous as some would suggest. Touristic travel is not, I would argue, in contrast to Palmer, "a taken-for-granted habit of life" (2005:11). There are still class based parameters around who can afford to participate. And while middle class access to tourism as leisure practice has increased dramatically in the last 50 years, those in the lower, even lower middle classes of Euro-American society have at most limited access to the economic and cultural capital necessary to actively pursue the practice. The extensive travels of those whom I interviewed served to distance them from those lower down the social scale for whom such a pastime was only sporadic at most.

What becomes a "habit of life" for many travelers, particularly those who have never doubted their ability to travel, is a desire to remain separate from a burgeoning middle class touristic horde. This escape is something that has been documented and mused upon in writings about pleasure travel, the latter being once something only the wealthy upper classes could afford. They, of course, were only ever travelers, never mere tourists (see for example Turner and Ash 1975; Fussell 1982). Abundant leisure time and surplus monetary resources facilitated this travel (Veblen 1998 [1899]). Members of this elite were (and are) able to bypass local infrastructures designed to serve large numbers of middle class tourists. In today's world this translates to such things as large multinational hotel chains, large group tours, and theme park displays of culture and history – all things the travel enthusiasts avoided once they became seasoned travelers. Such patterns of avoidance allude to their affinity with a more sophisticated "taste culture" reserved historically for the wealthier classes. As Ehrenreich (1990) would suggest, these travel enthusiasts were always reaching upwards to secure their class position.

However, most of the travel enthusiasts I met did not, as suggested earlier, have overly abundant economic resources. Yet these travel enthusiasts possessed sufficient cultural capital with which to launch their trips, something acquired through their higher education, their employment histories, and middle/upper middle class roots. Samuel, a retired civil engineer in his early 60s, who had had a successful professional career in sanitation management, lived in a modest, rented apartment with Donna, his wife of 35 years. He proudly claimed, "You do not have to be rich [that is in economic terms] to travel". The secret lay in knowing "how" to travel, and strategically committing financial and personal resources to it. For Samuel and Donna, this involved analysing options for any particular trip using tools such as a spreadsheet. This allowed them to shop comparatively, drawing on the services of "good" travel agents and, more recently, scouring the web and utilizing web based information exchange communications about good deals on hotels, local transportation, and restaurants to ensure that they got the "best" package for each trip.[7] Using such strategies allowed them to reap, said Samuel, the pleasure of travel historically afforded only to "the wealthy". The tone of his comments hinted that he and his wife saw themselves as successfully outsmarting the rich at their own game.

Susan and Fred told me that they were well "branded" among their friends as a couple who were well traveled. Such notoriety gained them admiration for their experiences, their adventuresome spirit, their worldliness, and their tireless energies. They were obviously fit mentally and physically, something envied and desired by one's peers as one grows older. They gained an elevated status, firmly securing them from slippage down the social scale.

However, Susan and Fred would likely have agreed with Noy's (2004:83) assertion that "stories one tells of oneself are probably the best possible approximation of who one is". They knew that much of their individual "selves" was encapsulated in the stories of their travels. Several of the couples interviewed expressed a belief in a sense of a shared individuality; they saw themselves as "one" in their mutual responses and understandings of their travel experience.

The details of how Susan and Fred coped when they found giant cockroaches in their beds in northern China, or how they navigated their rented car in places where they could not read the maps or the road signs, were stories that said much to them about who they were as individuals. Their ability to cope in these situations was a matter of personal pride, something they would want to share with friends and family. Nevertheless they knew that sharing these experiences could elicit varying responses: either admiration for their capabilities and resilience or criticism of their wisdom and judgment, prompting worry and anxiety about them when they took off on another "crazy adventure". They wanted only the former, but in the end they were rarely offered an opportunity to face either. Within their immediate social circle rarely did anyone want to know the details of a trip beyond the simple fact that they had taken it.

Susan proudly showed me the shelves that lined a long wall in their house, crammed full of photo albums, each one narrating a trip. She acknowledged that nobody was really interested in looking at them and hearing the stories these prompted. The silencing of their stories through their friends' and families' lack of interest outwardly narrowed what defined them to a simple practice – i.e., they traveled a lot. But it was not the volume of their travel that they felt defined who they were. What they experienced on their travels and how they came to know themselves, "warts and all", through these experiences was what was important to them.

When I began this research project my own friends and colleagues could not imagine that I was setting myself up to endure hours of hearing endless travel stories and viewing countless photographs, slides or videos of other people's travels. To them this would be some bizarre form of torture. When I interviewed Monica she boldly admitted that as a child she was the only one in her family that gleefully watched the hours of slides that her aunt, an inveterate traveler, annually forced her family to suffer through. She was not content, however, just to absorb what her wealthy spinster aunt's slides and stories revealed to her about the world. She hoped that just once she too might see the cathedrals of Europe and the pyramids of Egypt. She wanted to feel her aunt's passion for these experiences, not just to hear about it. By the time we chatted, Monica was in her early 40s, and she had seen the cathedrals and the pyramids, in some cases more than once. What she came to realize in doing this was that what her aunt had seen and experienced was something quite distinctive from her own very personalized journeys to these places.

The unassailable void that an outsider has to cross in order to grasp even minimally the deeply personal nature of such travel experiences was something well known to the travel enthusiasts. Can anyone else ever be expected to comprehend the most intimate experiences: the revelation of self to oneself? For many of the travel enthusiasts this reality was initially frustrating, but in the end was affirming – a shift that happened progressively as they became seasoned travelers, as they amassed more and more untranslatable experiences. This accumulated "private capital" clarified a distinctive position for them in their social world at home. It further buffered them from any fear of slippage down the social scale.

Utilizing citizenship

Pico Iyer marveled at a friend who provided him with no less than 33 phone, fax, mobile, and email contacts in order that Iyer might reach him promptly, no matter what corner of the globe his friend might be in. After writing all of these details in his address book, Iyer observed that he had no room remaining for his friend's name (2000:113). The irony of this absence was not lost on Iyer, who as the "poet laureate of the global soul" leads a similarly mobile life as a "global citizen" (Saro-Wiwa 2005).

The phrase "global citizen" has a range of meanings as any search on the Internet suggests.[8] The meaning attributed to its usage here is someone who most regularly would call international airports and hotels "home" as much as anywhere else. It is someone whose work/travel may take her or him in any given week from Hong Kong to Nigeria to London and then to Los Angeles. And it is someone who takes great pleasure and pride in this mobile life, seeing himself as a resident in "the transnational village that our world has become" (Iyer 2000). The passports of these "global souls" are as much a document to facilitate a continued leaving, as any coming home (Iyer 2000).

The tourists I interviewed, no matter how much they enjoyed each trip they took, wanted nothing to do with such mobile and transient realities. Their world was not the "transnational village". Their travels fostered, in contrast, a grounded identity, one linked intimately to a national identity and their Canadian citizenship.

They would have agreed with Saro-Wiwa (2005), that "'at home in the world' is ok as an idiom but you still have to know which house you live in and on what street".

Traveling away from a place regularly seems like an unusual way to demonstrate one's attachment to it. And yet, the repeated departures from Canada that these tourists made affirmed a citizenship of which they were very proud and thankful to be able to claim (Harrison 2003). The Canadian passports they carried were, in fact, vital documents in the facilitation of their widespread travels. In the pre-9/11 era, a Canadian passport eliminated the need for visas to many countries. And while in the post-9/11 climate this has changed somewhat, such a passport still allows relatively uncomplicated access to a wide range of countries around the globe. It always facilitated their coming home again. Ironically in the case of the Syrian-born Canadian citizen, Maher Arar, such a passport did not facilitate his coming home. Arar was detained by American officials at a New York airport and deported to Syria where he was kept in jail and tortured for a year.[9] Canadians with such phenotypes and of Middle Eastern ancestry, such as Arar (who himself was returning from a family vacation when he was detained), were not represented among the travel enthusiasts I interviewed. As a result these travel enthusiasts' comings and goings, even in the post-9/11 era, were never scrutinized with such disastrous results. Hence, Canadian passports, combined with their "white" appearance, highlighted a particularized, and ultimately privileged, notion of what being Canadian was/is.[10] This was not a reality recognized by such a "well-traveled" collective.[11]

Most critically for many of the tourists I interviewed, their Canadian passports set them apart from their American neighbors, a group with whom they were often confused when abroad. Not that they all universally disliked all Americans – quite the contrary. But a Canadian passport was a symbolically dense document that plucked them from being one of 300 million to one of 30 million, the latter a group associated with an ostensibly more benign position in the world order, featuring Canadians as peace keepers, as defenders of democracy and minority rights. Depictions of Canada as a bilingual, safe and welcoming place with a high standard of living were underlying understandings of who they were, and what their home was that were played back to them in touristic encounters around the globe. Such qualities became uncritically absorbed into their sense of who they were as people, who they were as individuals. Each of those persons I interviewed took personal pride in laying claim to such virtues. It made them more than "not-being-an-American"; it made them distinctively Canadian.

A CONCLUDING THOUGHT

Based on research with a small number of committed individuals, I have argued here that touristic travel is one way for these persons to explore their individuality, to say who they are, even if the statements they make about themselves are only partially comprehended by those immediately around them. They are internalized as meaningful realities, shaped by the dynamics of time and experience. These statements are made against a complex backdrop, only some of which is self-reflexively acknowledged despite the claims of worldliness of these travelers. Personal characters, collective subjectivities such as class and national identity, and global power relations, all shape the touristic experience and responses to it no matter where in the world it happens.

I would argue that touristic travel is both a globalized social process integral to the twenty-first century and a deeply personal one. Is there space in this dynamic to examine the individuality claimed by those within locales that global forces have poised to receive not selected individual visitors but rather hundreds, if not thousands, of tourists every year? "Visitors" such as these are not necessarily perceived as being individually distinctive but rather are read as signs of the inequities of the global system. For those on the receiving end, the encounter with every tourist could be narrated as an equally personalized journey running in tandem with those experienced by tourists such as the travel enthusiasts. That narrative might often tell a very different story.

NOTES

1 I do not engage here with Urry's (1990) suggestion that the touristic posture is one many in the West have assumed in their everyday life, that is, we are tourists all the time. Discussion of this point would extend beyond my scope here.
2 See note 10.
3 See Harrison (2003) for more details on these travel enthusiasts.
4 See www.world-tourism.org/facts/barometer/WTOBarom05_1_en_excp.pdf. Last visited June 10, 2005. The steady increase in numbers of touristic travels was briefly interrupted in 2001 by the events of 9/11. Analysts of the tourism industry suggest that there has been a full recovery from this event, with people returning to touristic travel in ever larger numbers.

5 Those I interviewed, as Uriely (2005) argues, slide between the modern and the postmodern. Analytical frames that come from both of these contexts are thus legitimately used to discuss their travels and responses.
6 I use the term "new middle class" to include both Bourdieu's (1984) "new bourgeoisie" and "new petite bourgeoisie". Munt convincingly argues that in relation to matters of travel "the boundaries between these new middle-class fractions are blurred ... " (1994:108).
7 Informal travel information exchange mechanisms have been around for at least a couple of decades. One such early example was the reader driven magazine, *Travel Scoop*, which has been in publication since the early 1990s. Blogs are a contemporary variant of such information exchange mechanisms for travelers.
8 A search on Google generated 23,400,000 hits, June 10 2005.
9 See www.ctv.ca/servlet/ArticleNews/story/CTVNews/1082635956328_6/?hub=Canada. Last visited June 13, 2005.
10 Families of the 325 people who died in the 1985 Air India crash and who carried Canadian passports have argued that if these victims had been of Caucasian ancestry the event would have more readily been seen as a Canadian tragedy.
11 The stories of Arar and the Air India crash (see note 10) highlight a glaring gap in the discussion of claims of distinctiveness and individuality among tourists such as those I interviewed. Whiteness, as a racial type for this touristic population, is a silent backdrop by which these tourists define both difference, and their own individuality. Gender can be read as a homogenizing rather than distinguishing frame against which the tourists sort out who they are (see Harrison 2003:47). Discussion of these two was beyond the scope of this chapter and my current research.

REFERENCES

Amselle, J.L. (2002) 'Globalization and the Future of Anthropology'. *African Affairs*, 101:213–29.

Asad, T. (2003) *Formations of the Secular: Christianity, Islam, Modernity*. Stanford, CA: Stanford University Press.

Betz, H. (1992) 'Postmodernism and the New Middle Class'. *Theory, Culture & Society*, 9:93–114.

Bourdieu, P. (1977) *Outline of a Theory of Practice*. Cambridge: Cambridge University Press.

Bourdieu, P. (1984) *Distinction: A Social Critique of the Judgement of Taste*. London: Kegan Paul.

Bruner, E. (1991) 'Transformation of Self in Tourism'. *Annals of Tourism Research*, 18:238–50.

Clifford, J. (1992) 'Traveling Cultures'. In L. Grossberg, C. Nelson and P.A. Treichler (eds) *Cultural Studies Reader*. New York: Routledge, pp. 96–117.

Cohen, E. (1989) '"Primitive and Remote": Hill Tribe Trekking In Thailand'. *Annals of Tourism Research*, 16:30–61.

Edensor, T. (1998) *Tourists at the Taj: Performance and Meaning at a Symbolic Site*. London: Routledge.

Ehrenreich, B. (1990) *Fear of Falling: The Inner Life of the Middle Class*. New York: Harper Perennial.
Elsrud, T. (2001) 'Risk Creation in Travelling: Backpacker Adventure Narration'. *Annals of Tourism Research*, 28:597–617.
Feifer, M. (1985) *Going Places: The Ways of the Tourist from Imperial Rome to the Present Day*. London: Macmillan.
Fussell, P. (1982) 'Introduction'. In R. Byron (ed.) *The Road to Oxiana*. New York: Oxford University Press.
Gadamer, H.-G. (1975) *Truth and Method*. New York: Seabury.
Gadamer, H.-G. (1976) *Philosophical Hermeneutics*, D. Linge (trans. and ed.). Berkeley, CA: University of California Press.
Giddens, A. (1991) *Modernity and Self-Identity: Self and Society in the Late Modern Age*. Stanford, CA: Stanford University Press.
Harrison, J.D. (2003) *Being a Tourist: Finding Meaning in Pleasure Travel*. Vancouver: University of British Columbia Press.
Iyer, P. (2000) *The Global Soul: Jet Lag, Shopping Malls, and the Search for Home*. New York: Vintage.
Jacobsen, K. (2000) 'Anti-Tourist Attitudes: Mediterranean Charter Tourism'. *Annals of Tourism Research*, 27:284–300.
MacCannell, D. (1976) *The Tourist: A New Theory of the Leisure Class*. New York: Schocken.
MacCannell, D. (1992) Cannibalism Today. In MacCannell (ed.) *Empty Meeting Grounds: The Tourist Papers*. London: Routledge, pp. 17–73.
Munt, I. (1994) 'The "Other" Postmodern Tourism: Culture, Travel and the New Middle Classes'. *Theory, Culture & Society*, 11:101–23.
Nash, D. (1996) *Anthropology of Tourism*. Oxford: Elsevier Science.
Noy, C. (2004) 'This Trip Really Changed Me: Backpackers' Narratives of Self-Change'. *Annals of Tourism Research*, 31:78–102.
Osbourne, L. (2005) 'Letter from New Guinea'. *New Yorker*, 18 April:124–41.
Palmer, C. (2005) 'An Ethnography of Englishness: Experiencing Identity through Tourism'. *Annals of Tourism Research*, 32:7–27.
Prebsen, N., Larsen, S. and Abelsen, B. (2003) 'I'm Not a Typical Tourist: German Tourists' Self-Perceptions, Activities and Motivations'. *Journal of Travel Research*, 41:416–20.
Richards, G and Wilson, J. (2004) *The Global Nomad: Backpacker Travel in Theory and Practice*. Toronto: Channel View.
Saro-Wiwa, K. (2005) 'What's in a Name? It's Who You Are and What Battles you Fight'. *Globe and Mail*, online edition, May 21.
Saul, J. (2005) *The Collapse of Globalization: And the Reinvention of the World*. Toronto: Viking Canada.
Scarles, C. (2004) 'Mediating Landscapes: The Processes and Practice of Image Construction in the Tourist Brochures of Scotland'. *Tourist Studies*, 4:43–67.
Sennett, R. (1998) *The Corrosion of Character: The Personal Consequences of Work in the New Capitalism*. New York: Norton.
Thurot, J. M. and Thurot, G. (1983) 'The Ideology of Class and Tourism: Confronting the Discourse of Advertising'. *Annals of Tourism Research*, 10:173–89.
Turner, L. and Ash, J. (1975) *The Golden Hordes*. London: Constable.

Uriely, N. (2005) 'The Tourist Experience: Conceptual Developments'. *Annals of Tourism Research*, 32:199–216.
Urry, J. (1990) *The Tourist Gaze: Leisure and Travel in Contemporary Societies*. London: Sage.
van den Berghe, P. L. (1994) *The Quest for the Other: Ethnic Tourism in San Cristobal, Mexico*. Seattle, WA/London: University of Washington Press.
Veblen, T. (1998 [1899]) *Theory of the Leisure Class*. Amherst, NY: Prometheus.
Wang, N. (2000) *Tourism and Modernity: A Sociological Analysis*. Oxford: Pergamon.

7

Becoming Educated, Becoming an Individual? Tropes of Distinction and "Modesty" in French Narratives of Rurality

Deborah Reed-Danahay

INTRODUCTION

The ways in which a life story displays or claims individuality are ambiguous. In anthropology, the field of life history research has featured a tension between, on the one hand, an emphasis on the individual as a creative social actor, and, on the other, the shared cultural themes also expressed in the telling of a life (Whittaker 1992; Rapport 1997; Coffey 1999; Brettell 2002). Most scholars agree that the life narrative conveys both, but anthropologists have typically been more interested in the convergence of self and culture, rather than in focusing upon the idiosyncratic nature of the individual. Anthropologists are also increasingly interested in the ethnographic encounter between anthropologist and informant, and on the personal narratives of anthropologists. While earlier attempts to find representative or emblematic members of a society to tell the life story were made, "experimental" life histories frequently focus on a marginal character, as in Vincent Crapanzano's (1980) book about the Moroccan, Tuhami.

The person who comes forward to share his or her life is, for various reasons, often someone on the margins of the communities studied by anthropologists, and it is often the encounter between the two people (anthropologist and "native") that becomes the story. The figures of Nisa (Shostak 1981) or Esperanza (Behar 2003) display a strong individuality at the same time, however, that these women are meant to represent at some level more general aspects of women's lives. Anthropology as a discipline has approached the issue of individuality through longstanding debates about biographical methods. One sign of the ongoing tension in anthropology associated with autobiographical approaches is Ruth Behar's recent caution (2004) that we may be entering a new era that devalues subjectivity. Self-reflexivity on the part of anthropologists about the claims we make about individuality in the life narrative approach may be helpful in further explorations of this method, but we might also look more closely at the claims to individuality made by our informants.

In a review essay of some life histories that appeared in the early 1980s, Vincent Crapanzano evoked Victor Barnouw, who "remarked once that the main difficulty with life histories, fascinating as they are, is knowing what to do with them" (1984:959). In the collaborative volume *The Weight of the World* (1999), Pierre Bourdieu and his colleagues collected life stories and personal narratives from a wide range of members of the "dominated classes" (urban and rural underclass). Recalling C. Wright Mills, who had written about the intersection of personal troubles and public issues (but without explicitly evoking him), Bourdieu remarked in this volume that "narratives about the most 'personal' difficulties, the apparently strictly subjective tensions and contradictions, frequently articulate the deepest structures of the social world and its contradictions" (1999:511). For Bourdieu, the analysis of life histories should focus on the ways in which they display these wider structural features. This begs the question, however, of why some people continue to tell their lives as if they are unique while other life narratives are more modest in their claims about individuality, and focus more on the shared, collective nature of experiences. In some ways, this is about the tension between claims to authenticity and claims to distinction.

In this chapter, I consider the ways in which published life stories based on childhoods in rural France deal with individuality, and balance a foregrounding of the self that is part of a first-person narrative with a desire to demonstrate authentic, shared peasant roots. One of the issues is that those who write memoirs and autobiographies have become educated and thus distanced from their origins, so that the act of writing such a text is symbolic of this distance. Becoming educated and literate is implied in the act of becoming sufficiently conscious of oneself as an "individual" to write a first-person narrative. I am particularly concerned with interrogating the ways that one can make claims about individuality in a life narrative while simultaneously seeking to be representative of a way of life. I will analyse four childhood memoirs from the French region of Auvergne that are part of a larger corpus of memoirs and autobiographies that I have been collecting and analysing over the past decade.[1] This is also the region in which I have conducted fieldwork on and off over the past 25 years, and I read these texts in light of this experience.

These books are not life histories in the ethnographic sense of interviews and the transcription of a life story. Only one reads like a conventional autobiography, as a linear narrative of one person's life experiences; the other three are organized around vignettes and shorter stories. All four books use first-person narrative, and were written by their subjects. All are autoethnographies, in the sense of combining life stories with ethnographic descriptions, and each authenticates the "peasant" voice of the writer through a demonstration of insider status and intimate knowledge of rural life. Pierre Bourdieu's theoretical approaches to biography, and his own narratives of rurality, are particularly relevant to the study of French rural autobiography given his own childhood origins in rural South Western France. Later in this chapter, I will briefly discuss Bourdieu's rural roots and autobiographical reflections upon them, and show the ways in which his "auto-analysis" displays some of the same tensions found in the rural literature discussed here.

THE BIOGRAPHICAL ILLUSION

For Pierre Bourdieu, the individual is an illusion and the privilege of the bourgeoisie, the class that imagines they have choices and "tastes" that distinguish them from the lower social strata. There are two related ways that Bourdieu discussed individual identity and its illusions. First, he argued (1982) that our identity is shaped by "rites of institution" that give us, through such mechanisms as official state paperwork and identity cards, the illusion of a fixed identity that does not vary from situation to situation, but only in terms of social and biological aging. This is the identity associated with the proper name. Second, Bourdieu argued that our everyday sense of "identity" and of our "individuality" (which are somewhat different from the public and official identity conferred by the state) are mediated by the habitus, which is a set of dispositions shared by others in a similar class position. Our individuality is expressed through our "tastes", which we perceive to be a matter of choice, but which Bourdieu maintains are not really choices, but rooted in our habitus (1984).

In *Distinction*, Bourdieu explored the relationship between habitus and lifestyles. He defined "taste" as "the propensity and capacity to appropriate (materially or symbolically) a given class of classified, classifying objects or practices" (1984:173) and offers as an example the traditional cabinet maker and his world view (an expression of his habitus):

> ... the way he manages his budget, his time or his body, his use of language and choice of clothing are fully present in his ethic of scrupulous, impeccable craftsmanship and in the aesthetic of work for work's sake which leads him to measure the beauty of his products by the care and patience that have gone into them. (1984:173–4)

For Bourdieu, such attributes of lifestyle are not freely chosen and cannot be adopted or cast off at whim. Rather, they are based in the habitus, which is an inculcated system of thought, feeling, bodily gestures, etc. that remains at the preconscious level. Taste is a matter of "necessity" for Bourdieu, and the expression of different tastes and the distinctions between them result in social differentiation and social class distinctions. Social classes, and the finer distinctions within broader social classes, are evident primarily, Bourdieu argues, in terms of taste. Therefore, the Right Bank intellectual has a different taste in art than the Left Bank intellectual, and also different philosophical approaches to life, cooking, house decor, etc. (1984:292).

In turning to biographical methods in social science, Bourdieu offered a criticism of taken for granted assumptions about the life trajectory that did not sufficiently analyse the constructed nature of individual identity as a unique and coherent entity. In his essay, 'The Biographical Illusion', he wrote that "to produce a life history or consider life as a history, that is, as a coherent narrative of a significant and directed sequence of events, is perhaps to conform to a rhetorical illusion" (2000b:298). He felt that lives needed to be understood in the contexts of the social and physical spaces in which they were situated, and that to ignore these spaces was tantamount to a description of a subway route that did not take into account the different stations that were part of a network structure. Bourdieu noted that during interviews to collect life histories, interviewees "constantly lose the thread of strict chronological order" (2000b:298) and that this must be constructed afterward by the biographer. He noted also that it is only those subjects who, due to their own position in social space and trajectory, have an "interest" in the "biographical enterprise", would be most inclined to follow a linear and coherent narrative in telling their life story.

FRENCH AUTOBIOGRAPHY AND THOSE "WHO DO NOT WRITE"

The genre of autobiography in Europe moved historically from a story about an emblematic life steeped in religious significance, as in the *Confessions* of St Augustine, to more of a focus on the individual and secular self, a transition usually considered to be marked by Rousseau's *Confessions* in the late eighteenth century (Conway 1998). The nineteenth century, a time of both growing capitalism and associated notions of individualism, was also a time of great interest in autobiography and the production of autobiographical texts. Autobiography is often viewed primarily as a bourgeois genre. Philippe Lejeune, who has been working to expand the canon of autobiography, writes that the word "autobiography" was imported to France from England in the early nineteenth century. He cites the Larousse dictionary of 1866 as defining it as the "life of an individual written by himself" (Lejeune 1989:123). Lejeune has, however, also traced an early discussion of the term that permits more room for ambiguity and greater recognition of the different intents of a writer and a reader. Thus Vapereau, in the *Universal Dictionary of Literature*, wrote in 1876 that autobiography refers to a "literary work, novel, poem, philosophical treatise, etc. whose author intended, secretly or admittedly, to recount his life, to expose his thoughts or to describe his feelings" (Lejeune 1989:123). For Lejeune, these definitions still represent the two ways in which autobiography is considered – one more narrow and literal than the other. He has proposed what he calls the "autobiographical pact" as a way to refer to an agreement whereby "the author proposes to the reader a discourse on the self" (1989:124).

Lejeune has observed that French peasants are among those who "do not write" autobiographies. According to Lejeune:

> This discourse on their life remains contained within the memory of their group (village, trade-guild) and rarely goes beyond this circle. Enclosed in one and same milieu, their life does not have the type of individuality needed to arouse interest, and which is often linked to social mobility and success. (1989:199)

It is more often those who have "emerged from these milieus" and who are no longer peasants, who write their life stories. Therefore, the life of peasants is imagined by those from more dominant sectors of society. Lejeune borrows from Pierre Bourdieu's (1977) observations that peasants are among the "controlled classes" who do not speak, but are spoken (in public, dominant discourse by intellectuals and journalists).

Lejeune implies that a certain type of individuality will "arouse interest" but does not explore that idea, and thus leaves the impression that only those who have experienced social mobility will exhibit individuality. This assumption about French peasants is one shared by Bourdieu, who described a peasant habitus as one characterized by taking for granted the lifestyle of the farmer and of being "empaysanné" (entrenched) in a certain milieu. Such a person lives in harmony with traditional peasant life; for the peasant, the social group is paramount and the individual is subject always to its control and gaze. This idea is very similar to that of Lejeune in his description of those who do not write as "enclosed in one and the same milieu". In some ways, this was an ideal type, since Bourdieu wrote mostly about peasants who were no longer in this state, having been exposed to social and economic changes that disrupted this tradition. This was true for his writings about both rural France and post-colonial Algeria during the 1960s. However, both Lejeune and Bourdieu convey ideas about peasants that confer more individuality on those who have experienced social and geographical mobility out of the peasant milieu.

While there have been few studies analysing such French peasant narratives, the topic of working class autobiography in France has received the attention of several historians, most notably Lyons (1991, 2001), Traugott (1993), and Maynes (1995). In his introduction to a collection of excerpts from nineteenth century worker autobiographies, Traugott notes several important issues of relevance to understanding their relationship to rural memoirs. In discussing various genres of autobiography, he argues that the genre of the "representative life" is the most common one for working class autobiographers. He also addresses the issue of what prompted these people to write their autobiographies, and has found two main factors: that they had become members of worker organizations that provided them with resources, and that they had experienced geographic and social mobility (Traugott 1993:33). Here, Traugott's findings are in line with the view of Lejeune that mobility is a major theme for autobiographical writings, and that those who are not mobile, "do not write". While asserting the representative claims of these autobiographers, Traugott also, however, finds that "these memoirs likewise show signs of having been hand crafted, for they bear the marks of their authors' individuality" (1993:37).

This tension between being representative and being an individual, between the structurally shared features of existence and the social agency of a worker or peasant, are also displayed in the popular autobiographies (using the term broadly, in Lejeune's sense) to which I will now turn. In my discussion, I will critique the notion that peasant lives lack individuality and "interest" by looking at the claims these authors themselves make in their writing.

AUVERGNAT LIFE STORIES: COLLECTIVE MEMORY AND INDIVIDUAL LIVES

The four books I will discuss evoke the region of the Auvergne in the telling of personal narratives by authors who all claim a peasant childhood in the rural Auvergne. Each author, however, lived in a slightly different part of this vast region that now officially encompasses four departments but was even larger in its historical definition. Although it names one large region of France, the Auvergne is recognized at the local level to be composed of several smaller subregions marked by different terrain and history. Overall, the Auvergne is imagined in both regional and national consciousness primarily in terms of its stark landscape and high mountain plateaus. It represents *"la France profonde"*, and, like Brittany, is known as a region in France that retained its peasant identity longer than others. As with any identity, however, that of the Auvergne is fluid and used differently in different situations.[2] Life stories associated with an Auvergnat identity, and which foreground the regional aspect of the subject's identity, tend, however, to share a focus on the historical poverty of the region and its difficult mountain landscape and climate. The wily Auvergnat who has been able to thrive in such an environment is a common trope in the oral and written literature of this region, and I have written elsewhere of the use of the term *se débrouiller* to connote the ways of "making do" (coping) and also of "making out" (outwitting a situation), evoked by my own informants in the rural Auvergne (Reed-Danahay 1993, 1996).

The first two books I will discuss are distributed by the same Clermont-Ferrand publisher, La Dorée. La Dorée publishes rustic novels and memoirs. A paragraph preceding a list of its publications in the front matter of the book by Verdier (to be discussed below), explains the intent of the series in the year 2000:

> Regional novels and memoirs (*les romans et récits du terroir*) keep alive the collective memory across the history of one family or one village of our regions. It permits the reader to rediscover his own childhood memories or to reconstitute a slice of life of his ancestors. Destinies cross, feelings merge and offer us a living saga, a valuable testimony at this turn of the century.[3]

This description foregrounds the ways in which the story of one life or of one family becomes representative of a way of life. The focus is on collective memory. The first three books I discuss here share this vision of regional literature, while the fourth is a more conventional autobiography that emphasizes the distinctiveness of the individual.

Tintinou, Paysan d'Auvergne by Justin Bourgeade

This book was first published in 1936, but reissued in 1997. Bourgeade was born in 1895 and spent his childhood in a mountainous village in the department of Cantal. He left to eventually become a writer and columnist for the major regional newspaper *La Montagne* and spent the rest of his life in Clermont-Ferrand, the major city of the Auvergne region. He died there in 1967, 30 years before the reissue of the book. He would have been 41 years old, and in mid-life, when the book was first published. The nickname in the title of the book (*Tintinou*) draws from the diminutive version of his name: "tin" from "Justin", with the patois ending "ou". This use of a nickname, or, as Sheringham (1993:7) puts it, a form of avatar in an autobiography, has been common in French autobiography and used by such writers as Sartre (*Poulou*) and Duras (*la petite blanche*).

The cover of the more recent paperback version shows a stark photo of an isolated old stone house in a high mountain setting, with an inset photo of a boy of about ten years of age. The back cover has a photo of Justin in old age, with coat and tie, sporting the typical beret worn by men of his generation. The blurb on the back cover tells us that "these memories are of lived scenes that share with us an existence at once rugged and rich, and vividly capture the secrets of the Auvergnat soul". This book is not referred to as an autobiography, but as both memories (*souvenirs*) and testimony (*témoignage*).

In his preface to the book, Bourgeade tells the reader that these are childhood memories, based on everyday life in a village at the time of his childhood (which would have been at the turn of the century). He writes also that he does not intend a psychological study of peasants, nor to generalize about all villages in this region of Cantal, but to focus on only one. At the same time, however, he writes that life in these villages is more or less similar – a frugal life centered on dairy farming with Salers cattle (the typical breed in the Cantal because of its hardiness and ability to withstand the cold and wind of the high mountains). He suggests that others who spent childhoods in similar villages, and then left as did he, will relate to his memories with "the same emotions". Bourgeade writes:

> Youth experienced here the same rustic pleasures, certainly more varied than those of youth in the cities. Seemingly deprived of everything, little villagers are however a thousand times more satisfied than the urbanites ... all native or uprooted Auvergnats who, in their youth, lost the nails of their clogs on the rocky paths of the villages, witnessed the same scenes and lived the same half-savage existence in the bosom of wild nature. (1997:v–vi)

Bourgeade tells his childhood memoirs as a series of vignettes, some of which are personal narratives of his own boyhood experiences and others of which are portraits of events or other people in the village. The sections of the book display typical Auvergnat themes of the rustic nature of life in the mountains, with one section on old legends, while others are associated with geographic locations like the mountains, the prairie, and the river. Other sections deal with what are presented as typical people and scenes of village life. These stories are told with a touch of irony and most often humor, which is also a common theme in Auvergnat regional writing. His memories of childhood center on common experiences, like guarding sheep in the mountains or going to primary school, shared by many of his generation. While most of the vignettes draw from his childhood, Bourgeade explains in the preface that some are more recent observations but that little has changed since his childhood. A timeless quality, therefore, is associated with village life at this period before World War II, in the mid-1930s. And a shared experience and collective memory of village life is assumed and perpetuated through this type of book. Bourgeade's own life experiences become representative of a shared, collective peasant experience at the turn of the century. The colorful local inhabitants of Bourgeade's childhood village are narrated in ways that show their own distinctive quirks while also pointing to a shared sense of villages that include a diversity of such types. Bourgeade displays his own individuality through his facility of storytelling as a writer or raconteur, who amuses his readers and evokes in them recognition of aspects of their own lives. He makes local village life interesting and somewhat idiosyncratic.

Mémoires d'un Papi Auvergnat by Henri-Antoine Verdier

Verdier, like Bourgeade, is a man whose childhood was spent in a rural village in the Auvergne region but who left and had a career elsewhere. Verdier was born in 1911, and the book jacket cover explains that since he was the youngest in his peasant family, he had no choice but to leave, to "exile himself" in the city. He had a career in the civil service but also wrote a rustic novel (*Les Lentilles Vertes*) before undertaking this book of childhood memories. Both Verdier and Bourgeade depend on the virtuosity of their use of language for the success and appeal of their books. Bourgeade, writing much earlier, however, wrote his book exclusively in French, albeit a colloquial form of French. Verdier, however, writing in the 1990s, after the movements of language revitalization in France, makes generous use of the regional patois and authenticates his Auvergnat identity through his facility with this dialect. His book begins with a poem he wrote, titled "The mold was patois" (*Le moule était patois*). Verdier writes that his first cry was in patois; his mother's first kiss to him was in patois, and so on. A guide to patois for the reader appears at the start of the book, explaining some issues of pronunciation, and differences between French and the patois.

Verdier's book, like that of Bourgeade, is organized into a series of short vignettes or stories, amusingly referred to on the jacket cover as "*petites histoiriettes*". Each story is published in both French and patois, with French appearing on the right hand page, and patois on the left. The blurb on the book jacket tells the reader that this book is full of "humor, peasant anecdotes, stories and poems evoking an earlier era in the countryside ... The oldest will rediscover the language of their parents, the others will savor these moments stolen into oblivion. Quiet! ... the spectacle begins". The stories are presented as the type of stories the author would have heard during his childhood at the evening *veillées* common at that time, where villagers would gather in homes to sit around the hearth and hear stories. In the collective memory of this region, and in other provinces of France, this time is often associated with an era before TV and is generally one marked as pre-World War II.

The stories in Verdier's book are usually told in the third person but some are in the first person. These are told as if they are his own childhood memories. One personal narrative is about his little sister, from the perspective of a boy who has to look after her, another is about his mother's soup, and another recounts a snowy day when they didn't have to attend school. There are no stories about school or church per se, although these institutions in the village are mentioned and taken for granted as part of the landscape. One story, for example, concerns the bellringer at the church (bells are still typically rung in French villages to mark events such as deaths). This is similar to Bourgeade's book, in which one story recounts how he and a friend skipped school one day, but no story centers specifically on the teacher or events within class. Neither is the village priest a figure in these stories. As in Bourgeade's book, the stories are organized into sections of the book – the seasons, the hearth, the fields, trades of yesteryear, and neighbors (similar to Bourgeade's section labeled "Typical villagers"). The main characters in these stories are the "insiders" (peasants, merchants, artisans), rather than outsiders like the priest and teacher. Verdier and Bourgeade avoid controversial topics or overt political commentary in their memoirs. The focus is on collective memories and a romanticized, nostalgic look back to their childhoods and the colorful people and events they remember.

D'une fougère ... à l'autre: une siècle de vie rurale près du Sancy by Eliane Meallet

Eliane Meallet was born in 1938, in the department of Puy-de-Dôme, not too far from the villages in which I have conduced ethnographic fieldwork, but a little farther up into the higher mountains. I am familiar with the places she mentions in her book, and she evokes for me as a reader the style in which local history is recounted that I am familiar with in the everyday lives of the people I know and have lived with in the Auvergne. Meallet is an autodidact, and has written and self-published at least two rustic novels in addition to this memoir. Her book is known and has been read by some of the inhabitants of the *commune* I call Lavialle. I did not read it myself, however, until I found a used copy in the flea market in Clermont-Ferrand in 2001, the same year in which I also purchased the books by Bourgeade and Verdier at bookstores in Clermont-Ferrand. Meallet's book is an autoethnography in the sense that she recounts her own experiences, but is also trying to evoke something of the local region and its history through the story of her own family. Meallet herself is not part of the story until she gets to her birth and entrance into the family mid-way through the book.

Meallet's narrative is, like the other two, organized through a series of short vignettes. However, her book follows a linear trajectory, tracing a period from the early nineteenth century to the 1960s, when she had herself come of age. It is organized around several themes for each time period, but not according to the type of themes used by the other two authors. Meallet alternates sections outlining the major national and international events of the decade with technological and other changes in the region, and then the life cycle events and everyday life on the farm for her own family (starting with her grandparents' experiences, as she has reconstructed them). This book is self-published, using a printing firm in Clermont-Ferrand. The preface to it carries some authority because a local dignitary, who was the former mayor of her village as well as the former Deputy to the Regional Council, wrote it. He endorses the book by saying that as the second generation offspring of a modest peasant family from the region, he can attest to the changes in the region Meallet writes about, and to the region's endurance.

While irony or humor is not entirely absent from Meallet's book, it is a more serious chronicling of a family, a region, and a way of life, than the other two books. Meallet includes a short notice to her grandchildren in the preface to the book, telling them that they will be adolescents at the turn of the twenty-first century. She writes that she hopes they will find this story of the twentieth century interesting and, looking towards the future, mentions her wish that she would be able to know the twenty-first century and look back on it in the same way. The author tells the reader that "I made sure to write this history by using very simple words and phrases, true and natural, as I am myself, and as was my life and my surroundings" (1992:1). The value of being "simple" and natural is one espoused in the villages of my fieldwork, and I have written about this in my ethnography of the region (Reed-Danahay 1996). Putting on airs or acting superior to others is a highly transgressive form of behavior. Meallet, therefore, asserts her authenticity and veracity by appealing to this aspect of her self and her life. It is also a gendered vernacular, since males in this region are the more prominent public humorous raconteurs of Auvergnat life (as with Bourgeade and Verdier). To be "simple" (meaning modest), and natural is a value for both men and women, but for women, to be "serious" is especially valued.[4]

While Meallet tells her story in French, she does occasionally include some of the local patois, as in her use of it to recreate a conversation between her mother and another woman in a local market (which gives some sense of the rivalry between them as each one assesses and comments upon what the other has purchased). There is also a comment at the end of the book noting that the pronunciations and transcription of the patois are based on the ways of speaking in her own *commune*, and that this can vary from village to village. Meallet's own adult life is not chronicled in the book, and she ends her story around the time she and her brother each got married. He got the farm, and she left for her own "destiny", as she puts it. One assumes from the book that she continued to live in this region, but we don't know if she married another farmer. She does, in fact, still reside in a rural village in this region, but not in the *commune* of her birth. Meallet ends her chronicle with a list of changes since the 1960s, such as farmers now being called "agriculturalists" rather than "peasants" and says that it will be up to her grandchildren to decide if the changes in rural life have made people happier.

Meallet's book differs from the memoirs of Verdier and Bourgeade because it is both past and future oriented, while theirs only look back. She does not address her present, perhaps because it is self-evident to her and her readers, and therefore situates the past of her region and her family in a trajectory leading toward an unknown future. Her own individuality is claimed not through the unique qualities she displays – she insists upon her honest and modest approach to life – but through her attempts to chronicle the local history in this way. As a writer, she claims a voice that can narrate the lives of her family and neighbors. The texts of Bourgeade, Verdier, and Meallet depend more on the testimony of others they have known, and the lifestyle they experienced as a child, than on their own individual life stories. They are an expression not of a collective mass of undifferentiated peasant lives but of individuals who lived, spoke, and acted. While these people may be "entrenched" peasants, "enclosed in one and the same milieu", their lives are still claimed by these authors to express forms of individuality.

Toinou: le cri d'un enfant auvergnat, pays d'Ambert by Antoine Sylvère

While the first three texts seem to work against the claims of Lejeune and Bourdieu, this book works with them and underscores the role of mobility and education for the individual. The author of this book was born to a poor sharecropping family in 1888 and died in 1963. Sylvère was thus a contemporary of Justin Bourgeade, although they spent their childhoods in different parts of the Auvergne, with Bourgeade living further south and in a much higher mountain climate. The title of this book (*Toinou*), like that of Bourgeade's, evokes the diminutive childhood form of the author's name: Antoine. Sylvère, like Bourgeade and Verdier, left his childhood surroundings when he came of age, but he tells the story more in terms of fleeing than of reluctantly having to leave. The subtitle of this book ("The cry of an Auvergnat child") foreshadows the narration of everyday physical and symbolic violence suffered by the author as a child as well as by others in his milieu. *Toinou* is not a book of colorful village characters and humorous anecdotes, like those of Bourgeade and Verdier, nor a straightforward chronicling of the life of a peasant family in the twentieth century incorporating a mix of difficulties within an overall story of progress, like that of Meallet. It is a story of hardship and suffering in turn of the twentieth century France. I have had this book in my possession since purchasing it during my original fieldwork in France right after it came out, and significantly, I bought it in Paris.

This book is more of a conventional autobiography than the other three books, but like them, it tells a story of childhood and youth, stopping the narrative when the author comes of age. This is a book intended for a more national and intellectual audience, and was published by Plon in the well known series Terre Humaine (in which also appeared Lévi-Strauss' *Tristes tropiques* and Hélias' *Le Cheval d'orgueil*), Plon being based in Paris and this series featuring a strong focus on ethnography. A recent review of the series (Savin 2005), marking its fiftieth anniversary, notes that along with *Tristes tropiques*, one of the first volumes to appear, *Le Cheval d'orgeuil* and *Toinou* are among the most popular titles. *Toinou* is very much the story of an individual life. Although the text reads as a straight autobiography it is nonetheless a highly mediated text. Antoine Sylvère narrated the story into a tape recorder in the 1960s, and it has thus been transcribed by others into the autobiography of Toinou, which was published almost 20 years later. In his introduction to a recent book about the collection of works in the Terre Humaine series, Pierre Auregan (2001:19) casts *Toinou* as opposing the romanticization of the rural past, which places it in contrast to much of the rural memoir literature steeped in nostalgia. Auregan uses the phrase "*rurolâtrie ambiante*" to signify this, using a pun with idolatry to suggest a worship of rural life. He writes that *Toinou* is "caustic, ironic, demystifying, breaking with the unanimity that prevailed in the vision that the 1970s had of rural society, seeing in it a sort of golden age" (ibid.).

The individuality of Sylvère is immediately emphasized in the preface to the book written by Pierre-Jakez Hélias. Hélias fashions Sylvère as a sort of Horatio Alger figure, a self-made man. He notes that the appeal of the book is based primarily on Sylvère's personality, writing in the first paragraph:

> This was an autodidact starving for knowledge, having acquired by his own means a level of instruction and of culture that few privileged by fate are capable of attaining with all the help possible. This was a being of hunger and misery, born in the starkest of surroundings, not even speaking French, peasant child, worker adolescent, who made himself, by successive stages, schoolteacher, engineer, factory director, cooperative founder . . . (Sylvère 1980:vii). Hélias points out the autoethnographic nature of this book, calling Sylvère "a native who produced a work of ethnography" (1980:viii), while also applauding his avoidance of scientific jargon or the stereotypical vocabulary associated with his eventual position as a social and political militant (of the Left).

Antoine Sylvère begins his story with his birth, and explains that his mother left soon after to be a wet nurse for a bourgeois family in Lyon, leaving him with his grandparents and only cow's milk to drink. His father was working at the time in Normandy as a sawyer. The stage is thus set for a childhood of deprivation, with parents needing to leave the region to seek work elsewhere. Schooling experiences and religious instruction, as well as other experiences in his childhood, are told with much criticism of the way of life endured by Toinou. Although the narrative stops in late adolescence, we learn from a short summary written by his children that Toinou went on to join the army, take part in the French Resistance, as well as to educate himself and work for militant leftist causes. The memoir of his childhood is followed in the text with documents added by the editors of the book, including some extracts of a journal he kept while a soldier, some documentation on the legal and social conditions of workers during the nineteenth and early twentieth centuries, and a short essay on the patois of the Ambert region. An essay contributed by Sylvère's children, on the "personality" of their father, underscores his unique qualities.

MOBILITY, INDIVIDUALITY, AND EDUCATION

To return to the question that I cited earlier in this chapter, what are we to do with these memoirs? They are marginal texts, with minimal interest in and of themselves to most readers beyond France or even beyond those readers with a particular interest in rural France or the Auvergne. For an ethnographer, however, they are of interest because they display twentieth century forms of rural narrative within a context of declining rural life, and because they bear some tensions between the individual and collective experiences they recount.

The memoirs by these four authors point to the ways in which the agrarian past of France continues to mark the imagination of a country even though it is increasingly comprised of immigrants as well as an internally mobile population within the context of Europeanization. Current policies of neoliberalism emphasize mobile individuals within a globalizing economy, and concepts of a "new" European citizen less rooted in national identity are emerging in this context (at least among the mobile, educated elite). Very recent discussions in Europe, as I write this, following the collapse of the ratification of a new European Constitution with the veto of France (and the Netherlands), touch upon the protection of farmers associated with French agricultural policy. The Europe of farmers (France) is contrasted with a more modern or neoliberal Europe (represented by Britain). The peasant past in France has been a national preoccupation throughout the nineteenth and twentieth centuries and into the present, marked by different ideologies at different moments, but frequently opposing the traditional self, rooted in a local collectivity, to a modern, "individual" self. Anxieties about individuality and mobility have been expressed through the turn of the twentieth century popularity in France of published life histories written by peasants or former peasants. While only one of these authors, Eliane Meallet, did not leave the region, the other three (all male) wrote their memoirs of childhood from the perspective of someone who "left home". For Bourgeade and Verdier, the look back is one entrenched in nostalgia; for Sylvère, it is one of bitterness and emotional pain.

These texts stand in contrast to other contemporary artifacts of popular culture in France that deal with identity formation, such as the recent feature film *L'Auberge Espagnole* (Klapisch et al. 2003), which highlights the ways in which individuality is expressed through national identities in a contemporary, urban and bourgeois Europe of mobility. The regional identity expressed in the "peasant" memoirs gives way to national identities in this context. *L'Auberge Espagnole* is ostensibly the personal narrative, or memoir, of a young French student who, as part of the Erasmus program for university exchange and study sponsored by the European Union, was studying abroad in Barcelona. At the end of the film, we see that Xavier, the protagonist, turned away from a planned career in finance, which was the reason for his studies, to become a writer, thus writing the story of his experiences. In the apartment he shares during his year abroad with students from other European nations, Xavier encounters various people with different personalities that are all based on the national identities they respectively display. There is the neurotic but sweet English girl, the fastidious German, the free-spirited Belgian lesbian, etc. Xavier claims his individuality by breaking away from the career path set for him by his father and turning instead to the life of a writer. His travel to Spain and his "European" experiences there, his coming of age and education in the broadest sense, free him from certain constraints of traditional bourgeois French culture and enable his "true" self to emerge. The mobility of Antoine Sylvère is not so different in the sense that he, too, broke away from the milieu into which he was born and, through travel and both social and geographic mobility, was able to carve out a distinctive life that departed from that of his family and neighbors. Both subjects express a desire to escape a fate that seems overly determined and to reinvent themselves: to make claims of individual expression.

Lejeune's linking of individuality and social mobility is of interest here, particularly when viewed in the context of education. Rural French discourse frequently disparages those who try to "distinguish" themselves, and this is a theme in much of the literature on peasant societies more generally. This is a common theme in narratives of becoming educated, because the person who becomes educated and leaves farming is distinguishing themselves in transgressive ways. Since the simple person who does not "put on airs" is valued, someone who singles out his or her individuality in writing or narrating a life history must tread a delicate balance. This can create a dilemma for the person who becomes sufficiently educated to write their own autobiography, or to write about their childhood, because they have adopted an "interest" in the biographical enterprise that separates them from the group they seek to speak for in their memoirs.

In a previous essay (Reed-Danahay 1997), on education and autoethnography in two French memoirs by Emilie Carles (1977) and Pierre-Jakez Hélias (1978 [1975]), I focused on the ways in which these two figures narrated their experiences of becoming educated and leaving "home". This social mobility (primarily through education) was associated with the distance that permitted them to train an ethnographic gaze on their rural roots and so to produce life stories that were part autobiography and part ethnography. The ambivalence about literally and figuratively leaving home, expressed in both of these stories and in educational narratives more generally, was a major theme of my analysis. I also pointed out that these narratives had to be seen as part of a dominant discourse about rural life in France, when viewed in the contexts of their production, publication, and educated authors.

In that earlier essay, I did not focus specifically on the ways in which individuality was expressed or claimed in published life stories. But I was interested in issues of social agency in the texts and, in particular, the ways in which the subjects discussed their own volition in having acquired an education and left peasant life. I noted, for instance, that Hélias' story was written in such a way that his own experiences seemed somehow inevitable and a product of wider social changes affecting rural Brittany and the rest of rural France. Carles' story, as framed in the American version translated into English through a feminist lens, can be seen to fashion Carles as a unique woman who fled the rural oppression suffered by her mother, and who found a way to express her individuality and difference through education even though she returned to the village as a schoolteacher. Emilie Carles became an environmental activist, an educator, and a free thinker as a socialist and atheist (breaking away from Catholicism).

The theme of social mobility, of "leaving home" that is part of the stories told by Hélias and Carles, provides a vehicle for accentuating the uniqueness of the person who leaves and the origins and experiences shared with both those who did not leave and those who, like them, left. According to Lejeune, those who do not write did not leave and, therefore, individuality is associated primarily with the educated (either through formal education or self-education) or otherwise socially mobile person. Autobiographies, like those of Hélias, Carles, and Sylvère, that focus on the life trajectory of an individual person who experiences social and geographical mobility, reinforce the gap between those that left and those they left behind. They have acquired new "tastes" and abilities of narration through their mobility and new social positions that encourage them to foreground their own individuality and personality in their life stories. For Bourgeade, Verdier, and Meallet, whose memoirs are either self-published or published by smaller regional presses, and hence, in Lejeune's terms, have less "interest", the self of the narrator is being expressed through the act of telling the story and not through the unique qualities of their lives or personalities per se. This satisfies the need to be modest about oneself that is central to rural values, and thus places claims to individuality in a different register from that expressed in more conventional forms of autobiography.

In his own autobiographical writings, Pierre Bourdieu was reluctant to write conventional autobiography.[5] The epitaph to a reflexive essay published after his death reads "this is not an autobiography" (2004:5). Bourdieu wanted to distance himself from what he viewed as the narcissism of autobiography and also titled another of his personal narratives (2000a) as *Pascalian Meditations*. He was also uncomfortable on theoretical grounds with life stories that stressed the individual as hero without sufficient social analysis – the biographical illusion. Bourdieu felt that a truly scientific sociology depended on the reflexivity of the researcher, by which he meant being able to analyse one's own position in the social field and one's own habitus. He came to label this "auto-analysis". Bourdieu had rural origins, like the authors I have discussed above, and was born in 1932 in South Western France to the son of a sharecropper. He was roughly a contemporary of Meallet, born in 1938, and experienced many of the same changes she did as a child in prewar rural France. Bourdieu was, however, one generation removed from peasant life, since his father did not work in farming and was a postal worker. Nonetheless he did grow up around farmers and spent time on the farm of his grandfather and uncle.

Bourdieu wrote about his own departure from a peasant milieu, through education, and described himself as having a "split habitus" due to a life trajectory that crossed the boundaries of traditional rural society and the urban intellectual milieu he would eventually enter. Bourdieu is an example of a person of rural background who became educated, "left home", and yet claimed an authentic knowledge of rural life. The tension apparent in Bourdieu's life writing and in the published memoirs by others of rural origins in France is that if a peasant is one who does not write and who is entrenched within a milieu in which he or she does not distinguish themselves, then how can a writer claim an authentic peasant habitus? If we follow Bourdieu's theories of habitus and distinction, such writers have a split habitus, in which they cross borders between different milieus and have acquired a different habitus from that of their childhood that enables them to write about it. But does this mean that one needs to become educated in order to become an individual?

NOTES

1 See Reed-Danahay (1997, 2002, 2005b). I would like to thank the National Endowment for the Humanities and the University of Texas at Arlington for research support for this project. A Fulbright Research Award enabled me to further explore such texts in the context of European Union expansion.
2 I have written elsewhere about Auvergnat identity and its meanings at the local level, based on my ethnographic fieldwork in the region (see Reed-Danahay 1996).
3 All translations of previously untranslated French texts are my own.
4 The distinctions drawn between urban and rural women in France, in the view from the village, often portray the rural woman as more serious, modest, and prudent than the urban woman whose morality is more suspect (see Reed-Danahay 2002, 2005b).
5 I have explored Bourdieu's autobiographical expressions in more detail in Reed-Danahay (2005a).

REFERENCES

Aurégan, P. (2001) *Des récits et des hommes. Terre Humaine: un autre regard sur les sciences de l'homme*. Paris: Nathan/HER.

Behar, R. (2003 [1993]) *Translated Woman: Crossing the Border with Esperanza's Story*. Tenth Anniversary Edition. Boston, MA: Beacon.

Behar, R. (2004) 'Foreword'. In D. Freedman and O. Frey (eds) *Autobiographical Writing Across the Disciplines: A Reader*. Durham, NC: Duke University Press.

Bourdieu, P. (1977) 'Une classe objet'. *Actes de la Recherche en Sciences Sociales*, 17/18:2–5.

Bourdieu, P. (1982) 'Les rites d'institution'. *Actes de la Recherche en Sciences Sociales*, 43:58–63.

Bourdieu, P. (1984) *Distinction: A Social Critique of the Judgement of Taste*, R. Nice (trans.). Cambridge, MA: Harvard University Press.

Bourdieu, P. (2000a [1997]) *Pascalian Meditations*, R. Nice (trans.). Stanford, CA: Stanford University Press.

Bourdieu, P. (2000b [1986, 1987]) 'The Biographical Illusion', Y. Winkin and W. Leeds-Hurwitz (trans.). In P. du Gay, J. Evans and P. Redman (eds) *Identity: A Reader*. London: Sage, pp. 297–303. Reprinted from R.J. Parmentier and G. Urban (eds) (1987) *Working Papers and Proceedings of the Centre for*

Psychosocial Studies, pp. 1–7. Original French version Bourdieu, P. (1986) 'L'illusion biographique'. *Actes de la Recherche en Sciences Sociales*, 62/63:69–72.

Bourdieu, P. (2004) *Esquisse pour une auto-analyse*. Paris: Raisons d'Agir.

Bourdieu, P. et al. (1999 [1993]) *The Weight of the World: Social Suffering in Contemporary Society*, P. Parkhurst Ferguson et al. (trans.). Stanford, CA: Stanford University Press.

Bourgeade, J. (1997 [1936]) *Tintinou, paysan d'Auvergne: Scènes vécues de la vie rurale sur les hauts plateaux du Cantal*. Clermont-Ferrand: La Dorée.

Brettell, C.B. (2002) 'The Individual/Agent and Culture/Structure in the History of the Social Sciences'. *Social Science History*, 26(3):429–45.

Carles, E. (1977) *Une soupe aux herbes sauvages*. Propos receuillis par Robert Destanque. Paris: Simeon. Translated into English as *A Life of Her Own: The Transformation of a Countrywoman in Twentieth-Century France*. Harmondsworth: Penguin, 1991.

Coffey, A. (1999) *The Ethnographic Self: Fieldwork and the Representation of Identity*. London: Sage.

Conway, J.K. (1998) *When Memory Speaks: Reflections on Autobiography*. New York: Knopf.

Crapanzano, V. (1980) *Tuhami: Portrait of a Moroccan*. Chicago: University of Chicago Press.

Crapanzano, V. (1984) 'Life-Histories: Review Essay'. *American Anthropologist*, 86(4):953–60.

Hélias, P.-J. (1978 [1975]) *The Horse of Pride: Life in a Breton Village*, J. Guichemaud (trans.). New Haven, CT: Yale University Press.

Klapisch, C. et al. (2003) *L'Auberge Espagnole*. DVD. US: Twentieth Century-Fox Home Entertainment. Original 2002. France: Studio Canal.

Lejeune, P. (1989) *On Autobiography*, Eakin, P.J. (ed. and Foreword), K. Leary (trans.). Minneapolis, MN: University of Minnesota Press.

Lyons, M. (1991) 'The Autodidacts and their Literary Culture: Working-Class Autobiographers in Nineteenth-Century France'. *Australian Journal of French Studies*, 28(3):264–73.

Lyons, M. (2001) *Readers and Society in Nineteenth-Century France: Workers, Women, Peasants*. London/New York: Palgrave Macmillan.

Maynes, M.J. (1995) *Taking the Hard Road: Life Course in French and German Workers' Autobiographies in the Era of Industrialization*. Chapel Hill, NC: University of North Carolina Press.

Meallet, E. (1992) *D'une fougère . . . à l'autre: Une siècle de vie rurale près du Sancy*. Clermont-Ferrand: Pougheon.

Rapport, N. (1997) *Transcendent Individual: Towards a Literary and Liberal Anthropology*. London/New York: Routledge.

Reed-Danahay, D. (1993) 'Talking about Resistance: Ethnography and Theory in Rural France'. *Anthropological Quarterly*, 66(4):221–46.

Reed-Danahay, D. (1996) *Education and Identity in Rural France: The Politics of Schooling*. Cambridge: Cambridge University Press.

Reed-Danahay, D. (1997) 'Leaving Home: Schooling Stories and the Ethnography of Autoethnography in Rural France'. In Reed-Danahay (ed.) *Auto/Ethnography: Rewriting the Self and the Social*. Oxford/New York: Berg, pp. 123–44.

Reed-Danahay, D. (2002) 'Sites of Memory: Autoethnographies from Rural France'. *Biography: An Interdisciplinary Quarterly*, Special Issue on Biography and Geography, 25(1):95–109.

Reed-Danahay, D. (2005a) *Locating Bourdieu*. Bloomington, IN: Indiana University Press.

Reed-Danahay, D. (2005b) 'Desire, Migration, and Attachment to Place: Life Stories of Rural French Women'. In B. Straight (ed.) *Women on the Verge of Home: Narratives of Home and Transgressive Travel*. Albany, NY: State University of New York Press, pp. 129–48.

Savin, T. (2005) 'L'odyssée de Terre Humaine'. *Lire*, juin. www.lire.fr/imprimer.asp/idC=48567

Sheringham, M. (1993) *French Autobiography: Devices and Desires, Rousseau to Perec*. Oxford/New York: Clarendon.

Shostak, M. (1981) *Nisa: The Life and Words of a !Kung Woman*. New York: Vintage.

Sylvère, A. (1980) *Toinou: le cri d'un enfant auvergnat, pays d'Ambert*. Preface by P.-J. Hélias. Paris: Plon.

Traugott, M. (ed.) (1993) *The French Worker: Autobiographies from the Early Industrial Era*, M. Traugott (trans. and Introduction). Berkeley, CA: University of California Press.

Verdier, H.-A. (2000) *Mémoires d'un papi auvergnat*. Clermont-Ferrand: La Dorée.

Whittaker, E. (1992) 'The Birth of the Anthropological Self and its Career'. *Ethos*, 20(2):191–219.

8
An Anatomy of Humor: The Charismatic Repartee of Trevor Jeffries in *The Mitre* Pub

Nigel Rapport

AN ANATOMY: TREVOR JEFFRIES AND HUMOR

This chapter offers an account of Trevor Jeffries and his sense of humor and repartee, in particular the humor with which he treated himself, his society in *The Mitre* pub and the wider village community, and his way of life, in the Northern English valley of Wanet (Rapport 1993, 1994). It explores the fashioning of identity, of a public persona, by way of pub performances which are humorous in style.

Trevor took himself, his society and his way of life extremely seriously, cherishing and respecting his values; but at the same time he was able and very willing to satirize them: to hoist himself with his own petard. He was opinionated and yet even-handed and generous; passionate and yet ironic. The whys and wherefores of this habit of mind, and its implications, are my focus. They amounted, I shall argue, to a "life project" of constructing a village persona of great popularity, eccentricity and charm. By "life project", I intend an existentialist notion, encompassing the facility, through intention, of an individual giving his or her life a particular character, direction and force (see Rapport 2003). Trevor possessed an overridingly jolly demeanour. He was quite a tall man, but with a podginess which seemed to round off his angles. He carried himself in a round shouldered, semi-stooped fashion, too, which gave him an unforbidding, even vulnerable air. In his frequent appearances in *The Mitre*, with his beer glass in one hand, he seemed usually to be grinning or chortling, and his small eyes narrowed to slits as the mirth pushed up his fleshy cheeks. Trevor appeared sympathetic, and one who invited friendship.

When I first encountered him, as a new arrival in Wanet and in *The Mitre*, he addressed me, and his tone turned serious; then I knew that he was regarding me as a stranger: someone outwith the somewhat magical circle of camaraderie he provoked on his pub visits. I wished I could have been party to his strange self-parody, been included in the community of repartee, and been transfigured by Trevor's teasing eyes.

This chapter intends two things. Primarily to focus on Trevor's sense of humor: how I found him funny; what he achieved by way of comedy (I shall have recourse to a phrase of Goethe's that Nietzsche set much store by: "a general economy of the whole"). Secondarily I wish to consider the case study of Trevor Jeffries as instantiating more general truths concerning the "charisma" of humor. Weber's (1946) term was a complex one, and subtly placed. He wanted to signal an individual power: the individual above and beyond the normative (social, cultural, historical) milieus in which he or she was to be found: the existential actor. At the same time Weber wanted to mark the attractiveness of this individuality, the way others would want to mimic it, to join with it, and hence the authority which the individually powerful charismatic would accrue to transform the normative for others too. (Ken Burridge has written insightfully on the paradoxes this admits: the charismatic individual transforms the normative personhood of others, but, in his or her success, threatens the outward individuality of his or her own perspective (1979).) What I would point up here is the indexical or localized nature of Trevor Jeffries' humor. His humor was for insiders; it attracted villagers in Wanet to a consideration of local social life, to apprehend it from the perspective Trevor offered, to learn certain lessons – about imposture and camaraderie, about tradition and change – to do with social life as such, and finally to return from this position of global vantage to a village life vitalized by his signature.

TREVOR JEFFRIES' NARRATIVE THEMES

What I first found captivating about Trevor Jeffries – comedic, individual, endearing – was the way he managed to combine seriousness and satire in his self-expression such that unless you knew him well, you did not really know what to make of him; which then made his performance all the funnier to those who knew him best. But even for the latter there was a way that Trevor combined the serious and the satiric, and other discourses normally kept apart, such that it was at once funny and somewhat unnerving. This was also what made his pub performances entertaining; Trevor expressed common Wanet discourses (such as concerning the "hard times" of the past) in an uncommon and individual way. This was what made him, made him both a jolly personage and also a figure of knowledge and respect. His novel combinings of discourses made new discourses which were particular to him. In what follows I wish to identify a number of these discourses, as well as to describe their ongoing evolution; for they were key to his achievement, I would suggest, key to the popular persona that was Trevor Jeffries' life project. First, however, some further details of Trevor's life are introduced.

It was in the pub, *The Mitre*, especially, where I believe Trevor felt most relaxed. He would drink quite regularly, a few times per week, and always at weekends. He never drank enough in one session to become "legless" and incoherent, but he often drank enough to become happy and uninhibited; at weekends especially, he would usually end up singing and dancing, and kissing the women situated around the bar, until his long suffering but well loved wife, Hilary, would take him home. But there was certainly another and more serious side to Trevor which lived outside the pub – and from which the pub was a sometimes welcome escape.

Trevor was in his mid-40s, as I have mentioned, and worked as a foreman in Barber's, a large and long established joinery firm in the nearby town of Leyton. He was born in the Wanet hamlet of Robbgill and had lived there all his life. Trevor was the youngest of four brothers, all of whom became farmers except him, and one of whom now ran one of the biggest farms in Wanet (the union of his father's parents' farm, his mother's parents' and a third one he had bought). In the 1950s, however, going into farming as a profession had been discouraged, and so Trevor did not follow in the family tradition. Instead, he served his time as a joiner, then worked his way up the ladder at Barber's into management. He had since been offered (and accepted) a directorship, but he still enjoyed keeping the company of the men on the shop floor even if he no longer did any manual work himself. He also enjoyed traveling around the country for the firm, seeking out new contracts for work and checking on the quality of the finished products. Since Barber's employed up to seven "lads" from Wanet as joiners at any one time, Trevor was pleased to be able to call himself the dale's single biggest local employer. (Wanet might have its large farms (and wealthy farmers) but these remained mostly family-run operations, and, with much mechanization now in place, they employed few nonfamily labourers on a regular basis.)

Another reason Trevor enjoyed his trips around Britain was that it gave him the opportunity to develop further his collection of books – antiquarian, especially – on local (Wanet and Yorkshire Dales) life and themes; he was always on the lookout for the best bargains. There wasn't much to beat a good book, Trevor felt, and local history and custom was his favourite topic. He would try to buy a book per month, and always sought out the new auctions and sales. He could not bid as high as some, he acknowledged, but when he died what he had managed to accrue would be a valuable collection, and one he could imagine donating to a local museum – if ever one such came into being! If he could not buy a book then Trevor was also happy to photocopy it; there was a good photocopier at work to which he had easy access – and it did not cost Trevor a thing! Photocopying in his spare time, for nothing, Trevor felt, was one of the perks of the job.

Another reason to be photocopying at work was that that was where the Minutes from the Wanet Parish Council also came to be typed up and photocopied (through Trevor's offices) and by taking an early read he could thus keep abreast of the latest official happenings in the dale even if he had been unable to attend the meeting itself. And Trevor was keen for all such knowledge. It was known that he kept every newspaper cutting on Wanet that he could find (that was why, for instance, he remembered the names of all the local policemen who had ever served in Wanet – in the days when one was actually stationed in a village house, and since).

Finally, Trevor also worked as a local undertaker, supervising burials roughly twice per week, and worked as the local agent for the Prudential Insurance Company, signing up people from around the dale with the company and then assisting them with their claims and forms. All this, of course, is not counting his unpaid weekend work helping out on his brothers' farms in the dale, his weekly stint as church usher, his clerking on the School Governors' Committee, his "work" at reputedly being the best at keeping outsiders from hogging the dartboard in *The Mitre*, and his "work" at providing the last house stop on New Year's eve, after the pub had shut, after the last gate-crashers had left Pullens' house party and most people had given up the ghost, but some wanted just one more nightcap before retiring …

There was something in Trevor's humor when he relaxed in the pub which mirrored the diversity of roles and jobs he undertook in the workaday world. He mixed and combined moods and tones of voice, kinds of utterance, as he did jobs; he moved from storyline to storyline in his repartee, and one never knew just where he was "coming from". As he meandered around *The Mitre,* from room to room, with pint pot in his hand, almost like holding court between groups of people chatting on different tables, or playing dominoes or throwing darts, occasionally throwing darts himself, it was almost as if he were the resident landlord, or landowner, hosting guests in his parlour. As the night advanced, and his drinking did too, so Trevor's meandering became less steady. His jollity also increased. His small eyes, quite deep set, seemed to twinkle more mischievously, promising the imminent arrival of another bon mot.

But Trevor's humor was a dry one, even cynical at times; his humor was also anecdotal, and over the hours and the nights in the pub he would spin elaborate, ongoing yarns whose weird narratives, like nonsense poems, would transform the world of Wanet and *The Mitre* pub into even further removes from the everyday world of work. If juggling a diversity of workaday jobs and roles left him perhaps with a feeling of giddiness, then in his juggling with discourses and narratives, with his audience and his retinue in *The Mitre,* in juggling with discursive themes and registers (from history to humor to cynicism), perhaps he redeemed himself, achieved a kind of transcendence over his life, a self-control. Certainly it seemed to me that, however paradoxical, the more I recognized the diversity in his life and manners, the better I came to see the narrative of his life, his life project in Wanet (and focused on *The Mitre*), as a seamless whole.

One of Trevor's close friends was the farmer, Fred Harvey; they had known each other since their school days. One midweek evening when a darts match had taken a crowd from *The Mitre* to another pub further down-dale, *The Haywain,* Fred and Trevor found themselves dancing, at evening's end, with their respective spouses but within earshot of one another. *The Haywain* had a jukebox which was being fed with coins, and, long past the end of the darts (also long past the official pub closing time), the evening was closing with good humored dancing and singing, and some "friendly" collective kissing; Trevor had briefly pawed the landlady, Jess, and had now moved on to dancing with and fondling his wife. Moreover, when the jukebox needed more money and suggestions for selections, Trevor was in no doubt: "Lena Martell's 'One Day at a Time (Sweet Jesus)'", he shouted. Indeed, he went over to feed the machine himself before returning to resume his dance with Hilary with added verve; he sang along, too, with great gusto, to Lena

Martell's syrupy sentiments. And when Fred complained, from his nearby coupling with Doris – complained jocularly but with obvious feeling – that Trevor could not actually like this song, and how could Trevor have chosen it, and had he suddenly gone "religious" or soppy, Trevor shouted an explanation, while still singing along, that "'One Day at a Time (Sweet Jesus)' is my favourite record ... Because, you've really gotta take a day at a time – haven't you, Nigel? Isn't that right? That's what I do, at any rate".

Fred laughed and carried on dancing but I doubt he knew, any more than did anyone else, quite how seriously to take what Trevor was saying. Which was funny: Trevor was such a strange mixture.

But let me go back a bit, to the point where I first had a longish conversation with Trevor, one Sunday evening in *The Mitre* when I had been resident in the dale (via Manchester, via Cambridge, via Cardiff) for only a few months, and was helping out on Fred and Doris Harvey's farm as a part time farm lad. Trevor and I were leaning on the bar drinking, where he had found me after his games of darts were finished. In expansive mood, he elaborated on a favourite theme with few promptings from me:

> Are you a nationalist, Nigel? I'm a fighter for Yorkshire independence. [I grin, disbelievingly] Oh! ... I'm disappointed you're not in my camp, Nigel; I thought you were one with us: a nationalist ... I support a free Yorkshire. And why not? It's the largest county ... Why aren't you a Welsh nationalist, Nigel? [I say something about the disparities within Wales, North and South, Anglicized and Welsh] But why aren't you at one with North Wales? ... I'm a Wanetdale nationalist, too. You know there's a Wanet Liberation Army, at least in embryo. Its commander was here tonight: the Colonel. And I'm the recruiting officer; and all the rest are privates. But why shouldn't the Welsh burn second homes? I can understand it. Why shouldn't local second homes be burnt down when local people living here can't get houses and can't afford the prices and so have to move out? One day you just might see it happening here! [I say something about the difficulties of stopping people coming from the cities] No, I agree, Nigel, that legislation against second homes mayn't be possible, but the National Park could control purchases and sales and ensure locals have sufficient living accommodation. The Park should buy the houses themselves if necessary – just like the Welsh one should – and only let locals use them ... How's that "tent" you're living in? [I describe the cosiness of my one-seater caravan on the Harvey's farm] No: I'm not interested in either tents or caravans being in the dale! You know, Nigel,

I play darts with these boys, now – Ted, David, Ralph – 'cos they're all likely to grow up and leave the dale, once they're married, and not be seen again. Do you know how many local people have bought houses in the village in the last ten years, Nigel? [I shake my head] Three! ... Only two outsiders recently bid for Wether's house, mind you, so maybe the situation's improving. But then it might just be because Wether's is a council house and not an attractive cottage. [An auction is an auction, I suggest] ... By Nigel's mumbling he seems not to be in my camp at all! He's for Queen and Country. [Stung into saying something at least passingly constructive (about a situation of a shortage of affordable local properties which I feel is unavoidable) I bemoan the lack of local possibilities of earning a good living] Yes, the real problem is local work. There's not enough of it; and the process does not seem reversible. If you can get a house in Kendal, say, for £15,000 and also work, then why on earth live here? [I nod] ... You know, I can think right off of five holiday homes in Robbgill. When they were first bought the people came every weekend, or month, or at least holiday. But gradually they've come less and less, as the novelty wore off. And it's understandable; I'd soon get fed up if I had to go to Blackpool every time for my holidays. I'm not saying tourists are bad in themselves – and we probably couldn't survive without them, now – but these days the dale is full of "mystery men". [One of Trevor's erstwhile darts partners, Bill Radford, walks by us at this point, and grins at Trevor's mention of "mystery men"] "Colonel" Radford, do you remember how once there might have been 40 people drinking here in The Mitre of an evening – not the four there are now. [Radford nods, and grins some more, and keeps moving to the toilet] Astrid Proll was here once, you know Nigel, visiting a friend who was staying up the dale: the Baader-Meinhof terrorist who they later extradited. She was really here for a bit, and drank in the '*Wain*, and she spoke to me a bit. ["In English?", I ask] In good English, aye. ["What was she like!"] She was harsh, powerful; not an attractive woman. Her friend was better ... But she and I actually spoke for a bit. ["Did she pass on any guerrilla tips?!"] No, she didn't pass on any tips ... You've not really passed the test yet yourself, you know, lad. You're a bit of a mystery man yourself. The dale is full of them. Like James Hughes. What do you make of him? Is he Liverpool Catholic or Irish? ... People come here to hide from the past, or the police, you know, Nigel. Or to escape a wife or a girlfriend; or to find a wife or girlfriend! 'Cos there are so many beautiful women here to choose from – certainly enough girlfriends for me! [Leaning closer, he becomes conspiratorial] Look at how the parson's daughter's developed! Don't you fancy her? Twenty years ago, and I'd have been after her myself. [We laugh] Aye! The dale is full of mystery men now alright. Meanwhile all our parish records have gone over to Kendal for storage; so any old "Arab" can look at them ... .

At this point, Trevor is interrupted by his wife, who wants to leave, and our exchange is finished for the evening.

I came to recognize in the above, however, a number of narrative themes to which Trevor would return in his pub interactions and performances on other occasions; for he was certainly a figure whom a public, a "retinue", enjoyed watching and by whom it expected to be regaled. Let me try to isolate these themes and list them, without, hopefully, losing sight of the particular skill Trevor had of interweaving them, and the humor they gave on to.

THE FANTASTICAL

Firstly, there was a fantastical theme which Trevor narrated, concerning, for instance, the Wanet Liberation Army and the outsiders (including "mystery men" who had infiltrated the dale) against whom it would be, in some future time, deployed. The situation of an influx of newcomers to the dale (and its pubs), and the passing over of many of the powers of elected local government officials to appointed committee members of a "National Park" to which rural Wanet (for its "outstanding natural beauty") had been assigned, while its locals found it increasingly hard to stay, live and work in the place – all this was transformed here, by Trevor, into a comedic tale of intrigue, derring-do, and, by rights, the eventual triumph of the Good. On the occasion following the above interaction on which we met, then, again in *The Mitre*, Trevor greeted me thus:

> Ah, the mystery man ... The Commander is also here tonight, you know. And we're still unsure of you. We need to set you a test. ["Like what?", I laugh] You could be a spy, so we need to set you a test. ["Like what?"] You could find both kneecaps shot up – and that'd not be pleasant. ["I'm ready for whatever"] Okay: you should go and blow up the vicarage!

In fact, the theme became a closeness between us, something Trevor and I shared. For while it seemed to bespeak only my foreignness and suspiciousness, Trevor came to use it to transform my peculiarities and idiosyncrasies into things of local color and habit: "Those 'strepsils' Nigel has are probably full of dynamite ... You never know with mystery men!" "Mystery men! You never know what they might do!" [as I finish our game of darts with a surprisingly accurate winning flourish].

I also came to appreciate the subtlety with which Trevor could apply his theme. It could be used to spotlight and gently critique newcomers to the dale, as we have seen above, and again below, to the delight of his regular audience of locals:

> Any hired assassins or IRA men among all these "Arabs" in tonight? ... He must be, look at his lapels and tie. Look he's going out the back now to plant his grenades. Look! He's following me round this end of the bar! [he cringes in mock fear before the advances of the unsuspecting stranger] ... And there's another suspicious guy; he's a rum fellow! And there's Ronald Reagan's brother ... Lucky Bill Radford isn't here tonight; those assassins would shoot him on sight ... I'm going to go over and chat to that lapel-assassin. [I laugh appreciatively at the neologism] ... I'd chat to anyone, Nigel. Look! His eyes are gone. He's drunk. He's a teddy boy who's not grown up, that's it! Not an assassin ... .

But the theme could be used, too, to make gently disparaging remarks about fellow locals:

> Is Sid Askrig still keeping you in order on the farm, Nigel? ["Just about!"] Aye. That's why he's a General while I remain a mere private: his certain "tact" in dealing with people ... In fact, I'm surprised the General gave you the day off, today, it being Sunday and all ... You know, Nigel, Wanet sort of is a separate republic already! It's got its own General and Fuehrer ... ["And Colonel"] Yes and Colonel. But not many from Wanet make it to the rank of General, you know Nigel! Milden was just a sergeant, and Whistle too ... .

Consistency of content is not a priority in this theme (non sequiturs, indeed, being basic to its character), but in becoming a "mere private" in this utterance (as opposed to being a "recruiting officer" before), Trevor does bring into focus the bossiness of Sid Askrig, and aligns it with overbearing behavior from others such as "The Fuehrer" – alias Robert Milden, to his friends. My introduction of the name of "Colonel Radford" is inappropriate here, then, because there is nothing seriously critical Trevor has to say about his friend Bill. So Trevor soon passes over the "Colonel" and returns to his theme of "General Askrig". Except that it is not now really the fantastical theme of the Wanet Liberation Army that he takes up because it is the "real" Army and the real (Second World) War that he refers to. Milden (and Reg Whistle, too: another pompous soul) got to be mere sergeants in times of war, and yet, here is Sid Askrig, in relatively peaceable Wanet, claiming in his peremptory behavior the rank and status of General.

In short, Trevor was master of using the theme precisely to include and exclude, to build up and knock down its main personae. Likewise, he could suddenly leave the fantastical behind altogether and verge into something quite different. In particular, the fantastical and the "real" of Wanet past and present, and beyond, would be subtly interwoven so as to make a nuanced commentary on the latter; in fact, to espy it from a perspective from which it became something other, something wholly new and unique to Trevor's construction.

THE DYSTOPIC

Another theme which would on occasion follow on from the fantastical was that of dystopia. What was lighthearted now becomes cynical, especially with regard to life in the future. Again, Trevor and I are chatting at the bar, when Trevor begins addressing his fellows in general:

Nigel's a republican. I'm a monarchist not a republican. 'Cos the monarchy brings in lots of money to the country; I know many firms which are being kept open through the recession due to the monarchy alone ... You know, Nigel, I'm not sure if my firm'll survive this depression. I've not thought before how or who I'd lay off if there wasn't enough work. What an awful thought! 'Cos its like a family ... You know, it doesn't seem right: them at Ascot, while millions are unemployed. There should be more taxes on them at Ascot who can afford it, and more sharing out .... .

Bill Radford looked over from his game of darts at this point and called us both "Commies", and Trevor wandered over to pay him back by putting him off his throwing game. On other occasions, however, I found the dystopic theme taken up again:

People come around selling this and that, rubbish mostly, and I buy from them out of pity, to stop them going bankrupt. The trend seems to be for bigger farms and a worse standard of living! And it doesn't seem reversible ... Meanwhile, a house was sold here recently, two-up two-down, no backdoor, garage or garden, for £18,250! Crazy! And things are changing more widely, people becoming more violent. I'm frightened now to go into the cities. And the violence is going to spread ... But it can't all be dole problems and problems with the jobless, can it Nigel? 'Cos lots of the kids involved are too young to be at work. [I say something about their conditions at home and the root causes] You know, I didn't think this would ever get to Britain; I mean the English must be the least violent race around ... The real problem, I think, starts at home: it's the parents' fault. There's not enough strict discipline and strapping these days. Somehow there's less "discipline"; that's not the best word, but its okay: there's less discipline now than 20 years ago. Like in school too: more talking back to the teachers and less obedience. In fact, secondary education is a waste of time and money for most pupils, full stop. They should be out training as apprentices ... But the solution isn't simply more policing. You're right, you must look to the root causes ... But, you know, Nigel, the riots we've been seeing in the cities recently will cost the country so much. That's the worst part: it'll all just come off in insurance costs, and that's awful for all of us ... You know, I don't leave the door unlocked half as often as I did, even here. And I keep it locked at night now and when we're not there. Not like before ... .

THE RUSTIC

More usual than this maudlin projection into a dystopic future, however, was Trevor taking pleasure in a remembered Wanet past and charting its continuation into the present. This took two thematic forms. There was the narrating of an exaggerated rusticity, largely for the consumption of gullible outsiders (and a laughing local audience), and there was a more serious historicity, reserved for those locals in the know, who would appreciate that what Wanet had to offer depended on a proper respect for its heritage.

First the rustic, occasioned here by Trevor having heard that I was trying to ease a problem with moles on Fred Harvey's farm by suggesting the use of smoke pellets, such as might be employed in suburban gardens. We are in *The Mitre*, and Trevor catches me as I finish a game of dominoes; my fellow players, all locals, are still milling about:

Been "maudying", then, Nigel? Mole catching? I heard you were having some success at Fred's? [We laugh] You know, you should catch it with a long spike through the sod: a gavelock ... And then you can eat them! [I grin and people laugh] Well? Squirrel cooked in clay is a delicacy in some parts, so moles probably are too ... Isn't that what you eat in the Punjab, anyway? You come from "the Punjab", don't you, Nigel? The Punjab is Bradford, you know; that's by your way ... You know, as well as moles there are hairy potarses. They're very rare, and you need a hazel stick to kill them. [People again laugh] Nay, what a rum fellow you are, to be sure, Nigel ... maudying at Fred's. "Mother", [he calls over to his wife in another part of the pub] bring in the mole from the dustbin. Nigel wants it for his dinner!

Again, as with the fantastical, while bespeaking foreignness, the rustic theme became something by which Trevor and I ultimately drew close, as he was to repeat it on other occasions of our meeting:

Smoked any more maudies recently, Nigel? You need to put saltpetre on their tails ... Although its best with a gavelock when you see the earth coming up ...

Nay, you know Nigel's as wild as a hatter at throwing darts. As wild as a march hare. Imagine its a maudy you're after ...

Not leaving, Nigel? Where are you off? Going birding? "A bird in the hand is worth three in the bush", you know Nigel ...

Hello, Nigel. Been "wassacking"? Have you? Been wassacking lately [I look nonplussed as people laugh] Nay, Nigel's the rummest wassack ever seen in Wanet! Isn't he Stanley? [I explain I've been looking up some of the words he's been teaching me in my dictionary without success] Nay, I'm surprised all these dialect words aren't in the Collins dictionary, lad. "wassack"? "goosed"? "snape"? "jiggered"? ... I should dictate them all to you for you to write a book and become a university chancellor ... Thing is I'm not sure which are plain English and which aren't. Surely "jigger" is? ... .

THE HISTORICAL

The rustic, in short, Trevor employed to cock a snook at those outsiders who preyed on Wanet for its olde worlde charm and its "primitive" yokels. It also drew boundaries around those who immediately saw through it, and reminded them of the serious historical content that yet lay behind it. This latter historicity was also the more direct focus of other narrations:

No, *The Mitre's* a good pub, you know Nigel: always a good number in, always the best pub for locals. *The Eagle* has a different atmosphere altogether, though when I first drank there, it was different again. There was a whole room separated off, where the darts board is now, and it was possible just for locals to fill it; it could be full even if the rest of the bar was empty ... But I prefer *The Mitre*, always have done; *The Mitre's* always been my pub. There's an atmosphere here even with just twelve people on a weekday, when there isn't with twenty at *The Eagle* ... But I'm ashamed because I've only been to *The Eagle* once since Christmas. I must go. John and Wendy are always decent to me; you couldn't wish for a better couple there. It's just that I'd come to *The Mitre* whoever was the landlord ... I first came here when I was under age, and they served real ale, fetched from the cellar. Beer was 10d [ten old pence] in 1948. Better times, and better beer; from a cask, passed through a hatch there. Then, with Alfred as landlord, there was a small bar put in ... Alf's and my memories must go back 50 years, at least, here ... But all the pubs'll be choc-a-bloc on Saturday for Sports Day, you'll see. 'Cos it's the traditional time for those who used to live in Wanet to come back for a family get-together ... But what exactly is it that you're doing here, lad? [I explain my interest in local history and the changes that the dale has more recently undergone] Nay. Nowt changes here; that's why you fellows come to study us ... Nay, the history of the railway is the best time in the dale, lad. Find out about the railway archives from the old people, you should ... .

Indeed, Trevor was in the process of building up an historical archive of the dale and surroundings himself, as he liked to explain in detail on numerous occasions:

I've bought two new books. I found one in Leyton on the history of Wanet Grammar School. Cost a bit, you know! I've also got a handwritten letter to the Grammar School Governors, about 1830, in sort of Olde English (so I can't read all of it, maybe you could) going on telling the governors to pull their fingers out 'cos the school could be making a profit but instead it's losing money. And they did ruin it, you know, or it could still be going today; my grandma went to that school ... ["But there's still a 'School Committee', isn't there?"] Aye, the school still owns some land – a little farm up Riggdale and two or three pieces of land the other side of Wanet, and that brings in an income ... And I also bought a book about the life of a country solicitor. He lived at Kirkby Stephen, and he mentions the Thwaite family at Millwood and them issuing a notice and reward for the capture of a runaway slave – and he actually names the slave! That capped me 'cos I was sceptical till then about slaves here ... So maybe there were darkies in Wanet as well as in the cotton doings in Lancashire, it seems ... Phone Hilary if you're interested, Nigel – Charles'll let you use the pub phone – and ask her to bring the book in later when she comes. It's in the living room ... I bought that from the Kendal bookshop. On what we call New Road. ["Expensive?"] The only cheap books you'll find on the area are from far away. But I try to buy a book a month. There'll be a few new book sales round about soon, too; they're all advertised in the papers, registered, so there'll be some costly books: 50, 60, £75.

[Wow!"] You think £75 is expensive! I've got some right rare books, Nigel, and some of them are so valuable I have to lock them up. When I "go", I'll be worth thousands. And I'll donate it all to a Wanet museum! 'Cos I don't like private collections, where other people can't see them ... Did you see that book on the Postles that that bloke had in the other night? I photocopied a lot of it. It traced them back in the same house here as now to the 1680s! That must be a record! It was also possible to trace Hilary's lot through it 'cos her dad is Brian Postle Wether and his grandpa was a Postle. Hilary's great grandpa went to the USA, leaving his brother the farm. Then his wife died there and he returned to the old house in Wanet with his brother ... .

Lastly, it is in historical vein, also, that Trevor regards his part time work as undertaker:

I was called out at 1.30 last night! There was a phone call from the Leyton police to take a dead body to the mortuary. And I was downstairs and on the phone before Hilary stretched in bed to get it! Didn't get back to bed till 3 AM. ["Do you do that often?"] Well, no. There's not a big patch of funerals at the moment. I work on my undertaker's job about twice a week. ["Does it make you feel you've done your duty?"] Yes, I feel a sense of duty, and also respect if I knew the chap ... And you can spot them. Bob Hesketh, who was in tonight? He'll die within the year; he looked really bad. ["God!"] But I like to do the job well, Nigel. To know it's been done properly ... It doesn't pay; I'm only paid once a month.

THE LADDISH

The final theme I came to know well from Trevor's pub narrations was a laddish one. Often this expressed itself in off the cuff phrases as Trevor and I passed each other in the pub but were more involved with other people:

What's that book you've got, Nigel? A sex journal? ... A rum fellow is Nigel!

I misspent my youth, you know, Nigel, but there was nothing like this "Space Invaders" then ... But dominoes is an old man's game, Nigel: a sign of a misspent youth. This "Space Invaders" is also a sign of a misspent youth.

Look at all those moths flying out of Nigel's wallet! Getting as bad as Fred Harvey's! That's full of moths too ... Is Fred coming out, Nigel? No? He is one for changing his mind! Tell him I said he must be home counting his money. ["Shall I?"] I know him well and he'll not take offence. Tell him it's a joke ...

Look at the bad habits Nigel's picking up from Fred: keeping his darts in a 'baccy case! Nay: all these bad habits you've picked up here: darts and booze ...

Where were you gaffering today, Nigel? ["I was mixing cement for Sid Askrig"] Does the General keep you in order, then, Nigel? Is he above you in the hierarchy? I thought you were the gaffer .... .

The laddish theme spoke of a circle of intimates of Trevor's whom he made it seem very special to be part of; certainly I cherished it:

Come and drink in the back, Nigel: the pub is full of Herberts, and we're just organizing Sunday's fishing trip to the Irish Sea. ["Herberts?"] That's just what I've christened them. "Arabs" was last year's word and this year's is "Herberts". [I laugh. "Why?"] Just 'cos it sounds right ... Now, you must booze with me or you're not my friend. Shame you weren't at the '*Wain* the other night: I'd have given you a goosing ... Nay, but I wish you were on beer, Nigel, not gnat's pee. Lager is just gnat's pee. And it gives you a bad head. Bitter's the drink, or at least a bitter and mild mix if the bitter's off. No: you'd be a great mate of mine, Nigel, if only you were on beer. Look at the color of lager versus dark beer! ... Nigel needs a six pint initiation to bitter, doesn't he boys? [We join half a dozen of *The Mitre* regulars in the back of the pub] Now: everyone has to be in *The Mitre* tomorrow evening for eight pints so that we all start off on an equal footing on Sunday! ... And no puking on the boat, Nigel – or at least bring your own bag! [We laugh] Have you asked the General yet about the day off? He'll need a month's notice probably ... Have you got a rod? Then just cut a hazel bough outside, and Fred's got some ducks – there's y' feathers! .... .

THE IRONIC

Here, then, are some five themes, which I came routinely to recognize in Trevor's pub narrations, and which, for convenience, I have labelled: the fantastical, the dystopic, the rustic, the historic, and the laddish. Besides the humor contained in stories in particular voices, however (especially a fantastical, a rustic and a laddish voice), sometimes wry and sometimes more slapstick, there was the particular skill that Trevor had of humorously interweaving voices, so that one was never quite sure what was to be taken literally and what not; so that an irony imbued his pub persona as a whole. Before leaving the details of Trevor's utterances, therefore, let me return one final time with an instance of their ironic interweaving:

Not interested in the cricket results, then, Nigel? ["No. I can't stand cricket".] Typical Welshman! You dislike it 'cos you can't play it: there are no Welsh teams. ["What about Glamorgan?"] Oh yes, Glamorgan. But they're all Englishmen. Not like Yorkshire: all locals ... So how's your boss today, Nigel? ["Which one?"] You got two!? ["Yep. Fred and Sid!"] But only one paymaster! So what you been on with today? ["More digging, and then a trip to Gapton for the market and fish 'n' chips!"] Nay! Digging up fish 'n' chips at Gapton!? A rum fellow Nigel is. ["And I've just been at the Youth Club Committee"] ... Oh yes, you help with the Youth Club don't you. I couldn't be on the Youth Club Committee. The parents'd not allow it, soon stop it. ["Why?"] 'Cos of my reputation, or what I'd build up over the weeks. ["That's a rum do!"] What?! "Rum do", Nigel said! ... What a Sadducee and a Pharisee! ... So have you got a day off for the Royal Wedding? Negotiated with Fred? ["Not yet".] You should go and ask the real boss over there: General Askrig! You should go and give the General his marching orders! [We laugh] Where is Fred tonight? He's working all his youth away. Seated at home counting the loot, no doubt! ["He's tired".] Next, it'll be the National Park officer complaining about Fred's cowshit on the village cobbles. And "Mayor Milden" won't like it either; so you're going to stick a cork up the cows' arses in the street, Nigel, that's your next job ... Milden's been complaining 'cos he said he has an anarchist working for him on the building site: someone who's against the Crown and that. That was Bill Radford! ... Nay, I feel queasy and drunk. "A good puke is better than a poor breakfast", as they say. All darts players agree with that ... Will you phone the wife for me, and tell her you kept me? She doesn't like me staying out so late. [I grin] Do you want a fridge, Nigel? There's a real mess in our cellar. Hilary wants it cleared. Like a washing machine I bought from someone for less than £10. And antiques and fossils: a four poster bed marked 1674 that Hilary refuses to have in the bedroom (Hattie's interested in it though). And I've a good set of table and chairs to sell – just need reupholstering ... I saw Hattie's sister in Kendal market hall the other day, you know; I went to school with her: right vivacious girl! ... So what about that rag doll in the corner then for you, Nigel? ... How's about I come back to your place now, Nigel, for omelets. Got eggs? ["'Fraid not!"] Then we'll raid Fred Harvey's hen range: he'll supply the eggs! ...

TREVOR JEFFRIES' INDIVIDUALITY

In his combining of narrational themes, I would argue that Trevor Jeffries achieved that "general economy of the whole" which

Nietzsche pointed up as an exemplary individual trait. Here was an affirmation of all the world contained, a making sense of all that life had to offer, and a gaining of reflexive awareness of, and thus control over, all the diversities of his own character. Trevor Jeffries' individual life project, I suggest, took him to the ironic, nonconventional, fantastical edge of Wanet life so as to procure a perspective which made him a pivotal figure in local repartee.

As has been mentioned, in his mixing of the fantastical, the dystopic, the rustic, the historic and the laddish, Trevor fashioned a whimsical and also eccentric, often unnerving, pub persona. It was also challenging in its proffered transvaluation of local life: its disregard for conventional topics of conversation, politenesses, and the way conversation might be expected to flow. Sometimes under the guise of drunkenness (as if it was the expression of drunkenness) Trevor would construct a whole new utterance out of idiosyncratic parts and connexions:

> Where are you off? Going birding? "A bird in the hand is worth three in the bush", you know Nigel ...
>
> ... as well as moles there are hairy potarses. They're very rare, and you need a hazel stick to kill them.
>
> Have you got a [fishing] rod? Then just cut a hazel bough outside, and Fred's got some ducks – there's y' feathers!

Besides a creative bricolage, the construction also amounted to a topical and timely commentary. In its mixing and matching of themes, topics and phrases, it expressed the mixture of present day local life in Wanet: of oldtimers and newcomers, of continuity and change, of uncertainty and possibility:

> What's that book you've got, Nigel? A sex journal?
> Any hired assassins or IRA men among all these "Arabs" in tonight?
> Nowt changes here, so you fellows come to study us.
> Those "strepsils" Nigel has are probably full of dynamite.
> Look at the bad habits Nigel's picking up from Fred: keeping his darts in a 'baccy case!

Of course Trevor knew that my darts container, the 'baccy (tobacco) case, was the same old (empty) "strepsils" tin which he had before imagined contained dynamite filled throat lozenges. But he took great pleasure in his humorous elaborations of what went on around him and the new world in Wanet which they represented. While sometimes (unpleasurably) dystopic, his combination of a local life of past knowledge and present mysteries usually gave onto a pleasurably enjoyable conception of the potentiality, the crossroads of people, practices and relationships, which the future in Wanet would contain: "People come here to hide from the past, or the police, you know ... or to find a wife or girlfriend!" "You never know with mystery men!"

Trevor enjoyed weaving together attributes of local experience in Wanet into a whole new world.

And so did his audience; the pub persona which Trevor fashioned was a very popular one. He had a close circle of friends, almost a coterie, who would expect him to act as the wag and look to him to orchestrate their evening's pub activities and entertainment: drinking, playing darts, dancing and singing. When he was not present, tales would be recounted concerning his exploits and misadventures, in the pub and out, his proclivities and his aptitudes. When he meandered around *The Mitre*, pint pot in hand, chatting briefly to people at the bar or playing darts or dominoes, with local or outsider, then he might temporarily have left behind a group of close friends drinking at a table who would continue to follow his progress and laugh at his antics and exchanges. In other words, Trevor's audience might expect a humorous act from him wherever he and they were relative to each other in the pub. Indeed, there was a sense in which Trevor's utterances in the pub were always intended for a wider public consumption; he always spoke before an audience even when ostensibly he just spoke to you: "So what you been on with today? ... Nay! Digging up fish 'n' chips at Gapton!? A rum fellow Nigel is."

In short, the entire public space of *The Mitre* formed the stage for his potential clowning.

Other people enjoyed Trevor too: even if they weren't his close friends, and even if they became the butt of his jokes. For his clowning was not spiteful and his humor was good natured. The worst he became was a drunken nuisance – and a bit of an embarrassment for his usually patient wife. Somehow, the fact that Trevor did not take himself too seriously meant that his character and his antics could be enjoyed widely too. Trevor brought things together in *The Mitre* in such a way that nobody seemed to mind being a part of the show, whatever the role he afforded them.

Finally, this was very much Trevor's show; he was in control. It was Trevor's individuality that was on show and being appreciated;

it was consciously his act, his persona and his world that was being presented. The world in Wanet that he wove together in his narrations was a world in which he was the defining voice, and which he authored. He was very deliberate in his choice of word and theme, therefore, and taken aback when I chanced to mimic them: "What?! 'Rum do', Nigel said! ... What a Sadducee and a Pharisee!"

My mimicry calls forth a further novelty of expression, now bringing an old time Biblical reference into the pub context. Nor was Trevor afraid to lay claim to such novelties: "[Herberts is] just what I've christened them. 'Arabs' was last year's word ...".

When Trevor heard that I had a visitor to the dale, that my sister was coming to stay, he wondered whether I had "told her about him". Obviously he was a character in his own eyes as well as others'.

TREVOR JEFFRIES' CENTRICITY

In sum, Trevor Jeffries maintained and developed an individual vision of village life in Wanet – affirmative, whimsical – which others also found appealing and fed off. In this vision, he aligned Wanet past with Wanet present so as to portray a potential continuity into a Wanet future. He defined and christened the alien newcomers in the dale and their ways so that they were robbed of their powerful strangeness. And he gathered things around himself – books, news, claims, words, youth, quasi militaristic networks– so that the center of local life held together.

Inasmuch as he would "chat to anyone", Trevor fashioned a persona for himself in *The Mitre* pub which provided a center not just to his own life but to much of life in *The Mitre* as such. And this, it seemed to me, was what he set out to achieve. More than simply being a joiner in a country village, Trevor Jeffries' life project secured for himself and the audience of his performance an independent center of gravity. Transcending the narrowness of a peripheral milieu through ironic commentary and a narrative bricolage which linked local and global, past and future, tradition and change, he authored a Wanet identity which bespoke control over its fate. And inasmuch as others would keep chatting to him, acting as his talking partners, straight men, sidekicks and stooges, he assured for all that things would hold together; Wanet was a life apart, was life itself.

In my estimation Trevor Jeffries seemed to "love (his) fate", in Nietzsche's phrasing (1960:276); with good humor and a beguiling lack of seriousness he appeared to "redeem [his] life by transforming every 'It was thus' into 'Thus I wanted it'" (Nietzsche 1979:110). I certainly gained from the persona I found Trevor Jeffries presenting in *The Mitre*, and which I have sought to represent here. And when, after a year, I left Wanet, I was very pleased to have accompany me a spoof biography from him:

God Bless You, lad ... So, where to next? Had you been to Northern Ireland first before you came to join the Army here? ["No, not yet!"] Then where is Nigel to go next to spread the word? Bill Radford is already converted: he's beyond the pale ... So you're off now to be professor of philosophy, Nigel? [he grins].

REFERENCES

Burridge, K. (1979) *Someone, No One: An Essay on Individuality*. Princeton, NJ: Princeton University Press.

Nietzsche, F. (1960) *Joyful Wisdom*. New York: Ungar.

Nietzsche, F. (1979) *Ecce Homo*. Harmondsworth: Penguin.

Rapport, N. (1993) *Diverse World-views in an English Village*. Edinburgh: Edinburgh University Press.

Rapport, N. (1994) *The Prose and the Passion: Anthropology, Literature and the Writing of E.M. Forster*. Manchester/New York: Manchester University Press/St Martin's Press.

Rapport, N. (2003) *I Am Dynamite: An Alternative Anthropology of Power*. London/New York: Routledge.

Weber, M. (1946) *From Max Weber: Essays in Sociology*. London: Routledge and Kegan Paul.

9
Proclaiming Individual Piety: Pilgrims and Religious Renewal in Côte d'Ivoire

Marie Nathalie LeBlanc

INTRODUCTION

In this chapter, I examine the emergence of a group of young Muslim pilgrims in Côte d'Ivoire from the mid-1990s onwards. These young pilgrims construct renewed notions of the self, offering alternative sites of self-affirmation, or individualization. Notions of persons and selves have a long history in Africanist anthropology, a history tied to postcolonial processes of individual and collective positioning. Anthropological studies of selves, personhood, individualism and/or subjectivity can be roughly organized around two poles that correspond to different approaches to culture,[1] namely an experiential perspective that focuses on everyday life and practice (Jackson 1996) and a second position, inspired by the work of Marcel Mauss (1979), that describes personhood as a cognitive category that entertains close links to cultural complexes, rather than through subjective experience. This second perspective, developed to some extent by Dumont (1985), raises the issue of individuation, wherein societies range from being community based to individualistic. As such, the transition from community based to individualistic models of society has been tied to processes of modernization, framed in an evolutionary perspective.

This principle of individuation has had a significant impact on the anthropological understanding of African subjectivities, suggesting, on the one hand, that, historically, individual identities are embedded within collective structures, articulated around principles of genealogy and collective frames of reference. On the other hand, colonization and the emergence of independent nation states are considered to have destabilized this traditional order, bringing about a number of individualizing processes that express themselves through the creation of small enterprises, the individualization of family ties and residential choices or the diversification of social networks (Leimdorfer and Marie 1997, 2003). This perspective implies that African selves are primordially comprised of collective selves and not individual ones, contrary to Western atomistic notions of selves.

Here I want to return to an experiential notion of selves and to question the assumed community based dimension of African subjectivities as well as to examine the inferred ties between modernization and individuation. To do so, I will show that young pilgrims construct eschatological selves through an Arabized version of Islam that relies mainly on claims for individualized matrimonial practices and on a managerial style inspired by postcolonial models of modernity and bureaucracy.

The discussion is based on ethnographic field research conducted among young Muslim elites in Abidjan in 1998, 2000 and 2002. The analysis relies on interviews with pilgrims (a total of 40 interviews, 25 with men and 15 with women), participant observation within Islamic associations, interviews with association leaders and a material culture survey conducted in the households and workplaces of 25 pilgrims (selected out of the initial 40 interviewees). A local research assistant conducted the interviews, while I carried out the participant observation and the material culture survey (1998 and 2000). The survey engendered a detailed analysis of five pilgrimage photo albums, the significance of which is discussed below.

CHANGING ROLE OF THE *HAJJ*

Among West African Muslims, it is commonly anticipated that one's religious practice will change throughout one's life course. With age, one is expected to adhere more closely to the locally prescribed orthodoxy. Historically, some religious rituals have marked the transition towards a strict adherence to religious prescriptions. The *Hajj*[2] or yearly pilgrimage to *Makkah* is a significant marker in this passage. After performing the pilgrimage, Muslims are expected to follow religious prescriptions rigorously. Their religious experience is accompanied by the outward display of Islamic markers, such as special headdresses, that differentiate them from other Muslims (LeBlanc 2005a, 2005b).

Historically among the majority of West African Muslims, the *Hajj* has been regarded as an once in a lifetime event that was to be performed by elders, that is individuals typically aged 50 years old and older. While the performance of the *Hajj* is one of the pillars of

Islam, it is required only if one can afford to do so. Consequently, West African Muslims hope that with age they will accumulate the necessary financial means to perform the pilgrimage – the average cost in 2005 for a West African pilgrim was 2,500,000 CFA francs, or approximately 3,000 Canadian dollars. In a number of cases, older Muslims are sent on the *Hajj* by members of their families as a way to honor them or to thank them. During my research, for instance, I encountered cases where a more fortunate son elected to send his father to the *Hajj* rather than himself, or a grandson with a good income in Europe decided to send his grandmother to the pilgrimage to thank her for having brought him up while his mother was studying abroad.

From 1995 until 2002, the number of Ivorian pilgrims attending the *Hajj* increased, and during the mid-1990s the nature of those who undertook the pilgrimage changed (LeBlanc 2005a). It started to include a significant amount of young pilgrims, some performing numerous yearly trips to *Makkah*, up to three or four times between 1995 and 2002. The demographic changes affecting the selection of pilgrims can largely be explained by the increased participation of pilgrims aged between 30 and 45 years old. According to the Ministère de l'Intérieur and the Conseil National pour l'Organisation du Pélerinage à la Mecque (CNOPM), in 1995, 2,000 pilgrims left Côte d'Ivoire for Medina, whereas in 2000, 3,000 pilgrims did so. The quota for Côte d'Ivoire set by Saudi officials is close to 3,500 pilgrims; this quota varies according to past participation and to rates of international attendance. Moreover, according to the same sources, before 1998 Ivorian pilgrims were on average more than 45 years old and in 1998 the average age dropped to 30 years of age.

The number of pilgrims declined after 2002 due to the political and military situation in Côte d'Ivoire. In September 2002, military fighting broke out in Côte d'Ivoire that resulted in the scission of the country into two separate administrative entities: the North and the South. To some extent, this division marks a distinction between Ivorian Muslims and Ivorian Christians/animists. A large portion of Muslims is historically situated in the northern part of the country, except for the city of Abidjan (in the South). This scission discouraged participation in the *Hajj*, especially in 2003 and 2004. This was preceded by the violent prosecution of Muslims by a special death squad, the murder of prominent *imams* and the discovery of a mass grave in October 2000 in Yopougon, a neighborhood of Abidjan. Not surprisingly, Muslims became generally reserved about the public display of their Islamic identity. Moreover, since the trip to *Makkah* usually departed from Abidjan and the road between the South and the North regions was more or less closed between 2002 and 2004, Muslims living north of the city of Yamassoukro (where the French military has been stationed since 2002 to create a buffer zone between the North and the South) could not travel to Abidjan to take the plane. Some of them alternatively traveled to Bamako, Mali, instead.

Nevertheless, the cumulative demographic transformation of Ivorian pilgrims prior to these events was characterized in this way by one of the young male pilgrims interviewed:

> Before people thought that the *Hajj* was to be performed once during one's lifetime and people saved money and prepared for the *Hajj* all their life. You also need to know that once you have done the *Hajj*, your life is no longer what it was. You *have* (informant's emphasis) to become a good Muslim. You have to change your behavior, to change the way you dress, to do all the prayers, to respect the yearly holidays, etc. ... It is very hard to be a pilgrim. When you come back from *Makkah*, life has taken a new turn. Now, young people have become courageous. We recognize the importance of our religion and we can see that it is *the one* religion (informant's emphasis). We have learned; we read *al-Qur'ân* in Arabic; we study and we are ready to make this change earlier on in life. It takes courage to be a good Muslim, but it makes you closer to the real way of life. In fact, the *Hajj* that was a necessity for older people has become an obligation for younger people if they can afford it. (Abidjan, September 2002, translated from French by the author)

This statement shows how the *Hajj* has acquired a novel connotation among young Muslims. In contrast to their elders, for whom the *Hajj* is seen as a singular lifetime event, the pilgrimage is coming to be regarded as a trip that may be repeated on a regular basis, even annually in some cases, and a journey that may be performed earlier on during the life cycle.

The appearance of new pilgrims in the Ivorian religious landscape relates to the emergence, often spectacular, of youths in the public domain of most African societies during the 1990s (Cruise O'Brien 1996; Diouf 1996; Richards 1996; Abdullah et al. 1997; Meyer 1998; Maxwell 2001; Jua 2003). As Mamadou Diouf explains, the transformation of young African men and women as newly emerging social actors corresponds to innovative categories of self and identity:

> The new trajectory could be summed up as a radical transformation of the idea of citizenship, together with the conflation of the domestic and the public spheres, the production of new forms of identification which appeal to multiple resources, and a refashioning of the indices and signs of autochthony and membership, of inclusion and exclusion. All of these changes are associated with the reconfiguration of the national territory, domestic and sacred spaces, forms of organization, loyalties, and so on. In most cases, these developments, which are accompanied by the erosion of state and family obligations, suggest new avenues of political action and expression that may be violent or nonviolent, formal or informal. And they often are accompanied by new associative formulas, political commitments, and esthetic formulations on the margins of institutions and traditional codes of conduct. (2003:3)

The implosion of youths into the public sphere relates to their exclusion from centers of economic and political power, encouraging the creation of new forms of legitimacy and new spaces of self-expression. In their analysis of the social consequences of late capitalism, John and Jean Comaroff characterize these processes as follows:

> [I]n recent times, this segment of the population [youth] has gained unprecedented autonomy as a social category an *und für sich*, both in and for itself; this in spite, or maybe because, of its relative marginalization from the normative world of work and wage ... [A]long with other disenfranchised persons (notably the homeless and the unemployed), [they] constitute a kind of counter nation: a virtual citizenry with its own twilight economies, its own spaces of production and recreation, its own modalities of politics with which to address the economic and political conditions that determine its plight ... As a consequence, youth tend everywhere to occupy the innovative, uncharted borderlands along which the global meets the local. This is often made manifest in the elaboration of creolized argots of streetspeak and cybertalk that give voice to imaginative worlds very different from those of the parental generation. (Comaroff and Comaroff 2000:308)

Young Ivorian pilgrims, however, generally belong to the socioeconomic elite of their country. Then again, as in the case of other young African members of the middle class, from the 1980s onwards, they experienced a process of impoverishment. This adversity translated into ever increasing obstacles to penetrating the workplace of salaried employment and to attain an expected lifestyle, modeled on postcolonial ideals of modernization (LeBlanc 1998). It must be noted that due to the economic success of its plantation economy in the 1970s Côte d'Ivoire until recently held a specific economic status in the region. Accordingly, living conditions anticipated within the middle class were relatively high. Côte d'Ivoire remains one of the few countries in the region where youths can afford to visit *Makkah*.

THE NEW PILGRIMS

The new young pilgrims in question belong to two groups: the French speaking secularly educated elite of the country and a new set of Islamic clerics. In both cases, their level of schooling is quite high in comparison to the national average. Among the secularly educated elite, most have university degrees from Côte d'Ivoire or abroad, especially France, Morocco or the United States. As a result of their schooling, they have accumulated professional experience in both the public and private sectors. In popular parlance, these professionals are labeled "intellectuals" and are categorized as "civil servants",[3] even if they are not actually employed by the state. They endeavor to penetrate the centers of economic and political power in the country. However, since the early 1990s' debate on *ivoirité* and conflicts over national political control, attempts at socioeconomic advancement are limited on the basis of ethnic and religious affiliation. As Muslims, they find themselves increasingly at the margins of national instances of political decisionmaking.

This first group of secularly educated pilgrims includes both young men and young women, despite the fact that young women are less numerous. New pilgrims are usually between 25 and 40 years of age – an age cohort corresponding to the social category of youth (LeBlanc 1998, 2005b). In most cases, they are not yet married. In fact, most of the women who are part of this group are single professionals, a fact that is quite significant in the context of contemporary Ivorian society (LeBlanc 2005b). The presence of single professional women can be attributed to a process of gender democratization within the educational sector, which served to open the doors to education for many young women, and to a growing desire on the part of some young people to exercise control over their marital choices (LeBlanc 1998). The presence of a significant number of as yet unmarried men and women within this group of new pilgrims can also be explained by the diminishing access to marriage by young men due to harsher economic conditions since the 1980s in most West African countries.[4]

These young secularly educated pilgrims are heavily involved in Islamic associations and generally take literacy classes in the Arabic language. Their religious activism can be attributed to the fact that they were initially recruited into neighborhood Islamic associations through the Association des Elèves et des Etudiants de Côte d'Ivoire (AEEMCI), an association active in national, secular French-language schools (high schools and universities). The activism of secularly educated intellectuals has led to the creation or revival of several neighborhood Islamic associations linked to local mosques or to national organizations. In the early 1990s, most of these activities were centered in middle class and elite neighborhoods in Abidjan, such as Rivièra, Marcory and Cocody. Further, it must be noted that religious revivalism among the socioeconomic elite took place in the context of the reorganization of the Muslim community from the late 1980s onwards and of national conflicts regarding *ivoirité* and citizenship (I will discuss both elements in the following sections).

Activism in Islamic associations goes together with a shift in the religious performance of young Muslims. In effect, claims of piety by young pilgrims must be considered in light of the emergence of an Arabized version of Islam in Côte d'Ivoire in the 1990s.[5] The Arabized version of Islam draws from a notion of piety based on literacy in the Arabic language: on the strong criticism of Western modernity, which has been positioned since colonization as the main model for national development; and on the rejection of ancestral practices of Islam, accusing them of syncretism, namely of confusing religion and culture.[6] Among youth, claims of an Arabized Islam are directed against elders – as such the Arabized version of Islam acts as a space where youths can gain some form of social legitimacy in the face of surrounding gerontocratic relations of power, especially in terms of the capacity to gain control over one's standing as an adult, that is the passage from youth to adulthood (LeBlanc 2006). In numerous African societies, this takes place through the attainment of economic independence and/or marriage. Claiming an Arabized version of Islam allows one to assert control over one's choice of marital partner and timing of marriage by an appeal to the logic of the *ummah* (LeBlanc 2003).

The second segment of pilgrims is made up of an emerging group of Islamic clerics, locally acknowledged as *ulamah* (sing. *alim*, an Islamic religious scholar). They have been trained in *madâris* (plural of *madrasa*) in West Africa or abroad in Morocco, in Mauritius, in Saudi Arabia or in Egypt. *Madâris* are Islamic schools that expanded from the 1950s onwards and that adopted a curriculum based on literacy in the Arabic language and the teaching of subjects such as French, English, mathematics, geography, history and so forth (LeBlanc 1999). These *madâris* demarcate themselves from traditional mnemonic schools based on *morykalan* teaching, or the acquisition of the capacity to recite *al-Qur'ân* by heart under the supervision of *kalanmoro*, Mande clerics that acquired their scholarly status through hereditary descent. These *ulamah* are literate in the Arabic language, as well as in French in a number of cases. Some of them have lived abroad, for instance in France or in the United States. Some have also been employed as civil servants by the national bureaucracy in the 1980s. However, the majority of new religious scholars are financially independent from the state bureaucracy (Savadogo 2003, 2005). To a large extent, these clerics, or what Marie Miran has labeled the *"bourgeoisie de 'marabouts en cravate'"* (Miran 2006), partake in the post-colonial national modern economy. They transposed an acquired economic and managerial culture to their religious practice, bringing about the emergence of an Ivorian "modern Islam", distinct from ancestral forms of religious performance.

The public role of *ulamah* also signals a shift in style of religious authority, namely one in which the assertion of orthodoxy is based on claims of knowledge (in the Arabic language) rather than hereditary charisma (LeBlanc 1999). While clerics are not the most numerous amongst new pilgrims, they usually play central roles in newly created associative structures. They are *imam* or assistant *imam* in influential mosques; they hold executive positions in the numerous associations. The expansion of an Arabized version of Islam originated among them. In the majority of cases, clerics do not personally finance their participation in the *Hajj*. Their participation is usually paid for by the different religious structures. In effect, for many of the young pilgrims who organize religious activities and events, their active participation in Islamic associations is rewarded with financial support to make the journey to *Makkah*. They act as spiritual escorts for other pilgrims or undertake the logistical planning and realization of the *Hajj*.

Both groups of young pilgrims remind one of the secularly educated intellectual Muslims described by Hefner (1998). Elite groups such as these have emerged in numerous Muslim societies in the context of the "democratization of Islamic knowledge" (Eickelman and Piscatori 1996). Historically, Islamic knowledge was the prerogative of a restricted number of jurists, but in the contemporary context this is no longer the case. Several factors, such as the democratization of Islamic and secular schooling, the appearance of a large body of accessible Islamic literature and the creation of electronic Islamic media, account for this change. Accordingly, the present context has given rise to a mounting passion for religious knowledge among a growing population of Muslims.

RELIGIOUS REVIVALISM AND THE NEW STRUCTURE OF THE IVORIAN MUSLIM COMMUNITY

The early 1990s marked the profound transformation of the religious culture of the Ivorian Muslim community. It moved away from a parochial practice based on ethnocultural specificity towards a standardization of religious practice built upon literacy in the Arabic language and accessibility to religious texts. Besides the impact of global changes in the *ummah*[7] since the 1960s – including the international travel of students to Arab Islamic teaching institutions, the spread of Islamic media and the financial involvement of Arab Muslims in Sub-Saharan Africa – Ivorian Islamic revivalism took place in a specific political and economic context. Notably the 1980s and 1990s were decades marked by a significant economic decline of the Ivorian economy (starting with the crisis of the price of coffee and cacao in the mid-1980s), drastic measures of structural adjustment imposed by Mitterrand's French government and the World Bank, a process of democratization with the first multiparty election held in 1990, and a national debate regarding national identity, leading to civil and military unrest beginning in 1999. These dynamics led to the multiplication and diversification of Islamic associations, the strengthening of Islamic identities, as well as the frailty of the middle class.

The reconfiguration of the Muslim community in the 1990s marks a significant mutation in the national and international role of Ivorian Islam. As I have argued elsewhere (LeBlanc 2005a), it switched from a local religious culture to a transnational practice based primarily on material and spiritual links with *Makkah* as well as other centers of Islamic culture. As of the 1990s, Ivorian Muslims also became increasingly involved in transnational networks of migration and exchange of information. In addition, the internationalization of Ivorian Islam took place in the context of a specifically Ivorian bureaucratized managerial style. Three associations played a significant role in the religious revivalism movement of the 1990s, namely the Association des Elèves et Etudiants Musulmans de Côte d'Ivoire (AEEMCI), the Communauté Musulmane de la Rivièra (CMR), and the Conseil National Islamique (CNI).[8]

The AEEMCI dates from 1975. Its initial mission was to bring together all Muslim students in the country and to supervise their religious practice. As previously mentioned, it is mostly active in French speaking, secular schools. It organizes teaching seminars, weekly Friday prayers and special events for calendar holidays (such as *Eid Al-Fitr,*[9] *Ramadan,*[10] *Lailatul-Qadr*[11] or *Laylat Al-Baraa*[12]). Furthermore, its local members encourage the respect of religious prescriptions by students of Muslim origin by offering advice on dress codes for women, for instance, or on marriage rules.

The CMR was created in 1982 as a neighborhood association, based in one of the most affluent areas of the capital, Rivièra. It brought together Muslim intellectuals and high ranking civil servants claiming an Arabized version of Islam. During the 1980s and 1990s a Muslim middle class and upper class emerged on the national sociopolitical landscape. The CMR played a central role in the reconfiguration of the Muslim community. Keeping in mind the socioeconomic background of its membership, it is in the CMR that managerial styles were initially experimented with – through the creation, for instance, of administrative boards and bank accounts for mosques, *imam* with fixed salaries (as in the case of government employees) – and that discourses on Islamic social actions, charitable trusts and work efficiency emerged (see Miran 2006 for a similar description). Other Islamic associations quickly borrowed the managerial style developed by the CMR. By the mid-1990s, this managerial culture reproduced itself in the organizational structure of the *Hajj* with the creation of an investment fund (Plan d'Epargne Pélerinage or PEP), and travel and pilgrimage committees (Comité National d'Organisation du Pélerinage à la *Makkah* or CNOPM). The PEP, established in 1997, allows salaried Muslims to invest a portion of their monthly income into a fund that is put into the PEP bank account (SIB, CITIBANK ou ECOBANK, see www.cni-cosim.ci for a description of the PEP) allowing Muslims to accumulate the cost of the *Hajj* or the *umrah*[13] in a few years. It must be noted that only salaried civil servants or other professionals can afford to participate in the PEP investment plan – the minimum monthly investment is 25,000 francs CFA (see ibid.).

Lastly, the CNI, created in 1993 by members of the Arabizing elite, is a national Islamic association supported by the large majority of Ivorian Muslims. Following the first multiparty election in 1990 and the ensuing liberalization of the right to associate, it was created out of dissatisfaction with the longstanding Conseil Supérieur Islamique, the only Islamic association recognized by the ruling Parti Démocratique de la Côte d'Ivoire or PDCI (1960 to 1999) at that time. While in 1992, the PDCI had to recognize the right of other Islamic associations to exist outside of the organizational structures of the PDCI, it still supported the CSI into the late 1990s. Nonetheless, since 1993, the CNI has increasingly played a leadership role in the Muslim community by centralizing instances of Islamic power and assuming a role of political representative in the context of national ethnoreligious conflicts. The CNI is organized in a pyramidal structure. It has a national bureau in Abidjan and it has local branches in other cities and regions of the country. Its organizational purpose has been to unify Muslim associations under its directorate. Since its creation, the CNI has focused on activities aimed at promoting and strengthening the Muslim community in Côte d'Ivoire. On the CNI website, its goals and activities are described as such:

> Le CNI, Association Fédérative, regroupe plusieurs associations et communautés musulmanes oeuvrant dans des domaines aussi divers que variés. Sa vocation première est d'apporter à la communauté musulmane l'expertise nécessaire pour:
>
> - La formation spirituelle et intellectuelle des musulmans
> - L'encadrement de la jeunesse scolaire et universitaire
> - L'information la plus large possible des musulmans et des musulmanes sur les préoccupations de la Oumma et de l'environnement dans lequel ils vivent.
>
> Pour l'accomplissement de cette entreprise, le CNI s'est doté de plusieurs organes qui travaillent en étroite collaboration avec ses structures de base dans tous les domaines. Afin de mener ces nobles objectifs, le CNI maintient des relations cordiales, aussi bien avec les pouvoirs publics qu'avec les autres confessions. Il contribue ainsi au maintien d'un climat de paix et de convivialité entre toutes les composantes de la société ivoirienne.

Les réalisations du CNI

- L'officialisation des fêtes religieuses islamiques
- La mise en place du Comité National d'Organisation du Pèlerinage à la Mecque, qui encadre plus de mille cinq cents pèlerins chaque année
- La construction et l'équipement de la première radio musulmane de Côte d'Ivoire, AL BAYANE (2001)
- Acquisition d'un domaine foncier de plus de cinquante hectares avec un lac de quatre hectares (www.cni-cosim.ci).

The CNI also took over the management of the Islamic televised talk show *Allahou Akbar* in the early 1990s. Up until 1999, when the first coup d'état, headed by General Robert Gueï, occurred, the CNI was involved in promoting the integration of the Muslim community into the different national structures. For instance, under the rule of the PDCI, there was an attempted negotiation for the inclusion of Islamic schools within the national curriculum, as had been the case in Mali in the 1980s (Brenner 1991). Since the coup d'état in 1999, the CNI also became involved in defending the political rights of Muslims in Côte d'Ivoire by denouncing, in coalition with le Conseil Supérieur des Imans (COSIM), the exclusionary and oppressive practices exercised against Muslims as well as the imminent threat of ethnoreligious conflict.[14]

A number of regional associations subsequently established non-governmental organizations (NGOs) in the 1990s that play a part in the creation of Islamic schools and are active in the health sector. Some of these NGOs, such as ID-Pan (Intelligentsia de la Diaspora Panafricaine) took part in the peace process that was established after the 2002 crisis.[15] Other NGOs are linked to international Islamic organizations, notably the Fondation Djigui, an Ivorian Islamic association based in Abidjan that is involved in the promotion of women's and children's rights and welfare. Some young pilgrims travel to the United States to attend seminars and other religious training activities in the context of these international NGOs. For instance, members of Djigui's bureau traveled to Washington and Chicago in 2005 – they were invited by the American Cultural Service and the Islamic University in Chicago.[16]

It must be noted that, while the transnational ties of Islamic associations in Côte d'Ivoire are not a new phenomenon – some international Islamic associations in West Africa date from the 1930s (see for instance Gomez-Perez 1998; Soares 2004) – the organizational culture of these associations is relatively new. Interestingly, in addition to ties with Arab countries, due to *Hajj* and to the travel of Ivorian students to Islamic teaching institutions in the Arab world, new transnational ties between Islamic organizations are now oriented towards the United States rather than Europe. To some extent, the move away from European influence reflects both the growth of Ivorian migration towards North America and the presence of Ivorian intellectuals trained in the United States rather than in France. In effect, the recent internationalization of Ivorian Islam comes, on the one hand, from the travel of religious leaders to visit expatriate communities in Europe and the United States for fund raising events or for religious assistance. For example, in 2001, Koudouss Idriss Koné, Aboubacar Fofana and Djiguiba Cissé, leaders of the CNI and the COSIM, spent a month traveling between New York, Philadelphia and Atlanta to help Ivorian Muslims create a North American CNI.[17] On the other hand, as a result of the national crisis, a number of Islamic leaders and Muslim intellectuals migrated outside of Côte d'Ivoire, some of them to the United States. It must be noted that in the postcolonial context West African migrants to North America have generally been intellectuals, pursuing their studies in American universities or seeking employment in North American industries, businesses and government agencies.

"BEING AN IVORIAN MUSLIM" IN THE 1990s

Besides the reorganization of the associative structure of the Muslim community, the national political context in the 1990s significantly contributed to identity shifts in the Muslim community (LeBlanc 1999, 2006). "Being an Ivorian Muslim" took on a new political meaning in the Ivorian political landscape. In the context of debates regarding citizenship in Côte d'Ivoire, which started with the first multiparty election in 1990, Muslims felt increasingly excluded from the centers of state power. Muslims have redefined the boundaries of their identity to the extent that, for Muslims, their religious identity became central to their public roles (LeBlanc 2000b).

The relatively recent participation of young pilgrims takes place in the context of significant political changes in Côte d'Ivoire, notably the death of Félix Houphouët-Boigny in 1993 (who had served continuously as president since independence in 1960); the conflict over his succession between Henri Konan Bédié and Alassane Dramane Ouattara, resulting in the creation of a new electoral code in 1994; subsequent debates regarding *ivoirité*, and finally a series of coups d'état from 1999 that culminated in the effective scission of the country between the North and the South regions in 2002.

In this context of civil and military unrest, although Muslim leaders (especially members of the CNI and COSIM) maintained links with the ruling political parties (PDCI under Henri Konan Bédié, 1993 to 1999; Union pour la Démocratie et le Progrès en Côte d'Ivoire under General Gueï, 1999 to 2000; and Front Populaire Ivoirien under Laurent Gagbo, 2000 to the present), other Muslims turned towards new political structures, including Alassane Dramane Ouattara's Rassemblement Démocratique des Républicains, or more recently, Guillaume Soro's Forces Nouvelles. These two new political entities remained at the margins of political legitimacy as a result of debates regarding national identity. One could argue that, to some extent, political exclusion led to the public display of Islamic identities. In a context of more or less effective political exclusion, religious identity became a site where young Muslims could claim a social role in the Ivorian sociopolitical landscape. For a number of the youth, at the grassroots level, involvement with the youth branch of political parties was replaced by a commitment to newly created Islamic associations.[18]

HAJJ AND IDENTITY

Young pilgrims' enthusiasm for the *Hajj* is revealed not only at the level of its performance proper but is also expressed through its contingent impacts upon the daily lives of pilgrims. As I have already pointed out, the *Hajj* automatically entails the transformation of an individual's identity in that he or she must effect a change of lifestyle in order to conform more diligently to religious prescriptions. Pilgrims must modify their daily routines as well as their physical appearance in order to convey the strength of their faith. Thus, while this adjustment consists of elements related to religious practice such as strict adherence to prayer times, it also encompasses changes at the level of one's social behavior and of one's consumption of material culture. Behaviorally, young pilgrims are expected to stop frequenting youth spaces such as bars and discotheques and to focus on religious and family matters rather than socializing with their peers, and to respect basic rules of *purdah*[19] for women.

Materially, the dress style of an individual, irrespective of his or her age, is modified upon return from the *Hajj*. Certain elements of material culture traditionally mark one's status; for instance, wearing a white scarf, fastened with a black and gold cord, tied around the head, serves as a sign indicating the pilgrim's status. For women, irrespective of their age, the change in dress code requires that they wear a veil at all times. While for older women, it was a question of always wearing a prayer shawl (*langara*), for young female pilgrims, they tend to adopt Arab forms of headcovering, such as a *hijab*[20] or a knitted cap imported from Saudi Arabia and used to conceal the hair. It is because of these requisite changes that, in the past, young Muslims argued that they should wait until they have reached the necessary level of maturity, religious and social, before performing the *Hajj*; otherwise, they might not be prepared to assume the necessary changes in lifestyle.

While material, behavioral and spiritual changes are traditionally expected in the context of the *Hajj*, the appearance of new young pilgrims introduced a set of new social markers signifying one's status as a pilgrim. There are two central markers for young pilgrims, namely literacy in Arabic and the display of a newly defined Islamic material culture. Literacy in the Arabic language implies that new pilgrims, as well as other Arabizing Muslims that cannot afford the *Hajj*, increasingly attend literacy classes and wish to speak and read the Arabic language. In effect, the use of Arabic salutations, namely "*Assalamu alaikum*" ("Peace be on you") or "*Wa Alaikum Assalam*" ("And on you be peace") are very popular among young pilgrims to the exclusion of usual Dioula or Banmanan salutations. The same goes for Western inspired handshakes: young pilgrims touch their forehead rather than shaking hands when they greet one another. The privileged role of literacy in the Arab language as a marker of religiosity makes sense both in terms of the general context of Arabization in Côte d'Ivoire and in terms of the socioeconomic class of the majority of new young pilgrims – they are already literate in the French language and, thereby, locally categorized as intellectuals.

The display of a newly defined Islamic material culture brings about a shift in the traditional categorization of material objects between sacroreligious objects and secular objects. Historically, the *Hajj* has been connected with the consumption of both types of objects. The link between pilgrimage and trade is not a new phenomenon (Werbner and Basu 1998). Historically, in Islamic as well as in Christian and Hindu traditions, pilgrimages have always presented opportunities for economic and commercial exchange. Furthermore, in the West African context the entanglement of Islam and trading practices has a long history. From its inception, the trans-Sahelian trade engendered a process of Islamization of Sub-Saharan communities. These historical continuities suggest that the circulation of objects in the context of the *Hajj* is not a phenomenon initiated by the increase in the number of pilgrims attending the *Hajj* and the younger age of its participants. Nevertheless, significant changes did occur throughout the 1990s in terms of the type of objects exchanged between Côte d'Ivoire and Saudi Arabia, their categorization and the context of their consumption.

Sacroreligious objects purchased at *Makkah* and exchanged upon one's return include objects of ritual significance considered to embody spiritual powers, such as water sourced from *Makkah*, prayer mats, incense, rosaries and prayer/religious books. Secular objects bought for personal consumption or for the purpose of being resold include paintings/pictures/photographs/posters, clothes, perfumes, makeup, furniture and electronic goods. With the growing participation of middle class youth, secular objects intended for personal consumption or for resale purposes have come to be exchanged in growing numbers.

The cause of this growth in the consumption of goods from Saudi Arabia can be located in the fact that many of these young pilgrims have higher purchasing power on account of their status as salaried professionals. More significantly, with the appearance of young middle class pilgrims, the historical distinction between both categories of objects became blurred. Some secular objects acquired a sacroreligious status. Objects bought for personal consumption, or for the purpose of being resold, acquire a sacred character by symbolizing the transformation in a pilgrim's religious identity. These objects, put on display in people's homes and in their places of work, became public symbols of their faith. For instance, some pilgrims adorn the walls of their house with pictures of *Makkah* or posters with Arabic writing; others put wall units in their living room with a television set, a VCR, books in the Arabic language and knick-knacks, all bought in Saudi Arabia; still others decorate the walls of their homes and places of work with pictures of themselves during or right after their trip to Saudi Arabia.

The new sacroreligious meaning attached to these secular objects is derived from the fact that they come from *Makkah* and that they provide a symbolic testament of an individual's participation in the *Hajj*. At first glance, it may seem that these consumption practices serve simply to affirm the economic status of young pilgrims as members of the local middle class who are endowed with significant purchasing power.[21] However, in light of political and religious dynamics in Côte d'Ivoire, it is clear that this form of sacroreligious consumption reflects both a claim for an Arabized Islam and a revived religiosity among French speaking secularly educated middle class youth. Contrary to *ulamah* schooled in Islamic settings, for young French speaking secularly educated pilgrims religious knowledge cannot constitute the basis of their Islamic identity, especially the capacity to appeal to religious texts in the Arabic language. Rather, external signs such as dress code, household decoration, and activism in Islamic associations serve to publicly affirm their Muslim identity and the intensity of their faith, at least until their participation in Islamic associations and in literacy classes in the Arabic language will allow them to make founded knowledge claims.

CLOTHING AND SELF[22]

Fashion choices among women are telling examples of religious transformations.[23] Since the early 1990s, I have witnessed changes in Ivorian Muslim women's dress styles that are closely linked with the economic exchanges facilitated by the pilgrimage. It is possible to observe, first, the relinquishment of the African *bubu*,[24] characteristically associated with Islamic populations in West Africa, in favour of the adoption of Arab-style clothing, notably the *jalabiya* or *abaya* or *jilbad*, commonly referred to as "Moroccan dress" by Ivorians. Instead of wearing locally made *bubu*, many young women prefer wearing long gowns imported from Saudi Arabia by pilgrims – it must be noted that young Arabizing men also elect to wear *jalabiya* – style gowns with a small head cap (or *kufi*). Female pilgrims buy their own, give them to their mothers, sisters, female in-laws and friends as gifts, or sell them to their co-workers. Interestingly, Arab inspired fashion is also adopted by older women who, on the one hand, aspire to the level of religiosity seemingly attained by their daughters and granddaughters. On the other hand, older women are strongly encouraged by their daughters and granddaughters to imitate their dress code.

Another significant modification lies in the wearing of the Muslim veil – the equivalent of the veil for young Arabizing men would be the beard. Female office workers started wearing veils at their workplace at the end of the 1990s. Arabized youths, however, have taken after the styles of North Africa and the Middle East by covering their head with a scarf resembling the *hijab*. There are a number of ways to wear the *hijab*, and Ivorian Muslim women have also experimented with the style of doing so. Moreover, female office workers often wore a *hijab*-like veil with simple Western inspired attire, such as long skirts with long sleeved blouses or alternatively with loose fitting trousers complemented by long sleeved tunics.[25] From the 1940s, Muslim women working in offices began to cover their heads; however they generally wore a scarf or turban that covered their hair and local clothing such as a *bubu* or the *complet trois pagne* (three piece suit made out of local cloth: a wrap or skirt, a shirt and a scarf worn around the hips or on the head), rather than Arab inspired clothing.

Following the logic of the articulation between aging and religiosity, young, unmarried women do not automatically cover their head; they wear scarves or turbans covering their hair and they may wear a prayer shawl (locally known as *langara*) when they go out of their compound. Older women always wear a scarf or turban covering their hair and a *langara*, whether at home or outside of their compound. While wearing the veil at a young age,[26] Arabizing women have largely abandoned the *langara* for knitted caps or *hijab*-like scarves. Aside from wearing a veil in public and the choice of an Arab inspired veil by opposition to the West African scarf/turban and *langara*, young female pilgrims are also altering the local articulation between aging and religiosity. They exhibit external signs of religiosity earlier on in life, even before marriage in some cases.

HAJJ PHOTO ALBUMS: REPRESENTATIONS OF FAITH

In certain cases, young middle class pilgrims assemble photo albums chronicling their pilgrimage, which they then show to their family and friends. Some young Arabizing women, who have sent their parents to the *Hajj* rather than themselves, also create *Hajj* albums for their parents, mainly their mothers. Women are fond of such photo albums and spend a good deal of time looking over their *Hajj* albums.[27] In Côte d'Ivoire, *Hajj* photo albums started to become popular in the mid-1990s. They are a distinctly middle class, urban, Ivorian phenomenon that can be closely linked with the 1990s religious revivalism.[28] These albums mainly contain pictures of pilgrims, that is, of the owner of the album as well as other pilgrims who traveled together. In some cases, they also include postcards with religious writings in Arabic. It is worth noting that *Hajj* photo albums resemble personal albums put together by young West Africans, especially from the middle class. Personal photo albums are composed of portraits, with a distinct focus on the owner, his or her family, his or her friends, as well as some postcards of local or international stars from sport, cinema or music (LeBlanc 2004a, 2004b).

The presentation of self captured in these albums focuses on the piety of pilgrims. Their devoutness is exhibited by sporting Arab-style garbs and by displaying a body language that enhances religious modesty, including posed expressions of contemplation with eyes looking down, sitting on one's heels with hands on one's legs in a praying position or holding a prayer rosary. The inclusion of postcards with Islamic writings in Arabic in the albums reinforces these elements.

Most of the pictures included in the *Hajj* albums are taken in Côte d'Ivoire before the departure or upon the return of pilgrims. Some albums include pictures taken in Saudi Arabia in the context of tourist visits but not in the context of religious rituals. When possible, members of pilgrims' families, friends or colleagues accompany them to the airport in Abidjan for their departure to *Makkah*. When pilgrims come back from the *Hajj*, again members of their family, colleagues or friends welcome them. In some cases, local Islamic associations organize welcoming parties. Traditionally, it is expected that individuals who know recently returned pilgrims will pay them a visit. Especially in the context of *Du'a*, that is, when individuals perform the *Hajj*, they promise to carry out supplications invoking Allah for whatever they desire on behalf of a number of people in their family or immediate social environment.

When pilgrims return, people call on them and visit in order to receive a benediction. Such beliefs have been generalized into the standardized greeting of pilgrims at the airport, when possible. Returning pilgrims are popular social characters, and the Islamic televised talk show *Allahou Akbar* often features returning pilgrims who describe and discuss their experience.

Among middle class recent pilgrims in Abidjan, social visits and greetings have been transformed into large scale public celebrations, where hosting pilgrims frequently sacrifice a goat, a sheep or even a cow. A number of photographs may be taken in the context of these celebrations. Local religious leaders (*imam*, association leaders) are often invited to these celebrations. In some cases, they will take advantage of the occasion to pronounce a religious sermon.

CONCLUSION – INDIVIDUALIZED PIETY AND SOCIAL CHANGE

Among young middle class pilgrims, the frequency of the *Hajj* has become a condition for the expression of an Arabized Islamic identity. Participation in the yearly pilgrimage captures claims of a new Arabized orthodoxy centered on the use of the Arabic language in everyday life as a marker of modern Islamized selves. As such, Arabized modern selves are articulated in opposition to Western-style modernity, regarded as a bankrupt project embodied in the declining role of the postcolonial state as the main employer. Individualized piety is expressed in a renewed iconography, articulated through personal photography, fashion and gesture in everyday life. Participation in the *Hajj* relies on individualized choices made with the view of realizing the Islamic community, the *ummah*. For this reason, I refer to such practices of identification as the forging of eschatological selves, that is, the negotiation of moral selves in the face of the tension between community and individual choices. While religious transformations are expressed in terms of individual changes – individual experiences of faith – they are addressed to the community at large, including potential converts. The religious quest attained by the *Hajj* is seen as a progressive step within the global transformation of contemporary Ivorian society.

Following the logic of Arabization, in addition to religious conversion and *Da'wah*,[29] the transformation of Ivorian society requires, first, the establishment of a distance away from ethnic specificity for the profit of the *ummah*. This transition necessitates a move away from the ethnocultural practice of elders. For young Muslims, this distance is achieved through control over marital choices, that is individualized choices based on a disembodied global community, the *ummah*, contrary to practices of family imposed marriages (*balmafuru*) privileged by elders.[30] Arabizing youth rejects the social rules and obligations perpetuated by elders, actualized through family based marriage rules, on the grounds that in Islam one is required only to marry a Muslim, even a converted one. While claims for an Arabized Islam may not result in absolute individualized freedom, it certainly challenges notions of authority based on kinship and age by creating new sites of authority through religious knowledge and literacy in Arabic.

The discordant relationship youths develop in relation to the power of their elders that is expressed time and time again through a rejection of tradition, fetishism or syncretism, also involves a reconfiguration of the past or what certain authors have called nostalgia for the past or for memory (Meyer 1998; van Dijk 1998). The past, from which the Arabized version of Islam seeks to distance itself, is simultaneously what binds pilgrims to their elders and to daily practices seemingly lacking in religious orthodoxy. This version of the past calls into question the regeneration of morality, which is currently taking place in the elaboration of new forms of subjectivity based on the communitarian ideology of the *ummah*.

The linkage of religious devotion and intergenerational conflict is a recurrent phenomenon in African societies. Historically, religion acted as the social terrain where demands for change were made by youths towards their elders. Furthermore, it was often in the context of these demands that new religious movements took shape.[31] Despite the cyclical character of these conflicts, the experience of pilgrims discussed here suggests that the redefinition of religious subjectivity unfolds in a new sociopolitical space, permitting the assertion of alternative selves through the *ummah*. This collective identity relies on the movement of individuals across social and geographic borders with the aim of enhancing their purity and their religious status, allowing pilgrims to imagine the reorganization of society.

I conclude by suggesting that Ivorian Arabized selves force us to revisit notions of personhood that emerged in the study of African societies and to some extent in other locations. As noted in my introduction, we must revisit the idea that African selves are necessarily the antithesis of Western atomistic selves. In fact, Arabized selves question the classical Weberian thesis defended in *The Protestant Ethic and the Spirit of Capitalism* (1958) according to which Protestantism entertains a privileged relationship to modernity and the emergence of the modern self, a thesis already suggested in the case of Nigeria by Hackett (1995) and in the case of Congo-Brazzaville by Dorier-Apprill (1998). Young pilgrims claim a form of individuality, suggesting a modern self that lies between atomistic decisionmaking and community obligations based on the universal notion of the *ummah*. Arabized selves correspond to claims for autonomous, emancipated subjects who seek to rework their belonging to alternative social worlds. The issue is to find new inscriptions within the collective order that blend individual and collective allegiances. The emergence of young pilgrims alternatively raises the possibility that modern, individualized selves may not necessarily be fashioned according to Western atomistic principles, going back to the notion of multiple modernities proposed by John and Jean Comaroff (1990). Indeed, one of the central problems of modernity in African societies has been to grasp localized dynamics of the creation of individualized spaces of identification (Rowlands 1996; Leimdorfer and Marie 1997, 2003). Clearly, in the case described in this chapter, the reproduction of postcolonial social class and its managerial logic are central clues. New pilgrims fashion their religious performance on Ivorian bureaucratic logic, with highly structured hierarchical associative organizations, bank accounts, and paid *imams*, while shifting their collective references to a globalized space with symbolic references to the Arab world and material links with *Makkah*.

NOTES

1 See Corin (1998) for a detailed description of anthropological perspectives on the notion of self.

2 *Hajj* is an Arabic word which means the performance of pilgrimage to *Makkah* in Saudi Arabia. It is one of the five pillars of Islam. A Muslim is to perform *Hajj* at least once in his/her life, if means and health allow. There are rules and regulations and specific dress codes to be observed. It must be performed during certain specified dates of *Dhu al-Hijjah*. In addition to *tawaf* and *sa'y*, there are a few other requirements but especially one's standing (i.e., stay) in 'Arafat during the daytime on the 9th of *Dhu al-Hijjah*. It is to take place during the last month of the lunar calendar called the month of *Dhu'l-Hijjah*. *Dhu'l-Hijjah* is the 12th month of the Islamic calendar, during which the great pilgrimage to *Makkah* takes place.

3 *Fonctionnaires* in the French language.

4 See Dimé and Calvès (2006) for a similar argument regarding young middle class men, marriage and limited economic resources in Dakar, Senegal.

5 Other authors have referred to similar claims of piety in West Africa as reformists or Islamists (see Evers Rosander and Westerlund 1997; Miran 2006). I have chosen the term "Arabized" in order to signify the specificity of the Ivorian experience in the 1990s, which primarily ties orthodoxy with literacy in the Arabic language (LeBlanc 1999). I am using Louis Brenner's definition of Arabization, which encompasses the central role of the Arabic language, the appeal to reformed models of *Qur'ânic* teaching, and the adoption of pro-Islamic position in opposition to the Western world (Brenner 1993).

6 See LeBlanc (1998, 2000a, 2000b) for a detailed description of the Ivorian version of an Arabized Islam.

7 An *ummah* is a community or a people or a nation. It is used in reference to the community of Muslim Believers. *Ummah* is a special name given to Muslim brotherhood and unity. The *Qur'ân* refers to Muslims as the best *ummah* raised for the benefit of all mankind (3:110). At another place, (2:143), it calls them "the middle nation" (*Umma Wasat*), a unique

characteristic of the Islamic community which has been asked to maintain equitable balance between extremes, pursue the path of moderation and establish the middle way. Such a community of Muslims will be a model for the whole world to emulate.

8 To a lesser extent, other associations also played a significant role in the revitalization movement of the 1990s. Three national associations were unofficially created in 1988: the Conseil Supérieur des Imams (COSIM), bringing together religious leaders from all branches of Islam represented in Côte d'Ivoire (Tidjani-e, Sunni, Shi'ite, and so forth), the Ligue Islamique des Prédicateurs de Côte d'Ivoire (LIPCI), bringing together preachers, and the Association des Jeunes Musulmans de Côte d'Ivoire (AJMCI), bringing together young men and young women who were not in school. After 1990, these associations became official. After 1990, a number of other associations were also created, such as the Cercle d'Etudes et de Recherches Islamiques en Côte d'Ivoire (CERICI), similar to the CMR, but at the national level, the Secours Médical Islamique (SEMI), bringing together Muslim health workers, and the Association des Femmes Musulmanes de Côte d'Ivoire (AFMCI), though their actions remained limited (see Miran 2006 for a detailed description of the creation of these national associations).

9 *Eid Al-Fitr*: festival marking the end of *Ramadan*. It takes place on the first of *Shawal*, the tenth month of the Islamic calendar. In Côte d'Ivoire, it is referred to as *Tabaski*.

10 The ninth month of the Islamic calendar. Fasting is obligatory during this month for all Muslims.

11 *Lailatul-Qadr*: the Night of Power, concealed in one of the odd nights in the last ten days of *Ramadan*; the night on which the *Qur'ân* was first revealed by Jibraeel to the Prophet Muhammad (S.A.W.), and which the *Qur'ân* itself describes as "better than a thousand months" (97:3).

12 The term *Laylat Al-Baraa* means "night of repentance" and it commemorates the night when all who repent are granted forgiveness. Muslims believe that it is on this night that God sets each person's path for the coming year. Thus, Muslims ask God for forgiveness for past sins and for blessings in the coming year on *Laylat Al-Baraa*.

13 *Umrah* (Minor Pilgrimage) is an Islamic rite and consists of the pilgrimage to the *Ka'bah*. It consists essentially of *ihram*, *tawaf* (i.e., circumambulation) around the *Ka'bah* (seven times), and *say* (i.e., running) between Safa and Marwah (seven times). It is called minor since it need not be performed at a particular time of the year and its performance requires fewer ceremonies than the *Hajj* proper. West African pilgrims often combine it with the *Hajj*.

14 In 2000, along with the Conseil Supérieur des Imams, the Front de la Outma Islamique, the Confédération Islamique de Développement de Côte d'Ivoire, the Al-Coran, the Association Islamique pour l'Appel en Islam de Côte d'Ivoire and the Union Nationale d'Aide aux Convertis de l'Islam, it participated in the National Reconciliation Forum that aimed at reuniting the Ivorian population.

15 Personal discussion with Fatoumata Traoré, founding member and president of ID-Pan.

16 Personal discussion with Aminata Traoré, member of Djigui's bureau.
17 Ibid.
18 See LeBlanc (1998) for a more detailed discussion of the central role of Islam in the 1990s.
19 *Purdah* is the curtain, screen or veil shielding women from the sight of men or strangers in Hindu and Muslim communities. It refers to a system of social seclusion for women practiced by some Islamic and Hindu peoples.
20 *Hijab* is the word used in the Islamic context for the practice of dressing modestly, which all practicing Muslims past the age of puberty are instructed to follow in *al-Qu'rân*. *Hijab* has come to mean veil, referring to covering for women's head and/or body. The most common current style is a head covering that is a square of fabric folded into a triangle then placed over the head and fastened under the chin. In the Ivorian context, it refers to a style of veil associated with the Arab world.
21 See Soares (2004) for a similar argument regarding the middle class in Mali.
22 It must be noted that I observed the changes described here before Laurent Gagbo came into power in 2000. His leadership of Côte d'Ivoire has drastically altered dynamics between Muslims and Christians in the country, which were already quite tense after the death of Félix Houphouët-Boigny. As the situation of Muslims and Northerners has been more openly questioned since 2001 and in the context of the scission of the country into two territories in 2002, it is possible that Muslims in Abidjan have become more reluctant to display their religious affiliation.
23 See LeBlanc (2000a) for a more general discussion of dress choices among young Ivorian Muslim women.
24 A *bubu* is a long, loose fitting African garment. The *bubu* usually consists of a gown worn over a shirt and trousers for men, and over a wrapper with a headscarf for women.
25 It should be noted that a similar phenomenon developed in Egypt in the 1980s (see among others, Hoodfar 1997). As discussed by Homa Hoodfar, the wearing of the veil with Western inspired clothing allows women to access the job market while simultaneously preserving their status as "good Muslims". In the case of Côte d'Ivoire, such gender issues are certainly present, although women have been employed in offices since the 1970s. Furthermore, recent national debates have been centered on issues of religion and ethnicity, issues that seem to be of greater significance than gender.
26 Traditionally, the only young, unmarried females wearing a head-covering piece are *madâris* or *morikalanw* students.
27 It must be noted that generally West African women are fond of photo albums.
28 In 2003, I conducted ethnographic research on personal photo albums in Mali, with a focus on the cities of Bamako, Segou and Djenne. While personal photo albums are as popular in Mali as they are in Côte d'Ivoire, *Hajj* photo albums are significantly less popular in Mali; the few *Hajj* albums encountered were in Bamako (see LeBlanc 2004a). The difference is most likely due to economic distinctions between Mali and Côte d'Ivoire – where Ivorians are generally richer than Malians. The

sociopolitical context of religious revivalism in Côte d'Ivoire in the 1990s is also significant. It is also likely that return migration and the exile of Ivorians to Bamako as a result of civil unrest in Côte d'Ivoire from 1999 may have had an impact on the presence of *Hajj* photo albums in Bamako.

29 *Da'wah* means inviting others to Islam, sharing the message of Islam; it implies missionary work and proselytizing.

30 I have extensively discussed intergenerational relations elsewhere (LeBlanc 2002a, 2000b, 2005b, 2006).

31 See among others Peel (1968), Amselle (1985) and Last (1992) for historical examples.

REFERENCES

Abdullah, I. et al. (1997) 'Lumpen Youth Culture and Political Violence: The Sierra Leone Civil War'. *Africa Development*, 23(3–2):171–216.

Amselle, J.-L. (1985) 'Le Wahabisme à Bamako (1945–1985)'. *Canadian Journal of African Studies*, 19(2):345–57.

Brenner, L. (1991) 'Medersa au Mali: Transformation d'une institution islamique'. In B. Sanankoua and L. Brenner (eds) *L'enseignement islamique au Mali*. Bamako: Jamana.

Brenner, L. (1993) 'La culture arabo-islamique au Mali'. In R. Otayek (ed.) *Le radicalisme islamique au sud du Sahara: Da'wa, arabisation et critique de l'Occident*. Paris: Karthala and Talence/MSH.

Comaroff, J. and Comaroff, J. (eds) (1990) 'Introduction'. In J. and J. Comaroff (eds) *Modernity and Its Malcontents: Ritual and Power in Postcolonial Africa*. Chicago: University of Chicago Press.

Comaroff, J. and Comaroff, J. (2000) 'Millennial Capitalism: First Thoughts on a Second Coming'. *Public Culture*, 12(2):291–343.

Corin, E. (1998) 'Refiguring the Person: The Dynamics of Affects and Symbols in an African Spirit Possession Cult'. In M. Lambek and A. Strathern (eds) *Bodies and Persons: Comparative Perspectives From Africa and Melanesia*. Cambridge: Cambridge University Press.

Cruise O'Brien, D. (1996) 'A Lost Generation: Youth Identity and State Decay in West Africa'. In R. Werbner and T. Ranger (eds) *Postcolonial Identities in Africa*. London: Zed.

Dimé, M.d.N. and Calvès, A.-E. (2006) 'Du "jamonoy twist" au "jamonoy xooslu": le basculement dans la précarité de ménages de la classe moyenne à Dakar'. *Revue Canadienne d'Etudes Africaines*, 40(3), in press.

Diouf, M. (1996) 'Urban Youth and Senegalese Politics: Dakar 1988–1994'. *Public Culture*, 19:225–49.

Diouf, M. (2003) 'Engaging Postcolonial Cultures: African Youth and Public Space'. *African Studies Review*, 46(1):1–12.

Dorier-Apprill, E. (1998) 'Eglises et ONG caritatives à Brazzaville (Congo): Activisme sociopolitique ou religieux'. In J.-P. Deler et al. (eds) *ONG et Développement*. Paris: Karthala.

Dumont, L. (1985) 'A Modified View of Our Origin: The Christian Beginnings of Modern Individualism', W. D. Hall (trans.). In M. Carrithers,

S. Collins and S. Lukes (eds) *The Category of Person*. Cambridge: Cambridge University Press. Original French publication 1938.

Eickelman, D.F. and Piscatori, J. (1996) *Muslim Politics*. Princeton, NJ: Princeton University Press.

Evers Rosander, E. and Westerlund, D. (eds) (1997) *African Islam and Islam in Africa: Encounters between Sufis and Islamists*. Athens, OH: Ohio University Press.

Gomez-Perez, M. (1998) 'Associations islamiques à Dakar'. In O. Kane and J.-L. Triaud (eds) *Islam et islamismes au sud du Sahara*. Paris: IREMAM/Karthala/MSH.

Hackett, R. (1995) 'The Gospel of Prosperity in West Africa'. In R.H. Roberts (ed.) *Religion and the Transformation of Capitalism*. London: Routledge.

Hefner, R.W. (1998) 'Multiple Modernities: Christianity, Islam and Hinduism in a Globalizing Age'. *Annual Review of Anthropology*, 27:83–104.

Hoodfar, H. (1997) *Between Marriage and the Market: Intimate Politics and Survival in Cairo*. Berkeley, CA: University of California Press.

Jackson, M. (1996) 'Introduction: Phenomenology, Radical Empiricism, and Anthropological Critique'. In M. Jackson (ed.) *Things As They Are: New Directions in Phenomenological Anthropology*. Bloomington and Indianapolis, IN: Indiana University Press.

Jua, N. (2003) 'Differential Responses to Disappearing Transitional Pathways: Redefining Possibility among Cameroonian Youths'. *African Studies Review*, 46(2):13–36.

Last, M. (1992) 'The Power of Youth, Youth of Power: Notes on the Religions of the Young in Northern Nigeria'. In H. d'Almeida-Topor et al. (eds) *Les jeunes en Afrique: La politique et la ville, Tome 2*. Paris: l'Harmattan.

LeBlanc, M.N. (1998) *Youth, Islam and Changing Identities in Bouaké, Côte d'Ivoire*. PhD thesis, Department of Anthropology, University College London.

LeBlanc, M.N. (1999) 'The Production of Islamic Identities through Knowledge Claims in Bouaké, Côte d'Ivoire'. *African Affairs*, 98(393):485–508.

LeBlanc, M.N. (2000a) 'Fashion and the Politics of Identity: Versioning Womanhood and Muslimhood in the Face of Tradition and Modernity'. *Africa*, 70(3):443–81.

LeBlanc, M.N. (2000b) 'From Ethnicity to Islam: Social Change and Processes of Identification amongst Muslim Youth in Bouaké, Côte d'Ivoire'. *Paideumia*, 46:85–109.

LeBlanc, M.N. (2003) 'Les trajectoires de conversion et l'identité sociale chez les jeunes dans le contexte postcolonial ouest africain: Les jeunes musulmans et les jeunes chrétiens en Côte d'Ivoire'. *Anthropologie et Société*, 27(1):83–110.

LeBlanc, M.N. (2004a) 'Constructions identitaires féminines à travers la photographie et son usage dans la quotidienneté: Espaces urbains au Mali et en Côte d'Ivoire'. In J.F. Werner (ed.) *Entre global et local: Medias visuels et dynamiques identitaires féminines en Afrique de l'Ouest. Rapport final du programme de recherche collectif.* Paris: Institut de Recherche pour le Développement.

LeBlanc, M.N. (2004b) 'Staging Selfhood in Postcolonial Africa: The Use of Personal Photography in Mali and Côte d'Ivoire'. Opening lecture, 'Minds in Motion' Conference, Concordia University, Montreal, March 13.

LeBlanc, M.N. (2005a) 'Identités islamiques et mouvance transnationale: les nouveaux rôles du Hajj chez les jeunes musulmans de Côte d'Ivoire dans les années 90'. In M. Gomez-Perez (ed.) *L'islam politique en Afrique subsaharienne d'hier à aujourd'hui: discours trajectoires et réseaux*. Paris: Karthala.

LeBlanc, M.N. (2005b) 'Conversion, Faith and Proper Womanhood: Matrimonial Practices among Young Muslim Women in Côte d'Ivoire'. Paper presented at the biannual meeting, Society for the Anthropology of Religion, Vancouver, April 8–11.

LeBlanc, M.N. (2006) 'L'orthodoxie à l'encontre des rites culturels: Enjeux identitaires chez les jeunes d'origine malienne à Bouaké, Côte d'Ivoire. *Cahiers des Etudes Africaines*, in press.

Leimdorfer, F. and Marie, A. (1997) *L'Afrique des individus*. Paris: Karthala.

Leimdorfer, F. and Marie, A. (2003) *L'Afrique des citadins: Sociétés civiles en chantier Abidjan, Dakar*. Paris: Karthala.

Mauss, M. (1979) 'A Category of the Human Mind: The Notion of Person, the Notion of Self'. In Mauss, *Sociology and Psychology: Essays*, B. Brewster (trans.). London: Routledge and Kegan Paul.

Maxwell, D. (2001) 'Sacred History, Social History: Traditions and Texts in the Making of a Southern African Transnational Religious Movement'. *Comparative Studies in History and Society*, 43(3):502–24.

Meyer, B. (1998) 'Make a Break With The Past: Memory and Postcolonial Modernity in Ghanaian Pentecostal Discourse'. In R. Werbner (ed.) *Memory and the Post-colony: African Anthropology and the Critique of Power*. London/New York: Routledge.

Miran, M. (2006) '"La lumière de l'Islam vient de Côte d'Ivoire": Le dynamisme de l'islam ivoirien sur la scène ouest-africaine et internationale'. *Revue Canadienne d'Etudes Africaines*, in press.

Peel, J.D.Y. (1968) *Aladura: A Religious Movement Among the Yoruba*. London: Oxford University Press.

Richards, P. (1996) *Fighting for the Rain Forest: War, Youth and Resources in Sierra Leone*. Oxford: James Currey.

Rowlands, M. (1996) 'The Consumption of an African Modernity'. In M.J. Arnoldi et al. (eds) *African Material Culture*. Bloomington and Indianapolis, IN: Indiana University Press.

Savadogo, M. (2003) 'Muslim Religious Associations in the Collective Protest in Ivory Coast since 1990'. Paper presented at the conference 'Islam, Society and the State in West Africa', Rutgers University, New Brunswick, December 5–7.

Savadogo, M. (2005) 'L'intervention des associations musulmanes dans le champ politique et social en Côte d'Ivoire depuis 1990'. In F. Sow and M. Perez-Gomez (eds) *L'Islam politique en Afrique subsaharienne d'hier à aujourd'hui: discours, trajectoires et réseaux*. Paris: Karthala.

Soares, B.F. (2004) 'Islam and Public Piety in Mali'. In A. Salvatore and D.F. Eickelman (eds) *Public Islam and the Common Good*. Leiden/Boston, MA: Brill.

van Dijk, R. (1998) 'Pentecostalism, Cultural Memory and the State: Contested Representations of Time in Postcolonial Malawi'. In R. Werbner (ed.) *Memory and the Post-colony: African Anthropology and the Critique of Power*. London/New York: Routledge.

Weber, M. (1958) *The Protestant Ethic and the Spirit of Capitalism*. New York: Scribner's.

Werbner, P. and Basu, H. (1998) 'Introduction: The Embodiment of Charisma'. In Werbner and Basu (eds) *Embodying Charisma: Modernity, Locality and the Performance of Emotion in Sufi Cults*. London/New York: Routledge.

10
Claiming to be Croat: The Risks of Return to the Homeland

Daphne Winland

Since Croatian independence from the former Yugoslavia in 1991, Croats have been refashioning senses of self in response to changes in the homeland. The often strenuous efforts of Croatian historians to convey an image of an historic Croatian identity built on cultural and social continuity belies a reality marked by major upheavals in cultural and political identities, largely due to the influence of imperial powers and political forces – the Ottoman and Austro-Hungarian empires, Italian influence in Istria and, most recently, socialism. While bringing about Croatian independence and the efflorescence of Croatian nationalism, the breakup of the former Yugoslavia in 1990 has once again resulted in the unmooring of Croatian identifications and reference points, symbolic, political and otherwise.

Croats everywhere, but especially returnees to Croatia, have felt the impact of these changes. Although the changes initiated by the momentous occasion of Croatian independence have had an enormous effect upon Croats in Croatia and abroad, one of the main issues factoring into decisions to "return" to the homeland has been not only *how*, but *where* one can be truly Croat. This is no easy task as the meaning of "Croat" has gone through numerous incarnations throughout the centuries amongst Croats and in their interactions with non-Croats. Historically, the identifier "Croat/ian", particularly as nation, was often ignored by both domestic and foreign governments in lieu of imperial or state designations imposed by Austro-Hungarian or Yugoslav regimes. It also included vilification as a marker of East European inferiority or of Nazism (in the latter case, Croatia was part of the Axis regime from 1941 to 1945); of terrorism (due to incendiary acts between 1950 and 1989 committed by diaspora Croats in the name of independence from socialist Yugoslavia); and identification as suffering victim (of Communist oppression). The language of Croatian identity reveals the struggles endured over the years to stake claims to their uniqueness and their destiny.

In this chapter, I discuss the Croatian national imaginaries nurtured in the diaspora that inspire some diaspora Croats to "return"; the motivations of the Croatian government that has courted them; their reception and treatment by homeland Croatians, and the implications of returnee experiences for configuring the self in the analytical space usually reserved for diaspora. Research on the experiences of returnees reveals complex motivations and needs, a diversity of political and social conditions and their status as more than a discrete group defined by signifiers such as ethnicity, nation, class or region. In particular, the experience of returnees reveals fewer bases of commonality than are presumed to be characteristic of a group seemingly so deeply committed to Croatia.

The grounds and circumstances for claiming individuality examined in this chapter differ in certain key respects from the cases reported in many of the other chapters in this volume. Instead of featuring the proactive pursuit of personal distinction, the claims for individuality reported here ensue from failed attempts at collective affiliation. Actively encouraged by the Tudjman regime to expect warm acceptance as prodigal sons and daughters, returnee Croats found themselves at best ignored and at worst stigmatized as opportunistic outsiders. Fond expectations of national homecoming gave way to the loneliness of criticism and separation. What this chapter illustrates is not merely the experience of a de facto estranged particularity but also the wielding of individuality as a means to deflect and deny unacceptable categorical identification. Returnees came to embrace individuality as a rueful acknowledgement of the emptiness of national imaginings as well as a tactical insistence upon the primacy of purely personal preference.

The case of returnees (or *povratnici* as they are referred to in Croatian) is intriguing because of the challenges it presents to some of the premises upon which theorizing diaspora and, by extension, notions of ethnonational collectivity are based. Diaspora, for example, has become the axis around which discussions about displacements, multiple locations and border crossings have revolved (Gilroy 1987, 1993; Rouse 1991, 1995; Tölölyan 1991; Cohen 1997). But while the combined results of diasporic scholarship have enriched our understanding of contemporary configurations of identity, movement, nationalism and more, most scholars have fixed their analytical gaze on *diaspora as collectivity*, albeit "on the move". Despite the abundance of ethnographic work on the impact of global forces of dispersal, dislocation and deterritorialization, it is partial in its treatment of the complex experiences that shape specific transnational lives and identifications. Given the highly problematic nature of the conventional fiction that groups share a commonality of origins, cultures, political interests and statuses, it is important to assess critically what are presumed to be the shared origins, links and sensibilities of diasporas.

Dijaspora has become a meaningful category of self-representation and political discourse for Croats both in Croatia and abroad, particularly since the Croatian declaration of independence in 1991. It is found in the language of Croatian politics, commemoration, festivities and publications, religious sermons and public speeches. For some Croats, it has become emblematic of purpose and pride but for others, of ignorance, corruption and vulgarity. For most diaspora Croats though, the declaration of independence and the Wars of Succession catapulted the significance of the term *dijaspora* to new heights due not only to elevated levels of Croatian consciousness but also to the influence they had on the political program of the first Croatian government of Franjo Tudjman. The new kinship that diaspora Croats felt they shared *and* had earned (due to the extensive financial and other support they provided to the homeland) motivated many to contribute their resources to the dream of the homeland and, in some cases, to "return".[1]

The premise upon which much scholarly work on return migration is based is driven by international developments in migration and the production of refugees. Much of the academic and biographical literature on return – with the exception of that on Jewish returnees to Israel – also focuses primarily on the return from exile of those displaced by turmoil in their homelands (Malkki 1995; Ilcan 2002; Long and Oxfeld 2004). The conceptual parameters of most anthropological research on return are thus confined to a focus on "those who are actually returning or contemplating a return" (Long and Oxfeld 2004:4), meaning those who left the homeland at some time during their own lifetimes. It largely focuses, too, on the experiences of returnees as distinct groups characterized or united by political upheaval, based on ethnic, religious or other group designations. While this focus works well in contexts of forced expulsion, exile and migration caused by war and natural disasters, it does not allow for the consideration of second and subsequent generations of diaspora returnees who are not products of these circumstances, nor for a critical examination of the idea of return and its uses. What of those returnees who left Croatia voluntarily and now wish to return, as well as those who were neither born nor have ever lived in the homeland? The Croatian returnees considered here include not only first generations who originated in the homeland but second and third generation diaspora Croats.

One perspective that has become almost axiomatic in more symbolically focused discussions of return is the "myth of return". The ubiquitous "myth of return" embedded in diasporic narratives of homeland is seldom addressed in terms other than those that speak to its symbolic importance. Although the notion is regularly used in the literature on return migration, it arguably obscures as much as it reveals. According to Marc Israel, the "concept is both poorly theorized and potentially offensive, implying romantic delusion rather than political commitment, continuing yearning rather than evolving identification" (2002:27). This focus on subjectivities is reflected in Naficy's rendering of the "burning desire for return" (1993:16) of Iranian exiles in Los Angeles wherein they construct an imaginary nation that accommodates both the homeland and their own presence and exile. Similarly, Matsuoka and Sorenson speak of how Eritrean diasporas in Canada are "haunted" by myths of return as reflected in the book's title, *Ghosts and Shadows* (2001). For diaspora Croats, the desire to return to the homeland reflects generations of personal and political histories and social conditions both in Croatia and in diaspora, the excitement of new challenges and the spectre of new beginnings in familiar places.

Perhaps the most powerful of the many criticisms of the "myth of return" are those that draw attention to ideology and to the material and sociopolitical conditions (of host and homeland) that shape homeland imaginaries, as in the case of diaspora Croats. The ideology of return and/or repatriation is also central to the project of identity building in the host nation. As Said argues in his *Reflections on Exile* (2000), a meta-identity of exile is conceived in order to cope with realities of life in the host country. Exit from the homeland is often legitimated through discourses of remembrance and return in addition to practices of commemoration and the creation of institutions and political organizations devoted to the memory and experience of leaving "home". For Croats, this has been the case, especially for those who strongly opposed Communist rule.

The social contexts that produce the desire to return to Croatia *and* to stay are, of course, influenced in part by the particular conditions of life in diaspora – personal, professional or otherwise. For some, the sense of a mission to preserve the sacred homeland, now combined with post-Communist nostalgia, inspires a longing for return to some version of a pre-Communist homeland with the "originary tradition" still intact. For others, particularly young Croats, the draw is less ideological than the promise of employment and other immediate benefits. The impact of the Wars of Yugoslav Succession and Croatian independence on people's decisions to emigrate to Croatia must also not be overlooked. But, contexts aside, an analytical perspective that is based on the assumption that diaspora returnees are members of a distinct and unified group invariably leads to simplified interpretations of return as a process involving social connection, primordiality or fragmentation of the group writ large.

Returnees' experiences are shaped by personal encounters with and responses to the contexts in which they find themselves and the expectations they seek to reconcile. Willingly or not, Croatian returnees are both *products of* and *participants in* post-independence processes and their return to the homeland reflects the culmination of diverse interpolations of the idea of a unified and imagined national homeland and community that are not necessarily of their own making, or reflects their own personal ambitions, dreams and desires. More typically, returnees in Croatia experience varying degrees of shock, disappointment and encounters of the self as other.

Since 1990, political discourses around Croatness or *Hrvatstvo* have almost exclusively embraced ideas that convey a sense of collective Croatian identity, a new and invigorated sense of national belonging. This was most clearly reflected in the early strategies of the first post-independence government (1990–99). The "people production" (Balibar 1991) needs and efforts of the new state meant that diaspora Croats from Croatia and Bosnia-Herzegovina were implicated in the Croatian state building (*državotvorna*) program of Franjo Tudjman.[2] An integral component of the strategy was – although now to a lesser extent – an active campaign to attract diaspora Croats to the homeland. While Croatia has always been a nation of emigration, soon after independence it strove to be a nation of immigration, primarily geared to *attracting back* Croats living abroad.

The parallels between the 1951 Israeli Law of Return and Croatian efforts to attract its diaspora, both symbolic and procedural, are striking. The inspiration for the Israeli law stems from the historic Jewish religious ideology of return from exile and, as such, it carries tremendous symbolic meaning. The phrase "next year in Jerusalem" is heard in both prayer and song. The positive valuation of the process is reflected in the terminology as well. The process of returning to Israel is referred to in Hebrew as *aliyah* (to go up) while to leave is *yerida* (to go down) – the former a positive act, the latter, a source of derision.[3] Whereas the Hebrew term for returnees – *olim* – conveys a sense of historical destiny, i.e., return to the Holy Land, the Croatian term *povratnici* is more recent and was identified as a preferred category of immigration by the nationalist government of Franjo Tudjman. Although a law of return was never formally implemented in Croatia, key sections of Croatian constitutional laws on citizenship are devoted to returnees. Article 16 of the Croatian Constitution guarantees automatic citizenship to anyone who "issues a written statement that he or she considers himself or herself to be a Croatian citizen" (Law on Citizenship, Croatian Constitution).[4] Among the measures that President Tudjman undertook after he came to power was the creation of special government offices and the Ministry of Return and Immigration (*Ministarstva Povratka i Useljeništva*) to represent the Croatian population abroad.[5] Croatia began incorporating its "nationals" abroad into both national polity and market through a variety of measures such as supporting homeland associations, the extension of citizenship rights to diaspora Croats, voting privileges and most importantly, the promise of incentives to those who return.[6]

With the death of Tudjman in late 1999 and the subsequent Croatian elections in January 2000, the influence of diaspora Croats on homeland political and economic affairs diminished considerably, particularly given the resounding defeat of Tudjman's nationalist HDZ party, which was usually assured of a majority vote from diaspora Croats. Measures included the closure of the Ministry of Return and Immigration, delays in the tabling of a Bill of Returnees modeled on the Israeli Law of Return, and the scheduled closing of some consulate offices in countries with the largest Croatian diasporic populations such as the United States and Australia. Changes to electoral laws effectively shut out the diaspora constituency. For their part, returnees living in Croatia have been increasingly marginalised by the state and its vision of the new Croatia, one that differs from that conceived in diaspora. More importantly, returnees have been forced to re-evaluate their identifications and status in Croatia as well as their senses of self in relation to their new/old homes.

"GOING HOME": RETURNEES AND THE CROATIAN NATIONAL IMAGINARY

Who are the returnees or *povratnici*? Returnees include those Croats who were either born in Croatia or Bosnia-Herzegovina (hereafter referred to as B-H) and emigrated to North America or Europe in the years following World War I, as well as people of Croatian descent who were born outside of Croatia or B-H and who have chosen to return or emigrate to the homeland.[7] Croatian-born nationals who left Croatia for various personal, professional or political reasons and who have returned to Croatia after having lived overseas for long periods of time are also considered. Of the 38 interviews I conducted with Croatian returnees in Zagreb and Zadar, approximately one third were with Croats who had left Croatia or B-H at an early age and returned, and the rest were typically second and third generation Croats who were born in countries like Australia, Canada and the United States. Second and third generation returnees in particular who are not Croatian-born are often the children of native-born Croats who left Yugoslavia between the 1950s and the 1970s. I do not include Croats from the near abroad, namely Germany and other countries of settlement in Western Europe, given how different emigration experiences between the near and far abroad diasporas (Brubaker 1996) manifest themselves in often divergent formulations and discourses of identity, constructions of the past and visions of the future.

One of the main challenges in investigating the experiences of returnees is methodological. It is difficult both literally and figuratively to locate or to corral returnees as a group. There are no official gathering places or establishments, newspapers, associations, events or even websites where returnees regularly congregate. Furthermore, returnees are not visible in Croatia, seldom define themselves as such and are often not known to one another. Their distinctiveness as a group lies rather in their political and symbolic significance to Croatian government policymakers and diaspora Croats and this, as I will argue, is tenuous at best.

While the term "returnee" suggests an emphasis on those who have chosen to permanently resettle in Croatia, this is not necessarily the case. There is a complex array of transnational movements that must be considered in contemplating the meaning of "return". This includes, for example, retirees who split their year between Australia, the United States or Canada and Croatia, "returnee entrepreneurs" who, by virtue of their commercial activities, travel extensively and have several home bases; and humanitarian workers, students and others whose length of stay in Croatia is contingent on the demands of their professions and/or family circumstances. So the designation of returnee reveals a great deal of diversity and, as a result, different sensibilities about the nature of return and its meaning.

Although, for the above mentioned reasons, it is difficult to get a definitive estimate of the average length of stay for returnees and an estimate of the number of returnees who remain in Croatia for at least one year, older returnees are more likely to resettle for the long term, albeit with frequent forays back and forth to host countries from which they returned (mostly as retirees), while younger returnees vary widely in their commitments. The decisions of younger returnees to return and to stay in Croatia are mostly influenced by employment opportunities, personal relationships and their abilities to adjust. Furthermore, the conditions of return for most are voluntary, therefore the sorts of obstacles that characterized the experiences of some of their parents and grandparents (for example, as Displaced Persons), are not relevant to their motivations and/or political/ideological or other commitments.

HOME AND HOMELAND

"Home" is a term that for some first generation Croats piques highly personal memories of the sights, smells, and sounds of life in the homeland. According to Rapport and Dawson, " . . . it is 'where one best knows oneself' where 'best' means 'most' although not always 'happiest'" (1998:9). This was clearly the case for those diaspora Croats who left Yugoslavia under difficult circumstances. While the idea of return carries a heavy freight of symbolic meaning and emotion, the pull of romantic nationalist imaginaries which some cited for their decisions to return did not last long, at least for those who remained in Croatia. For first generation returnees, return often involves reconnecting with the space of the homeland and a time before emigrating, but one seldom recuperated. Sentiments of patriotism and belonging to the homeland thus resonate differently for second and third generation returnees born in Canada or elsewhere than for the generations of diaspora Croats who emigrated from the homeland. They come to the experience of return from a perspective informed less by the kinds of experiences, remembrances and longings typical of first generation diaspora Croats than by the desire for the imaginary real.

A crucial step in examining Croatian returnee migration is therefore to examine the contexts that help shape decisions to "go home". When the homeland was inaccessible under Communist rule, it provided a powerful reference point and a moral geography for many diaspora Croats – an explanation for what made them unique and different from non-Croats but similar to one another. Also integral to the returnee experience, regardless of conditions of return, is the use of "home" and/or "homeland" as a conceptual or discursive space of identification (Jackson 1995; Brah 1996; Rapport and Dawson 1998). But, while "home" refers to "a place of origin returned to" (Weil 1978; Hollander 1993), this would clearly not be the case for many second and third generation diaspora returnees. For those who had never lived in Croatia, home is less experienced than imagined through a series of symbolic mediations and representations reproduced through family and community.

What is striking are the ways in which ideas of home and belonging are narrated, reflecting a wide range of impressions and experiences, shifting interpretations and contrasting expectations of life in Croatia. Indeed, tropes of home and homeland inflected with narratives of longing are central to the language of diaspora Croat existence across generations. But the homeland that is recollected, memorialized, celebrated and even mourned by diaspora Croats is quite different than the reality of Croatia, which is itself a fragmented social and political terrain. This can refer to both remembered or imagined places of origin – a region, village or town, a farm – and selected memories, be they traumatic, pastoral or benign. Memories and experiences of home themselves are also fragmented and in some cases ambivalent, based on personal histories and experiences. As Khan states: "The place to which one returns is not necessarily the place from which one came" (1995:96), a sentiment echoed by many writers on exile (cf. Adorno 1974 [1951]; Said 2000; Boym 2001; Kundera 2003). The often unsettling effects of return on diaspora Croat senses of self are then telling of the relationships and sometimes the conflicts between one's hopes and desires for a new life in the Croatian homeland, however conceived, inspired or nurtured.

Perhaps not surprisingly, the most prevalent experience communicated by returnees of all ages and generations was a personal sense of alienation from the idea, the promise and the experience of return as imagined in diaspora. A significant response to this experience was mistrust. Although this was sometimes expressed as mistrust of particular individuals – employers, bureaucrats and politicians, neighbors – the tenor and substance of these complaints reflected distrust towards a Croatia that they had envisioned much differently. Returnees whom I interviewed often complained about particular obstacles to adjustment in Croatia that, rather than underscoring a collective sense of purpose, challenge, belonging or even betrayal, were almost exclusively personal. While this varied depending on the amount – and the quality – of time they had spent living in Croatia, their complaints bore striking similarities. These included negative personal experiences with Croatian bureaucracy, the high cost of living, political instability, day to day experiences with corruption, unfair employment practices and, most importantly, their reception by homeland Croatians.

While returnee complaints about Croatian bureaucracy are ubiquitous – a carryover from socialist Yugoslavia – as well as those about the high cost of living and corruption, the issue of returnee reception in the homeland is most compelling, given that it speaks to the relationship between national imaginaries and realities as perceived by returnees upon return. For example, only five of 38 participants I interviewed found the homeland welcoming. Many had expected generous state support and enthusiasm, if not gratitude, from homeland Croatians upon their return. After all, according to one returnee, "We were coming back to help, to show our faith in our new country. We gave up a lot to come home" (Marco, 29, November 2003, Zagreb).

Some also felt that homeland Croatians treated them differently – that they were resentful or simply ambivalent towards them. "Some of the hostility surprises me" (Jackie, 32, August 2002, Zagreb). According to van Hear; "[a]mong the reactions to returnees may be welcome, toleration, grudging acceptance, rejection, antagonism or conflict" (1998:56). Among the comments directed at them were criticisms for "not fighting in the War of Independence in 1991–95", being seen as "rich", or "failures" who came to Croatia to try their luck.

Evidence for returnee grievances dates back to the early 1990s. Aside from major administrative changes, benefits for returnees changed at least four times from 1990 onwards and each time, the number and scope of benefits diminished. Initially, returnees could bring all their assets with them. There are now limits on what returnees can bring and for everything new they have to pay taxes and custom fees that are prohibitively high. The absorption center of Velika Gorica on the outskirts of Zagreb, which was initially set up to house approximately 30 returnee families (particularly those who needed financial support), has also been closed.[8] During its existence, responsibility for it was shifted from the Ministry for Return and Immigration to the Ministry of Labour and Social Welfare. In commenting on the experiences of returnees, Niko Šoljak (head of the International Club of Croatian Emigrants, Returnees and Investors from Diaspora) dramatically emphasized the cost of return for some who had lost their life savings in Croatia: "Many people committed suicide because they could not deal with the tragedy of it all. They were too embarrassed to return to the countries from where they had come to Croatia" (Šoljak 2002:17). Elsewhere he states that: "It was only a small number of Croatians who actually managed to return to the homeland. Those who did come back and started working and earning money in Croatia soon went bankrupt" (Šoljak interview with Denis Rebi, www.croatia.ch, November 2003).

For their part, homeland Croatians routinely displayed a general lack of interest in returnees and in their experiences or difficulties. Mention of diaspora often aroused sentiments of ambivalence, antagonism or derision. It didn't seem to matter whom I was interviewing, mention of diaspora Croats elicited comments such as that from a 45 year old computer analyst in Zagreb: "Those diaspora peasants don't know what they want or what they are talking about" (Janko, 48, April 1997, Split). "Let's face it – our returnees are not the best or brightest there is on offer" (Mirko, 34, August 2002, Knin).[9] Homeland Croatians thus often judged returnees as a group tainted by the actions of those high profile returnees who had participated in corrupt government and business practices, by their origins (many referred to them as peasants), or by their perceived ignorance and anachronistic views of Croatia. Thus, while the designation of returnee or *povratnik* is commonly used in Croatian public discourse both in Croatia and in the diaspora, it soon becomes an unwelcome label for those upon whom it is bestowed.

Croatian returnees have thus had to reconcile the dream of return with their status in the homeland. Returnees were anxious to integrate but stated that they were not prepared for the degree to which the transition would be difficult. They therefore presumed greater affinities with the homeland and expected that their compatriots in Croatia would be more welcoming. This offended the sensibilities of returnees for whom emigration to the homeland was motivated by the desire to connect with something conceived as familiar. According to one woman who lived in Croatia for three years: "It was so cool to sit in a cafe and hear everyone speaking Croatian" (Karen, 32, November 2003, Toronto). Yet, when she spoke Croatian to friends and co-workers in Zagreb, they invariably commented on her accent and scoffed at the regional dialect she had learned from her parents in Toronto. According to most homeland Croatians I spoke to about returnees, it is easy to detect returnees by their accent or Croatian language skills. Returnees' general lack of proficiency with the language was frequently derided by homeland Croatians. Just as their parents who had emigrated to Canada had had to deal initially with the limitations of poor and/or accented English, so too do these returnees have to cope not only with reactions to their accented and sometimes poor Croatian, but with the stigma of their parents' often regional Croatian dialects. As a result of experiences such as these, returnees did not like to draw attention to themselves, but even these efforts were often unsuccessful.

Because returnees were faulted for their political views they were frequently lumped in with Tudjman-era nationalists regardless of their opinions or affiliations. Even Croatian-born returnees who came back to Croatia after having lived abroad for extended periods of time were not immune from these criticisms. Some returnees with strong nationalist feelings stated that they were determined to remain in the homeland because of the "duty" of all Croats to help forge a revitalized Croatian national identity in the homeland. Homeland Croatians clearly resented the implication that a newly configured post-Communist "pure" sense of Croatness was necessary, particularly one driven by diaspora Croat returnees. Other returnees I interviewed were quick to dissociate themselves from those with explicitly nationalist politics, claiming that their decisions to remain in Croatia were based on individual and personal circumstances, rather than on collective, nationalist notions of the Croatian homeland.

One possible explanation for the unusual goal of some returnees to reinvigorate Croatian identity in the homeland can be explained by the varied landscapes they have constructed over the years in diaspora and the transnational circuits (symbolically or otherwise) they have traversed. In cities like Toronto, identity as a member of a distinct ethnonational group has proved to be an ever ready reference point for diaspora Croats, underscoring varied experiences of adjustment to alien sociopolitical contexts, the difficulties of adjusting to life in Canada, and Canadian multicultural themes of unity in diversity, but also the significance of pride in (ethnic) origins and collective identity. For second and third generation Croat returnees, the countries in which they were born and raised or to which they emigrated from Croatia as young children are invariably marked by cultural politics of difference that differ substantially from those in Croatia. These contribute variously to returnee perceptions and expectations of life in Croatia. Thus, for example, all of the young returnee women from Canada I spoke to were struck by what they claimed is the particularly overt sexism in Croatia. Others reverted back to the criticisms often heard in the diaspora: for instance, the negative vestiges of the "Communist mentality" of their homeland compatriots, the absence of qualities valorized in the West, such as self-fulfilment and personal initiative, efficiency and business acumen.

It soon became clear that "returning home" initially had tremendous appeal for those returnees who were looking for a renewed sense of identity and belonging. But their stated reasons for remaining in Croatia most often included marrying a Croatian national or finding a good job. According to a male returnee from Canada who has lived in Croatia for seven years: "I didn't go there because I was like, patriotic or nationalistic or anything like that. I went because there was a job opportunity that sounded exciting. Hey, I'm adventurous!" (Marco, 29, November 2003, Zagreb). "I came here in the summer of 1989 and met my husband. I've been here ever since and would never think of moving back to Australia. My family is here now" (Lyn, 33, October 2003, Zagreb). The relative importance of reasons identified for return varies depending on contextual and personal factors, making it difficult to generalize returnee motivations for staying in Croatia or indeed, for having left their diaspora homes in the first place.

But while it was relatively easy to isolate collectivist discourses around which return to Croatia had been configured, imagined and worked out in diaspora, being *in* the homeland told a different story. Expectations of familiarity and commonalities with homeland Croatians and Croatia based on imaginaries constructed far off in diaspora were, in time, often replaced by awareness of divergences once returnees were amongst other Croatians in Croatia. The journey "back home" then reveals the poverty of overdetermined and often essentialist categories of diaspora, nation and identity and the experiences associated with them.

"FAILED" RETURN

The story of diaspora return, whether inspired by political visions, romantic imaginings, individual quests and/or pragmatic considerations, clearly then does not always end in a "happily ever after". Although their numbers are difficult to determine, there are those returnees who have abandoned their new lives in Croatia and have come back to Canada. Twelve of these returnees were interviewed in Toronto between July 2003 and September 2004. The parameters for their inclusion in this research included initial plans to live permanently in Croatia and length of stay (at least one year) and proficiency in the Croatian language. I chose young, mostly second and third generation diaspora Croats in order to assess the impact of formative homeland imaginaries constructed through family, community and other diasporic influences on their expectations and experiences in Croatia.

There are many cases of people who have emigrated to Croatia only to return to Canada disappointed and disillusioned. Their disillusionment stems from a variety of factors – personal, professional and political/ideological. Combined though, their overall experiences reflect a disconnection between their expectations before and after arrival in Croatia. By far the most common theme that emerged was profound disappointment. Most commented on difficulties in adjusting to life in Croatia and with complaints similar to those identified by returnees who have remained: excessive bureaucracy, attitudes of homeland Croatians in the areas of work, customs and habits, as well as returnee reception.

For many, their return to Canada was attributed to the unrealistic expectations that they brought with them to Croatia. These young people returned to a country that they were only partially familiar with – a familiarity defined primarily through imagined and symbolic means. Three returnees remarked that they moved to Croatia because they wanted to make a contribution to the new state. "I really thought I could make a difference" (Angie, 31, September 2003, Toronto). While this patriotic and ambitious sentiment provided some with the impetus to emigrate to Croatia, for most it was otherwise. "In the beginning I was patriotic as well. I was always 'Croatia, Croatia, Croatia'. And I still love Croatia, but the one thing I realized, they don't care about us so why care about them?" (Steve, 27, April 2004, Toronto). "I was raised to be really patriotic and Croatia was the center of our lives" (Joseph, 26, April 2004, Toronto). "When I got back to Croatia after the war, after Croatia was finally independent, people didn't care if it was called Croatia or not. That surprised me" (Mary, 28, August 2003, Toronto).

Being Croat, perhaps not surprisingly, entails a performative dimension. Furthermore, it becomes the basis upon which assessments and evaluations of *Hrvatstvo* are judged. The symbolic power of the homeland, as experienced in an upbringing often heavily influenced by immersion in Croatian culture and regional customs, common to many young returnees, is reflected in their views on the meanings of *Hrvatstvo*. Views on what constitutes Croatian identity then are often expressed through family/community rituals and formalized practices, as evidenced in the following statement from a 35 year old returnee who spent five years in Croatia: "When you were growing up here [in Canada] you were socialized to be very Croatian, so to speak, and very patriotic. The Croatian park and the Croatian church and the Croatian school, tambouritza ... and you go to Croatia and realize that wow, some things they don't even know about. I was shocked, I thought everyone knew how to do Croatian dancing. I got there and ended up teaching THEM!" (Ivana, 31, September 2004, Toronto). Another who returned to Canada in 1999 made a comment that at first glance seems absurd, but reveals an interesting perspective on perceptions of the true or real essence of *Hrvatstvo*: "It's sad that the Croatians there don't nurture their culture as much as we do here in Canada" (Mirna, 32, August 2003, Toronto). "I think that we are more Croatian than they are. Here we go to church. I mean that's something for us. That's what tied us together, the Croatian school and the church. And over there, nobody was really into that. Well, after the war, everyone started going but I think that it's winding down again now" (Ivana, 31, September 2004, Toronto). These views can be partly attributed to the efforts of their parents and church, recreational activities and peer influences to instil cultural values and practices identified as central to Croatian identity in diaspora. But more importantly, they speak to the anxieties and ambivalences of (not) belonging (Clifford 1997:14, 22), here organized around and expressed in the familiar language of culture and tradition.

Returnee impressions and recollections of their time in Croatia were greatly influenced by the degree to which they felt accepted by homeland Croatians. "They thought we came on a free ride, that we were getting everything we wanted from the government. That is the total opposite of what happened" (Mark, 35, September 2004, Toronto). A returnee who came back to Canada with her Croatian-born husband stated: "The natives think that the returnees are crazy. My husband did. Why on earth would you want to live here when the majority of young people just want to get out of Croatia? And then we say, 'Oh ya, I just returned here from Canada' and they just sort of look at you" (Danijela, 32, August 2003, Toronto).

There was, however, a recognition on the part of these returnees of often disparate renderings of the homeland based on generational, class and other differences. Regardless of their initial impressions of the Croatian homeland, they had come back to Canada with views of the Croatian homeland that diverged greatly from those of their parents and/or their Croatian friends in Toronto. "The picture my parents had of Croatia is very different than the reality. Croatians at home are not stuck back at the turn of the century, working in the fields and singing all the time. People now have heating in their houses, telephones, cell phones, things that my parent's generation didn't have especially if they lived in small villages. So their experiences of hardship are there but are not the same as people now" (Mary, 28, August 2003, Toronto).

Contrary to the expectations of most of these returnees, there were few resettlement resources available to help make them feel welcome. When questioned on their expectations, though, few had specific suggestions other than general efforts by homeland Croatians to help make their transition easier, particularly by being more accepting. Although their experiences did not, in many cases, have the desired result, that is, permanently resettling in Croatia, few expressed having felt like failures for having returned to Canada. Most often, their explanations for coming back were phrased in terms that reflected personal or professional decisions rather than having been forced to abandon their plans to remain in Croatia. While several stated that they would perhaps eventually return to Croatia, most planned to remain in Canada. The intensely personal, lived experiences of separation and belonging reflect the struggles between the personal and the political, the ideal/imagined and the real. Together, these experiences lay bare the paradox of the dream of return as against return itself.

CONCLUSIONS

When viewed together, the experiences of returnees dispel imaginings of an ingathering of peoples. The status and experience of returnees to the homeland remains problematic 15 years after independence was proclaimed in Croatia. They have been the pawns of a deliberate and sometimes aggressive process of nation building which started during Tudjman's regime, a process perpetuated transnationally through the diasporas that spawn them and homeland political/economic interests that benefit from or reject them.

But there are a multitude of other factors too, personal, political and otherwise that, combined, resulted in the return of diaspora Croats to Croatia from both the near and far abroad. Returnees coming together in the very location where many expected to find commonalities, community and a naturalized ethnicity, instead often experience difference, otherness, a sense of rupture and marginality. The strategies and choices they make once they get there seldom fulfill the dreams of return to a shared, communal home. Once in Croatia, the desire or need for "belonging" for returnees is worked out and configured individually and seldom with reference to a shared sense of what that belonging entails. Rather, most seek to constitute their senses of self without reference to the collective vision of a unified Croatian people or other imaginaries bred in diaspora. Any discourse having a vision of the integrity of the collective therefore is constantly insecure.

Perhaps most tellingly, when I asked returnees, both those who remained in Croatia and those who came back after having attempted to resettle in Croatia, what about the experience had changed their senses of *Hrvatstvo*, most replied that much had changed in them. On the whole, they felt that they did not really belong anywhere. According to one: "I don't think I'll ever fit in. I'll always be 'the Canadian' in Croatia, but here in Canada I'll always be the returnee who came back, although I don't feel like either anymore really" (Mary, 28, April 2004, Toronto). The intersections of individual particularities which find their sources in personal histories and narratives with ideas, sensibilities and lived realities of *Hrvatstvo* reveal more than motivations for return and prevent the easy categorization of returnees as, for example, "nationalists", "patriots", "militants", "entrepreneurs".

Following Nigel Rapport in his study of Jewish "*olim*" in Israel then, it is "through a distilling of the essence of their past American selves that new migrants begin to be at home and imagine futures for themselves" (Rapport and Dawson 1998:13). These, though, seldom fulfill the broader national imaginary conceived and nurtured in diaspora and featured in the state production of Croatian culture, in Croatian polemics and by Croatian politicians. The futures that they must negotiate are ones in which each returnee must carve out a niche specific to their needs, abilities and the contingencies of life in a new country, rather than what we presume to be the diasporic imaginaries and desires that not only motivate them to make the move to Croatia but sustain them in their new/old home.

NOTES

1 Returnees include high profile and sometimes wealthy diaspora Croats, some of whom had received plum government appointments or profited politically or financially under Tudjman's regime.

2 Early on in his mandate, Tudjman had embarked on a campaign to annex parts of Western Bosnia and called for its secession from Bosnia-Herzegovina, which had the effect (and does still) of further radicalizing political and religious militancy of the Croats there.

3 As the daughter of an Israeli mother who emigrated to Canada in 1952, I remember the term *"yoredim"* (emigrants from Israel) as one packed with negative connotations. I was amused by the fact that the term *"yored"* rhymed with *"boged"*, which translates from Hebrew as "traitor". I only became familiar with the Hebrew term for immigrant – *"hagira"* – as a result of my academic interest in the subject (cf. Shuval 1998).

4 www.sabor.hr/sabor/parliament/acts/propis13.htm, December 16, 1996.

5 The Ministry of Return and Immigration also published a magazine titled *Bilten* chronicling government programs and returnee experiences.

6 The Croatian government was clearly interested in encouraging those returnees who could bolster their image abroad by appealing to nostalgic remembrances, real or imagined. The following testimonial is interesting because it reflected the experiences of a few Croats I met. This one, concerning a Croatian returnee, was circulated through the *Dom i Svijet* (Home and the World) link to the Croatian national government website in 1996: "Although he no longer holds performances due to his state of health, Spralja now plays his guitar just for his own enjoyment and that of his friends. It all started some 40 years ago when Spralja moved from Zadar to Canada. Once there, he started singing in a coffee shop and met there the Israeli singer Malka. They formed a successful duo and made records and made appearances on TV and radio. Later, he abandoned his singing career to open up his own restaurant in Toronto. Out of his love for Croatia and Zadar, Spralja started renovating one of Zadar's medieval bastions, which also harbors an arsenal. Spralja always emphasizes the fact that he loves his city and that he was pleased when he was awarded in 1989 the license for the arsenal that he is still refurbishing and which is to harbor a gallery. He brought in works of art that he had made in Canada and is to stage several exhibitions. His wife Angelina has been by his side during the whole of his career and she was the one who looked after the family. She also says that despite living in Toronto for 36 years and having relatives there she was still driven by a wish to return to the city she was born in".

7 I do not focus on Bosnian Croat refugees or others repatriated from Bosnia, Germany or other European states after the War of Independence in the early 1990s.

8 According to a Croatian Foreign Ministry press release in 1999 (before Velika Gorica closed): "Naturally, there is a great interest in the reception centre where returnees from poor families live until they receive documents and find accommodation and employment. There are some thirty people living at the centre at present, most of them young people".

9 On a trip between Split and Zagreb, I met a young Canadian Croat, who told me that he had come to Croatia the previous year with plans to reignite Croatians' commitment to Catholicism. He said that years of Communist rule had weakened the Catholic faith in Croatia. He then proceeded to recite verses from his Bible, at which point an old woman sitting across from us yelled obscenities at him in Croatian, and several young people sitting across from him also fixed a disdainful stare on him. When we disembarked, a man who was also in our train compartment told me in Croatian: "This is *just* what we need!".

REFERENCES

Adorno, T. (1974 [1951]) *Minima Moralia: Reflections from a Damaged Life*, E.F.N. Jephcott (trans.). London: New Left Books.

Balibar, E. (1991) 'The Nation Form: History and Ideology'. In E. Balibar and I. Wallerstein (eds) *Race, Nation, Class: Ambiguous Identities*. London: Verso.

Boym, S. (2001) *The Future of Nostalgia*. New York: Basic Books.

Brah, A. (1996) *Cartographies of Diaspora: Contesting Identities*. London: Routledge.

Brubaker, R. (1996) *Nationalism Reframed: Nationhood and the National Question in the New Europe*. Cambridge: Cambridge University Press.

Clifford, J. (1997) *Routes: Travel and Translation in the Late Twentieth Century*. Cambridge, MA: Harvard University Press.

Cohen, R. (1997) *Global Diasporas: An Introduction*. Seattle, WA: University of Washington Press.

Gilroy, P. (1987) *There Ain't No Black in the Union Jack: The Cultural Politics of Race and Nation*. London: Hutchinson.

Gilroy, P. (1993) *The Black Atlantic: Modernity and Double Consciousness*. London: Verso.

Hollander, J. (1993) 'It all Depends'. In A. Mack (ed.) *Home: A Place in the World*. New York: New York University Press.

Ilcan, S. (2002) *Longing in Belonging: The Cultural Politics of Settlement*. Westport, CT: Praeger.

Israel, M. (2002) 'South African War Resisters and the Ideologies of Return from Exile'. *Journal of Refugee Studies*, 15(1):26–42.

Jackson, M. (1995) *At Home in the World*. Durham, NC: Duke University Press.

Khan, A. (1995) 'Homeland, Motherland: Authenticity, Legitimacy, and Ideologies of Place among Muslims in Trinidad'. In P. van der Veer (ed.) *Nation and Migration: The Politics of Space in the South Asian Diaspora*. Philadelphia, PA: University of Pennsylvania Press.

Kundera, M. (2003) *Ignorance*. New York: HarperCollins.

Long, L. and Oxfeld, E. (eds) (2004) *Coming Home? Refugees, Migrants and Those Who Stayed Behind*. Philadelphia, PA: University of Pennsylvania Press.

Malkki, L. (1995) *Purity and Exile: Violence, Memory and National Cosmology among Hutu Refugees in Tanzania*. Chicago: University of Chicago Press.

Matsuoka, A. and Sorenson, J. (2001) *Ghosts and Shadows: Construction of Identity and Community in an African Diaspora*. Toronto: University of Toronto Press.

Naficy, H. (1993) *The Making of Exile Cultures: Iranian Television in Los Angeles.* Minneapolis, MN: University of Minnesota Press.
Rapport, N. and Dawson, A. (eds) (1998) *Migrants of Identity: Perceptions of Home in a World of Movement.* Oxford: Berg.
Rouse, R. (1991) 'Mexican Migration and the Social Space of Postmodernism'. *Diaspora,* 1:8–23.
Rouse, R. (1995) 'Thinking Through Transnationalism: Notes on the Cultural Politics of Class Relations in the Contemporary United States'. *Public Culture,* 7:353–402.
Said, E. (2000) *Reflections on Exile and Other Essays*: Cambridge, MA: Harvard University Press.
Shuval, J. (1998) 'Migration to Israel: the Mythology of "Uniqueness"'. *International Migration,* 36(1):4–24.
Šoljak, N. (2002) *Zbornik: Prvog Sabora Hrvatske Dijaspore* (Symposium: The First Assembly of the Croatian Diaspora), Pore, May 21–23.
Tölölyan, K. (1991) 'The Nation and its Others: In Lieu of a Preface'. *Diaspora,* 1(1):3–7.
van Hear, N. (1998) *New Diasporas: The Mass Exodus, Expulsion and Regrouping of Migrant Communities.* London: UCL Press.
Weil, S. (1978) 'Anthropology Becomes Home: Home Becomes Anthropology'. In A. Jackson (ed.) *Anthropology at Home.* London: Routledge.

Notes on Contributors

Vered Amit is Professor of Anthropology at Concordia University in Montreal. She has conducted fieldwork in the UK, Canada and the Cayman Islands. Her research interests include youth cultures, the politics of ethnicity, transnational mobility, elites and community. Recent books include *The Biographical Dictionary of Social and Cultural Anthropology* (2004), *The Trouble with Community* (2002) (with Nigel Rapport), *Realizing Community: Concepts, Social Relationships, and Sentiments* (2002) and *Constructing the Field: Ethnographic Fieldwork in the Contemporary World* (2000).

Parminder Bhachu is Professor of Sociology at Clark University in Massachusetts, USA. She is a former Henry R. Luce Professor of Cultural Identities and Global Processes and also a Director of the Women's Studies program. She works on emergent cultural and commercial economies in border zones innovated by multiply moved global citizens. She is the author of *Dangerous Designs: Asian Women Fashion the Diaspora Economies* (2004), *Twice Migrants* (1985), and co-editor of *Enterprising Women* (1988) and also *Immigration and Entrepreneurship* (1993).

Noel Dyck is Professor of Social Anthropology at Simon Fraser University in British Columbia. The author of several books on relations between Aboriginal peoples and governments, he has subsequently conducted field research on sport, childhood and youth mobility in Canada. His recent books include *Sport, Dance and Embodied Identities* (2003) (with Eduardo P. Archetti) and *Games, Sports and Cultures* (2000). He is currently completing studies of adults and the social construction of children's sports.

Julia Harrison is Associate Professor of Anthropology at Trent University in Ontario. Her research interests include tourists and tourism, the representational practices of museums, and the history of Canadian anthropology. Her recent publications include *Being a*

Tourist: Finding Meaning in Pleasure (2003), articles in *Museum Anthropology* and *Journal of Museum Management and Curatorship*, and an edited volume titled *Historicizing Canadian Anthropology* (2006) (with Regna Darnell). Currently she is conducting research on "cottage culture" in Ontario.

Marie Nathalie LeBlanc is Associate Professor of Anthropology at Concordia University in Montreal. She has conducted fieldwork in Mali, Côte d'Ivoire and Montreal. Her research interests include religion in postcolonial contexts; visual anthropology and photography; youth and popular culture; women, family and marriage. She has published recently in such journals as *Anthropologie et Société, Canadian Journal of Ethnic Studies* and *Cahiers des Etudes Africaines.* She was co-editor of a special issue of *Anthropologie et Société* on Religion in Movement (2003).

Mattison Mines is Emeritus and Research Professor of Anthropology at the University of California, Santa Barbara. He has done field research in Tamil Nadu among the Tamil speaking Muslims, the Kaikkoolar weavers, and, in Chennai, among the Beeri Chetti and Komati Chetti merchants. His publications include *Muslim Merchants: The Economic Behaviour of an Indian Muslim Community* (1972), *The Warrior Merchants: Textiles, Trade, and Territory in South India* (1984), and *Public Faces, Private Voices: Community and Individuality in South India* (1994).

Karen Fog Olwig is Professor of Anthropology at the University of Copenhagen. Her main research interests are migration, family networks and intergenerational relations, and the Caribbean. Recent publications include *Work and Migration: Life and Livelihood in a Globalizing World* (2002) (edited with Ninna Nyberg Sørensen); *Children's Places* (2003) (edited with Eva Gulløv), and *Caribbean Narratives of Belonging* (2005) (edited with Jean Besson).

Nigel Rapport holds a Canada Research Chair in Globalization, Citizenship and Justice at Concordia University, Montreal, where he is Director of the Centre for Cosmopolitan Studies. He is also a Professor at the Norwegian University of Science and Technology, Trondheim. His research interests include social theory, phenomenology, identity, individuality, literature, humanism and cosmopolitanism. His recent publications include *I Am Dynamite: An Alternative Anthropology of Power* (2003) and (as editor) *Democracy, Science and The Open Society: A European Legacy?* (2005).

Deborah Reed-Danahay is Professor of Anthropology at the University of Texas at Arlington. Her research interests include education, personal narrative, citizenship and transnational identities, and social theory. She has conducted research in France and in the US (most recently among Vietnamese Americans in north Texas). She is author of *Education and Identity in Rural France: The Politics of Schooling* (1996) and *Locating Bourdieu* (2005), and editor of *Auto/Ethnography: Rewriting the Self and the Social* (1997).

Daphne Winland is Associate Professor of Anthropology at York University in Toronto. She has written extensively on Mennonites, Laotian Hmong refugees and, most recently, on transnational politics amongst diaspora and homeland Croats. The results of her Croatian research are also contained in her forthcoming book, *The Politics of Desire and Disdain: Croats between "Home" and "Homeland"*. Her current project investigates contemporary struggles of Croatians to reinvent themselves as Europeans in the changing political, social and cultural landscape of post-Communist Eastern Europe.

Index